HUNTING PREDATORS
FOR HIDES AND PROFIT

Dedication

For Janet, Brendan, Brad and Blair

HUNTING PREDATORS
FOR HIDES AND PROFIT

Wilf E. Pyle

Stoeger Publishing Company

PHOTO CREDITS
Major L. Boddicker, 60; Earl Chase, 24, 25, 40;
Robert Elman, 110, 138; Bob Gilsvik, 34, 44;
Patricia Gilsvik, 27; Mike Griffith, 20;
Jerome J. Knap, 35, 108, 185; Bud Lang, 46;
Pied Piper Calls, 30, 32, 98; Ed Sceery, 149, 238;
Chuck Spearman, 43 (courtesy Ed Sceery);
Johnny Stewart, 23, 33, 106; Ray Wells, 8, 14, 16, 220
(courtesy Garber's Fine Furs, Passaic, N.J.)

Published by Stoeger Publishing Company
55 Ruta Court
South Hackensack, New Jersey 07606

International Standard Book Number (ISBN): 0:88317-131-7
Library of Congress Catalog Card Number: 85-051163
Manufactured in the United States of America

Distributed in the United States by Stoeger Industries,
55 Ruta Court, South Hackensack, New Jersey 07606;
in Canada, by Stoeger Ltd., 169 Idema Road,
Markham, Ontario, L3R 1A9

Acknowledgments

A book is a long-term project, usually requiring some help along the way. This book is no different, and there are friends, old and new, whom I must thank for their assistance as the pieces came together.

First, I want to thank Ed Sceery and Bud Lindsey, both predator call manufacturers, for contacting me and offering their assistance. Both men provided photographs and vital information on calling.

Other manufacturers helped. Thanks to Faulks, Scotch, Lohman, Johnny Stewart, and Major Boddicker of Crit'R Call fame for their contributions.

A special thanks to Steve Repka and Glen Gentiles for their advice and interest in the project.

Mention should also be made of the several photo contributors: Bob Elman, Bud Lang, Jerome Knap, Bob Gilsvik, Earl Chase and Mike Griffith; and Ray Wells, who took the cover photo.

A big thank you to Project Editor Charlene Cruson, who edited the book and was responsible for what you see in final form; and to Vic Schwarz, who rendered the illustrations.

And a very special thanks to my wife, Janet, for her help in crunching through the manuscript. Her support, as always, was invaluable.

About
The Author

Canadian-born Wilf Pyle has hunted predators seriously since 1975 and has, as he says, "turned a handsome profit" doing so. He has also traveled extensively throughout western North America, from the frigid reaches of northern Canada to the arid prairies of Texas, in pursuit of indigenous big and small game. He has studied the animals, field dressed them and, in the case of long-haired fur bearers, has skinned them and taken them through every stage of the pelt preparation process. An avid outdoorsman from sunrise to sunset, Pyle also enjoys fishing and camping. But these of course are only seasonal activities.

Full-time Wilf Pyle serves as an agrologist for the Province of Saskatchewan. As a field agrologist from 1974 to 1980, his work frequently took him into Canada's scenic countryside, where he learned the ways of many a cunning coyote. Today, he is Assistant Manager of Support Services, specializing in land management. Before becoming an agrologist, he was a wildlife biologist in Alberta and in Saskatchewan.

And all this after having received an associates degree in business administration and economics (1966), a Bachelor of Science in agriculture (1970) and a Master of Science degree in 1972. His Master's thesis, incidentally, was a study of the winter food habits and behavior of the pronghorn antelope, one of the first winter studies of its kind up to that time.

His writing career? In 1975, Pyle began writing for *Western Sportsman* magazine as its camping editor, a position he held for eight years. In 1981, he wrote as contributing editor for *Survival Guide*, and in 1982 he co-authored with the late Bert Popowski *The Hunter's Book of the Pronghorn Antelope*. In addition, Pyle has bylined some 200 articles for publications such as *American Hunter*, *Field and Stream*, *Outdoor Canada*, *Fur-Fish-Game*, *Rifle* magazine, *Handloader*, and *Petersen's Hunting Magazine*. He is also former western director of the Outdoor Writer's Association of Canada.

Hunting Predators for Hides and Profit is Wilf Pyle's first solo book, which represents the culmination of his vast experience in the outdoors, his expertise in predator hunting and his knowledge of science and economics—not to mention that it is one of the most well-written hunting books in print today.

Pyle resides in Regina, Canada, with his wife Janet and their three children—Brad, Brendan and Blair—all of whom helped in some way with this volume.

The Editor

Preface

What makes a person want to hunt hides in today's modern society? Is it a wish to return to simpler times, or is it a heartfelt desire to be outdoors doing something productive? Some may hunt because they are interested in the animals or like to work with the equipment, the guns, the vehicles, the reloading. Perhaps a guy just likes to be alone for a few hours a week.

It really doesn't matter what motivates us to hunt. The fact is that hide hunting can be an extremely rewarding outdoor experience. If done right, with some planning and dedication, it can also be a money-making proposition that pays dividends in cash and experience. It can turn a good profit and it can be fun. For some, it can become an engrossing business in the old tradition of the fur trade.

Hide hunting can range from a full-time job to a seasonal hobby. Most states still retain predator control officers and varmint specialists. While many of these view the predators as destructive agricultural pests, they still develop a professional skill level that is akin to that of the old-time outdoorsman or backwoods character. Hide buyers exist throughout the country, pursuing pelts in association with other work or as a full-time occupation.

Long-haired furs have been very lucrative over the past decade. This has not always been so, especially in relation to coyotes and gray fox, which were often treated as varmints rather than valuable fur. However, the shift in fashion interest from short-haired furs to long-haired kinds has brought these species into prominence. Coyotes that were routinely discarded now bring three and four hundred dollars for a prized specimen. In addition, the decline in fox ranching, rampant just after World War I, has made wild fox fur increasingly valuable.

Heightened interest in the long-hairs has meant that the animals have also changed. Coyotes, foxes and "the cats" are more cunning and secretive in their ways than only 10 or 20 years ago. In turn, the hunter has had to improve his skills and hone his efforts in order to realize a return. It has resulted in the animals acclimating better at living next to man. Even the far north has changed sufficiently that foxes, coyotes and even wolves come into much closer contact with man and are greatly affected by his varied activities. Urban areas, especially in the East, are now home to foxes, and the extension of urban acreages has given the predator the opportunity to coexist together with man. These factors have altered the habits and habitat of predators for all time.

The changes have benefited the hunter in several

Many long-haired pelts are used for hats, collars and trim. This fashion trend has brought into prominence furs from such predators as coyote, fox, bobcat and lynx (above).

understanding the fur market all reach heights of excellence under this kind of hunting. What may be useful for whitetailed deer is not enough to outsmart a crafty predator in its own environment.

Hide hunting may be frustrating for the beginner. Long periods of driving, bad weather, no results from calling, and a few close-range misses—not to mention going days without seeing an animal—will test any hunter's interest. A major objective of this book is to take you through every step in the hide hunting process, familiarize you with every skill necessary to succeed, and to cover the dozens of pitfalls that even entrap some pros. All this is done to prevent beginner burnout and frustration.

If you're looking to make hide hunting a viable and profitable business, certain measures that follow the hunting stage are essential. Proper handling of the hide—skinning, fleshing, stretching and drying—is important in enhancing the appearance of the fur. Step-by-step instructions in the section "Preparing the Hides for Market" are fully illustrated to present the processes in as easy-to-follow a manner as possible. As you'll see, a well-prepared hide that grades well will ultimately bring you the best selling price. It would benefit any serious hunter of hides to read and understand all the criteria and the economic factors that are considered by the hide buyer when he grades your furs. To ensure your success in the marketplace, tips on where to locate buyers, how to sell your hides effectively, what large fur auctions have to offer and how to keep accurate records are outlined in the section on successful marketing.

In sum, this book is designed to give you everything you need—from coyote calling to bargaining with a local buyer—to become the successful hide hunter/businessman. Familiarize yourself with every phase of the hunting/selling process *before* you head for the prairie, and good fortune will be yours—not only in the taking of the furs, but in receiving the financial reward you will so aptly earn.

Wilf E Pyle

Regina, Canada
Autumn 1985

ways. It means that little travel is required to get to long-hair country nowadays. Unlike big game hunting, this type of hunting can be practiced anywhere. The seasons are generous and the opportunity to hunt is far greater than in the more restricted game seasons. Finally, it means that in every area of North America today, a predator carrying a long-haired coat exists that is both a challenging target and a valuable trophy.

Hides do not come easy. For the average hunter proficient in outdoor activities, hide hunting demands the learning of new skills and changing the application of old ones. Knowing the animal, selecting the right call, calling the predator, using the correct cartridge, being able to function well in the outdoors, knowing how to prepare a hide, and

Contents

Hunting Long-Haired Predators

Chapter 1

A Look At
Some Background

The fur trade is one of North America's oldest businesses. It has been in continuous operation since the country was first colonized in 1607. Indeed, the only reason the country received any attention in those early years was the large and abundant fur populations of the day. Hunted and trapped by the Indians, furs were traded for mere trinkets called shoddy, and produced huge profits for the traders and their companies. Since profit was the driving motive, the land was settled in an almost relentless fashion with large amounts of furs being processed and traded around the world by Yankee pedlars in clipper ships. The fur trade that gave rise to the country was a business that featured keen competition, rivalry and riches for those who persevered.

Today, as in the bygone days of early settlement, the fur trade is a thriving business in North America. The value of all furs sold in the United States during 1983 was close to three billion dollars. The economic spin-offs from this were enormous, estimated to be somewhere in the neighborhood of three to five times this amount. Add to this the revenues derived by states and governments for licensing, the value of equipment and money spent on such items as vehicles, it becomes clear that the hide business is alive and well.

The demand for hides still remains high. The recovery from the last recession has been dramatic and the effect of this is only starting to be felt throughout the buying public. The sales of durable goods (items such as refrigerators and stoves) has risen monthly since the depth of the recession. Along with this, the demand for luxury items such as furs has also increased.

While fur trading continues at a pace that nearly matches its historic highs, several changes have occurred in the busines over the intervening years. For example, the kinds of hides now demanded are much different from those sought in the olden days. At the peak of the fur trade, beaver skins were the major hide sought after for the manufacture of hats. One hundred years ago, a hunter would have treated a coyote as nothing more than a killer of sheep and young cattle. Unlike yesteryear, these hides are now valuable for use in the manufacture of coats and collars. In short, the demand has changed.

Foreign manufacturers have continued to shop the American fur production areas. Prices for raw furs have been down, in part because of the strength of the American dollar against other overseas currencies, and in part because of caution on the part of the buyers. Once these buyers better ascertain the direction of the American economy over the next two to five years and the dollar begins its

Strong demand for long-haired furs like coyote makes turning a profit from the sale of these hides a lucrative reality.

profits for those who happen to be in place.

The world economy can also greatly influence the direction of hide prices. John Jacob Astor, who headed the American Fur Company in the 1800s, traded furs that were not affected by the same market forces that operate today. In his time, the challenge was in the gathering together of the furs and bringing them to market, the same phase that brings excitement today.

The demand was already there and running high. However, today the economies of many countries are tied by trade agreements and pacts that have been lobbied for by dozens of interest groups and are guarded over by vote-sensitive politicians. This simply means that normal market forces may not always be free to operate in true supply-and-demand fashion. Add to this any kind of world crisis and it is not difficult to see that overall world conditions can easily influence where prices for a primary commodity such as raw furs may eventually settle.

The scope of this book is intended to deal only with the hides of long-haired predators. Many of the principles of marketing or trading in furs are the same for all types of hides. However, in the last few years, strong demand for long-hairs makes selling or turning a profit from these hides a lucrative reality. It also makes the buyer's task easier since he knows that he has some leeway should he make a mistake on one or two purchases. In the end, in a rising market, he will still make a mild profit and, in turn, so will you. Long-hairs have been in this enviable position for some time, and from the looks of things, will be for some time to come.

Which Predators To Pursue

Which animals should be hunted? This is a fair question, and considering there are over 50 different fur-bearing species resident in North America, some selection has to be made. Of that number, the long-hairs are currently the most profitable and occupy the broadest range. Long-hairs, in contrast to short-haired animals, are those mammals that have a pelage featuring long guard hairs that grow into place just prior to the coldest part of the season. Short-hairs, while many times living in similar cold conditions, do not grow this type of hair.

inevitable decline, hide prices of raw American furs will likely soar to new all-time highs. The point to be made is that the buyers have not stopped buying.

Fashion will also influence hide prices over the near term. This is one axiom of the fur business that has remained constant no matter how the world economies have performed. Fashion is totally unpredictable. A few years back, weasel pelts were in great demand; prices paid for prime ermine were way out of proportion to the effort required to take the animals. These pelts were used in fur collars and accessory items; they were nice to look at and had a pleasing feel to them. However, once this fad in fashion passed, the price of prime ermine dropped. This same type of erratic behavior can grip the fur industry at any time, resulting in good

Fox fur can be found in a wide array of colors. During the winter all species, and in particular the red fox shown above, grow thick luxurious pelage.

Of the two predator cats, the bobcat enjoys a wider distribution and carries a beautiful coat in prime season.

The lynx is an exotic-looking creature, equally evasive and difficult to pursue.

There is little wonder why a full-length coat designed of lynx fur is alluring to well-to-do fashion buffs.

The fur trade recognizes several long-hair species. These include the fisher (*Martes pennanti*), marten (*Martes americana*), wolverine (*Gulo luscus*), and the wolf (*Canis lupus*) common mostly to the far North with pockets in the mountainous terrain of the Southwest. The arctic fox (*Alopex lagopus*) is indigenous to only the very far north.

A shorter list of long-hairs lives closer to home and is known to southern hunters as predators or varmints. This list encompasses the dog-like critters from the large *Canidae* family—the coyote (*Canis latrans*) and the various foxes, most notably the red fox (*Vulpes fulva*) and the gray fox (*Urocyon cinereoargenteus*); and the wildcats—the bobcat (*Lynx rufus*) and the lynx (*Lynx canadensis*). It is these species that should be concentrated on by most serious hunters of long-haired hides.

In any fur season it should be possible to take 200 or 300 of these animals in most parts of the range. The coyote, fox and bobcat comprise the largest portion of the wild fur taken in the long-hair class across North America today. They are highly preferred, and a ready market exists for any number the average hunter can bring to the hide buyer's counter. Focus on these and from perhaps a dozen to several hundred will be yours for the taking in any one season.

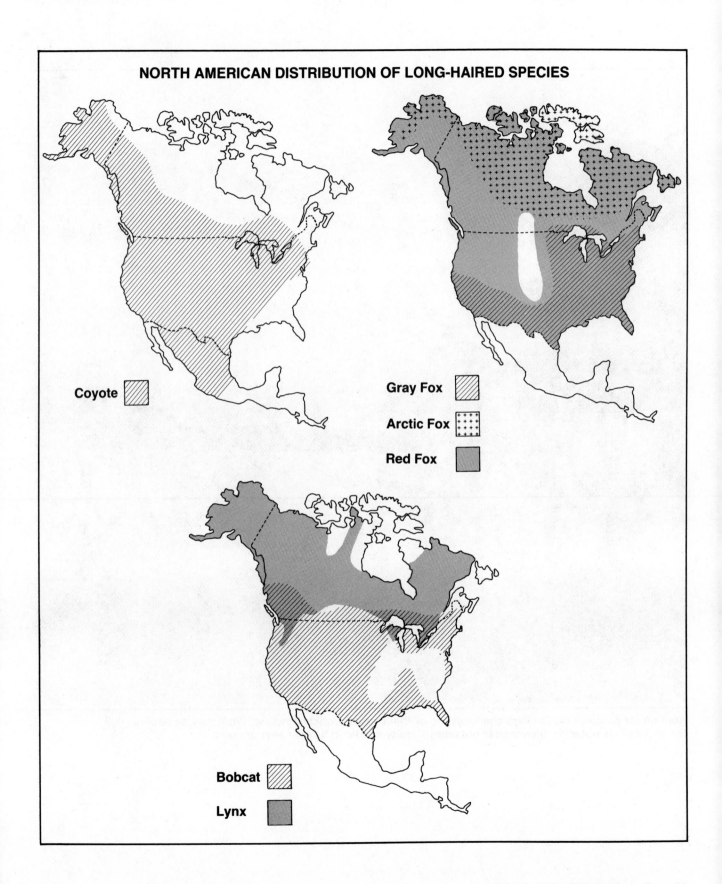

NORTH AMERICAN DISTRIBUTION OF LONG-HAIRED SPECIES

Coyote

Gray Fox

Arctic Fox

Red Fox

Bobcat

Lynx

Hunting for predator hides offers challenges to even the most proficient hunter. What may be useful for whitetails is not always enough to outsmart a crafty coyote in its own environment.

Chapter 2

The Cunning Coyote

Ask any school kid and he will tell you what characterizes the coyote: his plaintive howl. It is this howl that causes the hairs on the back of even an experienced woodsman's neck to stand on end as night descends; and it is this howl that has given the coyote names like "prairie yodeler."

Coyotes have long fascinated man. Ernest Thompson Seton, the famous naturalist-turned-writer, said that the number of primitive animals ranged in the millions. Bounties were paid on these canids up until recent times, and in some areas there is still pressure to kill the animal on sight. Even today the coyote is our most abundant long-haired species. Over one and a half million are harvested annually for fur. Uncounted-for others are shot by irate sheepmen and varmint hunters. In the face of this, the coyote still thrives and continues to populate our wild lands.

The scientific name for the coyote is *Canis latrans*, "Canis" meaning dog in Latin; "latrans" meaning barking—thus, barking dog. At various times in the history of the species scientists have recognized as many as 16 subspecies of this free-living animal. Coyotes, dogs, wolves and foxes are all members of the larger biological family, *Canidae*, and share similar anatomical traits, the most obvious of which is strong jaws with sharp-pointed teeth. Coyotes are basically smaller than wolves

and are often called "prairie wolves"; foxes are smaller than coyotes.

The coyote is easy to distinguish from the other species. The animal looks like a medium-sized dog, but it is grey or slightly reddish-gray with rusty to greyish legs, feet and ears. In general, the animal bears a warm sienna color with the belly area and throat off-white. When running, it carries its long tail (about a foot or longer) down between its hind legs.

The coyote is well equipped to carry out its scavenging existence. The jaws contain 42 teeth in the characteristic arrangement of canines and molars. This equipment has allowed the coyote to hold onto its ancient hunting grounds despite the intrusive activities of man.

Coyotes have remarkably good senses. Some studies have shown that a coyote can discern within one degree the location of any sound it may hear. This means that at half a mile, the animal knows within 45 feet where a sound is located. This has obvious effects on calling the coyote, and noises made by movement through brush can, unknown to the hunter, alert the animal.

The sense of smell is so highly developed that the animal can live by using this one sense alone. The coyote can detect odor in the air in as little as two or three parts per million. It is for this reason that these dog-like creatures will avoid fresh trails made by man, can sort out the location of carrion in the dead of winter, and can sniff out the homes of thousands of mice and other grass-living rodents.

Eyesight is extremely well developed—certainly better than man's and probably better than most other dogs. Part of this occurs after the pups are born, during the eight- to ten-day period in which they are blind. Nature has simply designed a method of allowing the eyes to develop after other organs have reached their highest degree of development.

The animal's instincts are so acutely developed that it appears to be able to think or reason its way out of a situation. Above all else, this animal can focus attention on any one sense and move that concentration between one sense and another.

With these abilities, it is little wonder that the coyote has survived, prospered and continues to hold man's fascination. It also means that the coyote is a tough quarry that must be thoroughly understood to be hunted successfully.

The coyote is a hardy animal and an efficient predator. It is really a lightweight. A heavy coyote would be 50 or slightly more pounds; most are around 30. A small adult could weigh as little as 20 pounds. This small size is efficiently distributed, the legs are well developed and muscled; the body is small and very lean. Even when a full supply of winter back fat is in place, the coyote is a small, sleek predator. These factors contribute to the animal's thriftiness and its generally tough resilient body.

A coyote puts this efficiently designed body to

As a member of the *Canidae* biological family, the coyote resembles the dog and shares the same general shape and characteristics.

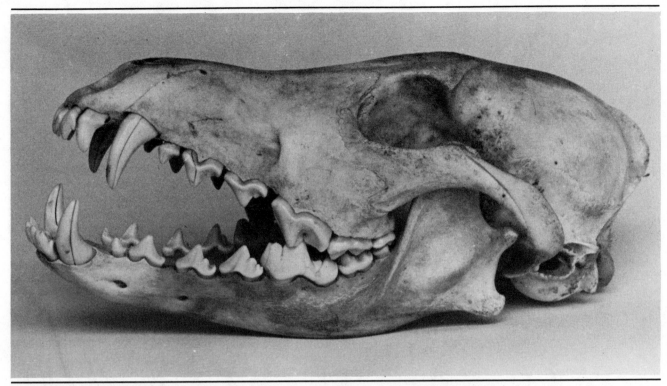

Large canines, well-developed molars and strong jaw muscles provide the coyote with the equipment it needs to handle any kind of meat-eating or scavenging jobs its environment has to offer.

use daily. Coyotes have been clocked at speeds of up to 40 miles per hour, the speed necessary to run down a young antelope or catch up to a snowbound deer. It is the kind of speed needed to overtake a large jack rabbit running for its very life. A coyote, once disturbed, can quit country quickly and will use its speed much the same way an antelope does. It puts distance between the hunter and itself, and it is known that a bothered coyote will run for two or three miles before settling down again.

The coyote is a very social animal. Scientists now recognize four types of groups most often seen in coyote life. The first group is called den breeders. This group, as the name indicates, carries out most of the repopulation that goes on each year. There are also den non-breeders that construct dens but fail to breed in any one year. Nomads are the third group and, basically, these travel the territories of other animals. The last group, called dispersers, will often be seen as the animals occupying new parts of the range or lone animals found in strange or uncommon localities.

Coyotes do not run in packs like wolves. Groupings seen in the field are usually members of the same family. Pairs are most often an adult male and female. Sometimes a yearling animal, usually a female, will be part of the family group. There are also instances where two females will den together and share the raising of the litter. In these cases, only one of the females has the pups. Lone coyotes encountered during hunting are most frequently young males or very old lone males.

Breeding Habits. Thought to be strictly monogamous, coyotes mate for life unless one of the pair is taken. The animals are usually seen in breeding pairs and will hunt, live and run together regardless of the season.

Many believe that the coyote will breed with the wolf. Given the mutual distrust each has for the other, it is difficult to believe that mating could occur. The wolf is twice as big. Besides, the behavior patterns of the wolf are very fixed, whereas the coy-

All the coyote's senses are extremely well-developed, but that of smell is so superior the animal could live by using this one sense alone. Here the animal sniffs along a familiar snow-covered trail.

ote can exhibit a broad range of behaviors and adaptive strategies.

Coyotes breed sometime in late February, and for them breeding and mating is a playful affair. The animals may chase one another, roll in the snow and perform a lot of mock fighting—accompanied by appropriate howling and barking. Re-mating will occur when one of the pair is lost.

The gestation period is about 60 days. Most sources quote 63 days as the upper limit. Anywhere from three to 18 young may be born in the litter, although the average is five or six. The male will usually move away from the den prior to the birth of the young, but does return to help in the feeding of the whelps after they are born. The pups open their eyes about eight days after they are born.

The early spring period is hardest on the animals. When lactation is well under way, stored food reserves are down and the long winter leaves the adults at their most physiologically vulnerable. In addition, as the season advances the pups demand more and more food. Sometimes carrion is carried to the den site. It is not uncommon to find the remains of a dead cow or deer dragged to the den where it is then pre-chewed by the adults and regurgitated for the young. All members of the dog family can regurgitate at will due to the special structure of the esophagus and upper part of the stomach. While for man regurgitation is almost a painful, uncomfortable experience, for the coyote it is a totally natural way to bring food to the young.

Denning is important since it can give a hunter a good indication of the presence of coyotes in an area. The coyote makes a den in the ground if it is relatively soft and easy to dig. The animals will also take over abandoned dens of badgers and sometimes gophers. They seem to prefer a warm, sunny slope. Dens may have several compartments, sometimes one for each of the young pups. There may also be several denning sites—as many as four or five. A smart female will move her young to another one of these prechosen sites if disturbance should warrant such action. Clearly the hunter must be able to distinguish between active dens and those that are only infrequently visited.

Hunters should not disturb such sites. Coyotes will tolerate some outside activity, but this should be kept to a minimum. Observation from a distance is wise. Sometimes coyote females will move den sites because of fleas and ticks. A large number of coyote dens is not always indicative of a good coy-ote population. One source indicates that a single female had 14 den sites, any ready to be occupied at a moment's notice.

The Capabilities To Survive

Coyotes have done well in the north. This is simply because they have evolved to survive the northern winters. The animal is light in weight so that it does not break through the snow. The hide is an incredibly warm, efficient insulator. Claws, teeth and the animal's virtual invulnerability to disease make it well outfitted for survival under these harsh conditions.

Unlike some animals, the coyote does not hibernate or undergo special biological adaptations to face the winter months. The animals do accumu-

The coyote's efficiently designed body enables it to run at speeds of up to 40 miles per hour; it is also capable of great endurance.

A pair is said to mate for life, although there is some evidence to the contrary. Here a mated pair fusses over the den entrance.

late fat prior to the winter season, but they do not go into a deep sleep of any kind. They can hole up for periods of two to three days without eating during the most severe storms and snow conditions. However, following this the animal is anxious to hunt and refill its belly.

The ability of the coyote to live on a variety of foods and its high reproductive rate make the coyote an animal with great biological potential. In good times, many young coyotes will survive to repopulate an area. This means population buildups can be dramatic, with many animals in areas where previously only a few existed years before.

It also means that the coyote can retain its status

A young coyote just out of its den. The short gestation and rapid development of the young means that areas can be quickly repopulated.

that varies from a few square miles to as much as 100 square miles. Later in this book the importance of home ranges and territories to the hide hunter is explained in greater detail. For now, it is enough to say that home ranges show considerable variation. Home range is the larger area over which an animal travels. A territory is the smaller piece of real estate that belongs to that animal only. Groups of animals may share home ranges. There may also be different kinds of territories, the most strictly fought over probably being a breeding territory. Territories encompassing foraging needs are usually large and extensive. They may follow drainages for miles where mice, voles and rodents are in short supply, or they may embrace a few acres where productive rodent patches and rabbit briars exist. They may also change with the seasons.

Tenaciousness is an important quality that enables the coyote to survive the exigencies of wildlife. The animal is tough and can move its sinewy

as a pest species, especially in sheep-producing parts of North America. Cattlemen become concerned when young calves or old, sick range cows fall to this king of the predators. On the plus side, coyotes account for the demise of many more field mice, rodents and voles that most farmers and ranchers would give the animals credit for. Rabbits are also a great coyote food. It is the potential for the coyote to be a menace that has let game managers give the nod to hide hunting and different forms of predator control.

As long as prey species remain in good supply, the coyote rarely becomes the problem it was once considered. In the West, the average coyote density is one animal to every two square miles. In mountain and forested areas, the population is somewhere around one animal per 10 square miles. Recent studies in Texas show that coyote densities vary over a large portion of their range. Animals ran from a low of one per three square miles to a high of one per square mile. In Wyoming on the National Elk Refuge, the population was slightly less than this. Food, weather and other local conditions will determine just how many coyotes live in any one area.

Normally, a coyote will maintain a home range

A young coyote tests its legs near the den site. Some dens may have several compartments, one for each pup.

The home range of a coyote may vary from a few square miles to as much as 100 square miles. Here a thick-furred animal is well-camouflaged in the dry brush of its home range.

body with remarkable speed, strength and endurance. An example that always comes to mind is the time I was working as a biologist in southeastern Alberta. A fellow worker and I came upon a hunter chasing a coyote in an old pickup truck. The chase went on for miles. The hunter, unaware that he was being watched by game officers, followed the animal in a steady half-mile circle over the frozen ground of a large native grass field.

The chase went on for some time, probably half an hour, but the coyote became smart to the whole process after about 15 minutes of intense, high-speed chasing. The animal would simply run 15 or

so feet in front of the truck, using no more speed than was required to keep ahead of the pickup. It would lead the truck in a circle and, when it felt that the truck was getting too close, would turn into the circle and run within a few inches of the truck in the opposite direction. Since the animal was getting winded, it would simply sit down. The operator would have to make a larger turn and then attempt to put the coyote up again. Meanwhile, the coyote had gained some rest and was able to continue the run for its life. The animal showed cunning and great endurance in keeping ahead of the truck. Incidentally, my partner and I intervened in the chase, and the coyote lived—no doubt much wiser about being caught out in the open—to run another day.

Accidents rarely seem to befall the coyote. Road-kill deaths are relatively rare. Drownings, broken bones and various types of hardware disease are quite uncommon. Coyotes have little trouble with fences or other devices unnatural to the animal world. Sometimes the odd coyote will get hung up in some man-made garbage. Coyotes have been found with metal rings or plastic collars around their necks, or have died from becoming entangled in some refuse. These are indeed rare cases—the result of the coyote's innate curiosity and the habitual scavenging of man-made garbage piles.

An external factor that influences survival is that the coyote has few natural enemies. Wolves and coyotes are highly antagonistic. Even though a large coyote is smaller than any adult wolf, these animals seem to have an inbred dislike for each other and either will kill the other given the right circumstances and a good opportunity. Also, the cougar will dispatch any coyote it might catch unawares, although their ranges rarely overlap and naturally occurring encounters are rare.

The odd coyote may become injured in a conflict

Tough northern winters make coyote hair grow long and thick. *Fur-Fish-Game* **writer Bob Gilsvik took this prize during the prime season in northern Minnesota.**

with a deer or elk. A female deer can kick the daylights out of a coyote that tries to get too close, especially during the fawning season. Antelope, too, will charge a marauding coyote. Yet this cunning animal can be successful in preying on big game under conditions of deep snow or when prey are sick or weakened by poor range conditions.

Porcupines are no friends of the coyote, either. Although rarely a problem, quills may be picked up by attacking a live porcupine or feeding on the remains of a road-killed animal. This greatly impedes the normal foraging habits of the coyote. Emaciated, lack-luster coyotes with two or three quills imbedded along the lymph tissue of the mouth and tongue may be found by a hunter who takes a good number of long-hairs during a season.

In some years, nearly half of the annual coyote population is lost to disease and starvation. Fortunately, this does not happen frequently, as the coyote is disease-resistant and a capable predator. In some areas, hunting and trapping can take a large number of the young, especially early in the season. Indiscriminate shooting by varmint hunters and big game hunters may hurt small populations of coyotes, but lack of food is probably the single major factor that limits the population. Shooting disperses the animal to new areas.

Hide Quality

The coyote produces an excellent pelt. The hide is best in the late fall and early winter, and can deteriorate very rapidly after that, depending on the winter and the temperature. The prime season can be very short, but in most years the definition of prime for the coyote is subject to some interpretation and extention by the buyers. Still, in some years, the hide is worthless by the end of December.

The back of the hide is the most important part of the hide. For years the hides were used for little else than decorations, but now long-haired coats have become fashionable items.

The neck and shoulders of the animal are the first to show any sign of rubbing or hair deterioration. This is downgraded by the buyer and becomes more obvious as the season progresses.

In the early years of the fur trade, the coyote was known as the "cased wolf." This was due to the way in which the hide was presented for market by the early Indians and traders. A coyote hide was skinned out like a tube, while the wolves of the day were spread out flat like a beaver or bear. Today, as in the olden days, coyote hides are only accepted in the cased skinned format, a complete description of which is detailed in the next section.

The coyote, more than any other animal, represents the blending together of modern society with an individual species' ability to survive next door. Its merit, in terms of interest to man and hide value, is great. It is an animal worthy of our admiration and our dedication in the hunt.

Chapter 3

The Colorful Fox Species

There are five distinct and recognizable fox species resident in different parts of North America. This in itself is a statement of the animal's ability to adapt and survive in diverse habitats. All of these, save for one, are probably more abundant today than at any time in their previous history.

Most hunters will have the opportunity to hunt primarily the red fox or the gray. In the South, the ranges of the two overlap, but the most widely dispersed is the red fox. The gray fox is confined to an area that solidly covers the eastern and midwestern U.S. The animal only rarely reaches central Canada. On the other hand, the red fox lives throughout all of North America, except for some of the Rocky Mountain country and parts of the central plains. Even in these areas, sightings are becoming more common than they were a generation ago.

The minor foxes, the swift (*Vulpes velox*) and the kit (*Vulpes macrotis*), occur on restricted ranges. The swift can be found on the central plains, while the kit fox prefers the desert country of the south and southwestern U.S. The kit fox is probably the least common of all the fox species. Poisoning campaigns have taken a toll on this animal and in some regions wildlife managers are attempting to restore it to huntable populations.

The arctic fox, a genus (*Alopex lagopus*) wholly distinct from the other foxes, is found only in the extreme north. Its habitat is confined to the great shield region of Canada and Alaska. For most southern hunters it will be a species only dreamed about, but for the serious northern hunter, the arctic fox is a valuable fur and a prized trophy.

In size, the red is the largest, with the arctic variety coming in second. Some gray foxes may be slightly longer, but in terms of body weight, the red and arctic would top out at 15 pounds. The lightest would be the kit, which would barely reach six pounds. Many large gray foxes would equal the reds, but the overall average would be slightly lighter.

The kit fox and its arctic relative are at opposite poles in anatomical development. The small kit fox features a slender body with long ears, long limbs and a thin coat. On the other hand, the arctic fox has a compact body, short, stubby, rounded ears, and is heavily furred. The other foxes are intergradations between these two extremes. The limb and appendage size is related to the surface area of the animal and the energy budget needed to keep the animals alive under greatly differing conditions.

Foxes are not particularly strong, and they have been compared to house cats in strength. As well, a fox does not have the endurance of the coyote or either of the wildcats. The fox relies more on escape

Although foxes are agile creatures, they are more fragile than either coyotes or wildcats.

routes and quick moves in its evasive strategies. It will roll out to the side of a pursuing coyote. On the endurance side, a pack of dogs can easily bring a fox to bay, although the animal may have covered several miles circling in the same territory.

Foxes are really delicate animals. Farm dogs, especially those with any hound breeding, are stark enemies of the fox. In the north, a lynx will take a young fox, and in the south, an adult bobcat will waste no time in dispatching foundling foxes. Cougars are also unfriendly, as are any of the birds of prey.

Eating Habits. The foxes are capable predators, however. Their long, sharp teeth help them survive throughout the summer on a mixed diet of mice, rabbits and the odd game bird. Where possible, woodchucks, chipmunks and gophers make up part of the catch. Foxes will feed on road-killed carrion, and nesting birds with their eggs are also taken when available.

All of the foxes will eat berries. In the north service berries are readily consumed, and in the south garden variety berries will be nibbled when the foxes pass on patrol for rabbits. Grapes, apples, pumpkin and potatoes have also been found in limited amounts in the diets of different foxes over the years.

From an agricultural point of view, foxes will stage forays into the chicken coop. Young pigs are also taken where the right conditions prevail. Livestock are rarely bothered by the fox, but any dead animals or afterbirth will be eaten. Dead chickens are frequently carried off to a den or cached for later use. A fox likes to roll in the remains of its various kills.

The fox probably does more good than harm, however. Great quantities of mice and voles are consumed. Insects and soil grubs are also eaten. Rabbits that do damage to farm gardens are kept in check, and rats that inhabit old and abandoned farm buildings are also cleaned up by foxes and their young.

All the foxes maintain home ranges that are commensurate with available food. A red fox will nightly cover three or four square miles hunting mice during the summer and fall. This quickly extends to several dozen square miles in the winter. Recorded known movements of red foxes have been over 125 miles. Gray foxes have been reported to move over 50 miles. Even though the gray will cover home ranges about the same expanse as the red, it prefers territories that are more wooded, marshy and enclosed.

The arctic fox has the largest home range and will follow lemming populations, moving into areas where these famous northern vole-like creatures are in abundance. This is especially true in the tundra regions. In more southern areas, arctic foxes will follow the habits of reds and grays.

Interestingly, arctic foxes usually display great movements. The early literature referred to these as migrations, but they were probably young animals responding to the need to establish their own home ranges. In 1978 I observed an arctic fox just ten miles north of the international boundary between Canada and the U.S. This is extremely far south for such a fox, but it was no doubt responding to the harsh winter environment farther north.

Breeding and Denning. The gestation period is just over 50 days for the average fox in all the species. Red fox are usually born in March and April, depending on the exact part of the range. Grays are born slightly later in April and early May. The arctic fox leaves things until June, which is understandable given the formidable winters of the Arctic. The swift and kit share April as the month for giving birth.

Litter sizes will vary greatly. At times of food abundance, litter sizes will reach the dozen mark in all the species. Averages are much lower, being around three or four. The pups make great demands on the adults and the male will usually help the female for the first few days after the young are born.

Like its other dog-like cousins, foxes also maintain several reserve dens for ease in flight from disturbances. A female will move her litter quickly and efficiently, with little provocation necessary to send her on her way.

Preferred denning sites are usually around old abandoned buildings, garbage dumps and farm sites. The spaces under the floor of some granaries and outbuildings are also sought after. Sometimes animals will go unnoticed by locals for years unless a chicken is found missing. Like the coyote, a fox will take over a badger den, especially one that has been built along the foundation of a building. Soft soil areas, rocky dens, old logs, hollow trees, dense

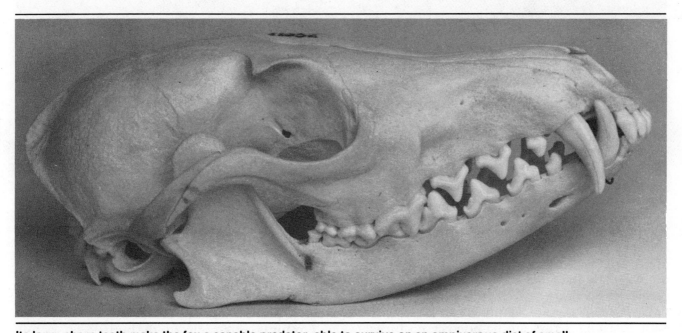

Its long, sharp teeth make the fox a capable predator, able to survive on an omnivorous diet of small rodents, birds, carrion, eggs as well as wild berries and other fruits and vegetables garnered at neighborhood farms.

Foxes are notoriously brazen, and even though they are leery of humans, they may be seen searching for food during the day despite their nocturnal or early morning preferences.

shrub patches and road cuts have all been used by the fox for denning.

Hunting Foxes

To the hunter, be prepared for a challenging experience. Of all the foxes, the red is most comfortable living next to man. Grays are certainly more secretive and the other foxes are very leery of humans. A red fox may be seen during any part of the day, although the animal prefers to hunt in the early morning. Grays are notoriously nocturnal. Red foxes will boldly walk into a farmyard and drink from the stock watering trough. Some have

been brazen enough to eat from the farm dog's bowl.

A gray fox will climb a tree when necessary to escape detection. The red will use fallen trees to break spoor in order to escape dogs in hot pursuit. Arctic foxes will trail wolves and bears for miles, looking for carrion. In short, all the fox species are very conscious about the trails they leave and the paths they walk. A fox will become much more familiar with a small area than a coyote or bobcat. They use this knowledge to escape from predators and in turn to prey on smaller mammals.

Fox fur is certainly worth the hunter's effort, but take care during calling, as the animal will often approach a caller in an uninhibited fashion. A thoroughly scared fox may inflict a nasty bite, and when a fox responds to a dying rabbit call, the animal expects to find its prey at the end of the trail. A cornered fox can give an incredible fight, with quick movements and much tail wringing. So caution should be exercised with this little predator.

Hide Color and Quality

For many years, fox furs were worth very little. They were decidedly out of fashion and suffered from the competition of ranch-reared furs. However, in more recent times the prices have risen, especially considering the size of the fur.

Since the *red fox* is by far the most widespread of all the fox species, the hide from this animal shows considerable variation among the different parts of the country. As with other hides, those taken from the areas farther north tend to grade better than those from the far south.

Generally, the fur is a reddish yellow being darkest on the back and grading into white on the belly. The reddish yellow tail is bushy and mixed with white-tipped black hairs. When properly prepared, these pelts are usually very silky.

However, the red fox can sport three additional color phases, all of which may be found in the same area, and are frequently found in members of the same litter. Some claim this great variation in color is due to the interbreeding of the European red fox with the original East Coast species that was na-

Although evasive and cautious, foxes respond well to calling.

Like the coyote, the fox adapts to harsh winter conditions by growing warm, thick pelage. Bob Gilsvik took this red beauty in southern Minnesota.

tive to North America at the time of the early colonists. No real scientific evidence supports this, but it does make for interesting reading.

Besides the reddish yellow phase, there is a pure *black* or *melanistic phase.* This pelt is similar in hair quality to the red, and the distribution of guard and underfur is the same. It is a very showy hide and the record paid for one of these is 2,625 dollars. That, by the way, was paid by a French fur house back in 1889. Within the black phase there is also a silver phase, so-called from the white-banded guard hairs found on the rump and head regions of the animal. Hides with less silver fur among the black are worth more to buyers.

Another version called the *cross fox* features a cross-shaped band of black hairs down the back and across the shoulders. These animals also have

much more black hair throughout the underfur, and these, too, can be very valuable.

Some areas seem to favor one phase or another. In the Sierra Nevadas, cross-type phases are common. In Alaska, half of the animals annually taken are of one of the phases other than red. Other regions of North America have suffered from the invasion of the natural strains by ranch-reared animals and a few strange color modifications have turned up.

Two other variations of red fox can turn up in the hide hunters take: a "bastard" fox and a "Sampson" fox. The *bastard fox* sports a coat color that is halfway between red and black. It can be described as a pale cross fox. Where the black cross is present on the cross fox, this is replaced by a red cross on the bastard fox. These pelts are handled and sold

Some ladies enjoy the fox hunt as much as the finished product. This fine-haired animal was taken in southwestern Ontario.

with the normal red fox type.

With the *Sampson fox*, Sampson is used to mean "in some respects" a fox pelt. A Sampson pelt lacks guard hairs, and is a curly-looking hide with matted underfur and no long-hairs. As such, it has no value to the hide trade.

In comparison, *gray foxes* tend to have finer hair than the reds. The underfur is usually not as thick and the average skin smaller; the hide is also not as thick. However, there is still a reasonable market for their hides because they can be dyed and used in many articles of clothing. A gray fox hide has a pepper-and-salt colored coat with buffy underfur and a long, bushy tail. There is a black strip down the center of the back and tail.

The *arctic fox* bears beautiful fur of high value,

with pelts that are very thick and silky. In the white phase, the rust-colored summer pelt turns pure white in winter. A blue phase also occurs throughout the range, but is most common on the Pribilofs and in Alaska proper. Its fur is slate blue, but is sometimes marked with brownish head and feet; it turns more brownish or gray in summer. It is worth more than the white, but is also much more scarce. The winter pelage reveals very dense, lush underfur, the most dense of the foxes. Since the white hair stains easily, the hide must be handled carefully and in a clean manner in order to bring top dollar. Both the back and the belly of the fur is used in manufacturing. This is uncommon in long-hairs and accounts in part for the high prices paid for these furs.

Hide buyers are quite cautious when buying fox furs, because the fine guard hairs and dense underfur can easily conceal damage from a bullet hole or a poor repair job. However, a properly repaired hide receives top grade, given good overall appearance. The top hair must have a silky feel, and an experienced buyer will base his decision as much on a quick stroke of the hand as on the appearance and color of the fur. A hide that lacks this silky touch is downgraded. A buyer can feel the wooly underfur as he moves his hand over the pelt. This fur tends to drag on the hand, whereas the long guard hairs let the hand pass quickly and smoothly.

As with all the other long-hairs, rubbing of the shoulder area is the first sign that the hair is starting to lose prime. On some fox, either through a nervous habit or from biting arthropods, bare patches about the size of a quarter show up when the fox bites that area. These batches will greatly affect the price of an otherwise perfect hide. As breeding season approaches, prime condition of the fur is also lost.

The fox species are definitely interesting, and collecting a fur from each species is the hide hunter's fantasy. Although the animals are small, their quick-actioned movements and pleasing colors add an expanded dimension to hide hunting. The fox will be with man for eons to come and in that time a prized fur will always be there for the taking.

Chapter 4

The Wily Wildcats

The two wildcat species of interest to the hide hunter share many similar habits, but differ in hide quality and habitat.

The bobcat is the more abundant species of the two. However, many lynx are taken every year and their fur is very valuable. Hunters throughout northern Canada will often have the opportunity to take both species within the same area. Indeed, in some areas great debate rages among hunters and wildlife biologists about the degree to which these animals interbreed and occupy the same ecological niches.

It is best to begin by distinguishing between these two closely related cousins of the wild. Actually, there are few easily distinguishable field markings that can be seen or sorted out at reasonable hunting distances. Lynx are generally larger, but where subadults are concerned, this is often not enough to separate the species satisfactorily. In the northern parts of the range, the lynx would be slightly paler than the bobcat. In general, the lynx has slightly longer legs, larger feet and longer ear tufts. Pelts taken in the southern areas of the range will show that the bobcat is more spotted than the lynx and slightly more brown in pelage. Again, color and markings show much local variation and no hard and fast rule of thumb can be given to cover all regions.

At close range, one feature does separate the lynx from the bobcat: the coloration of the tail. The lynx has a tail that is completely circled with black, whereas the bobcat's tail is black on top and white below. Other than the area in which the hunting is taking place, this is the only real criterion that can be used to differentiate the two species.

Neither cat is particularly large. A heavy lynx might tip the scales at 40 pounds, while an average weight would run around the 30-pound mark. A bobcat would weigh slightly less, averaging 15 to 30 pounds. The bodies carry very little fat, and most of the weight is tied up in sinewy muscle that is strong, capable and serves the animals well. A 20-pound cat could, for example, kill a big whitetail under the correct conditions.

A lynx or bobcat is not built for long, fast runs. Its compact muscle structure lets it run short distances only. Forty or 50 yards is about the farthest one of these cats will ever run. Many times the animals, if put up from a loafing spot, will run and stop, giving a final look back at the intruder.

Both cats have only 28 teeth, but these are almost as long as those of a 200-pound mountain lion. The canines are well pronounced and can clearly be used for hanging onto prey species. The jaws are muscled and short; the head, compact and strong. They have all the necessary equipment for a life in rugged back country or northern woods.

While the animals do not use their sense of smell to a high degree, the sense of hearing is acute. A call can be heard at greater distances by these animals than by foxes or coyotes. Live and easy meat at the location of the sound is very tempting on a cold winter night. It is also the reason predator calling works so well with the species. Rabbits are a major source of food and it is only logical that every cat has heard a dying rabbit squeak at least once before in its life.

One unique feature of both cats is the presence of ear tufts. For years, natural history buffs and scientists puzzled over the exact function of these little towers of coarse hair that adorn the top of the animals' ears. Some say these aid the hearing abil-ity, acting like antennae to catch and focus distant sounds. Tufts on the lynx are generally twice as long as on bobcats, and some southern bobcats may have only a few hairs serving as tufts. Today scientists are no further ahead in solving the true function of these hairs. Perhaps they serve some tactile purpose, just like whiskers, telling the animal when its ears are in close contact with brush or shrub.

The nocturnal hunting habits of the cats have led to the development of extremely keen eyesight. The diurnal sight of both the lynx and the bobcat is second to no other predator's, and their night vision is on a par with such species as the great horned owl. The cats' eyes adjust quickly to nightfall. In the light of day, the pupil reduces to a nar-

Lynx are generally larger than bobcats, with slightly longer legs, larger feet and longer ear tufts. Note the black tip of the tail, a distinguishing feature from the bobcat.

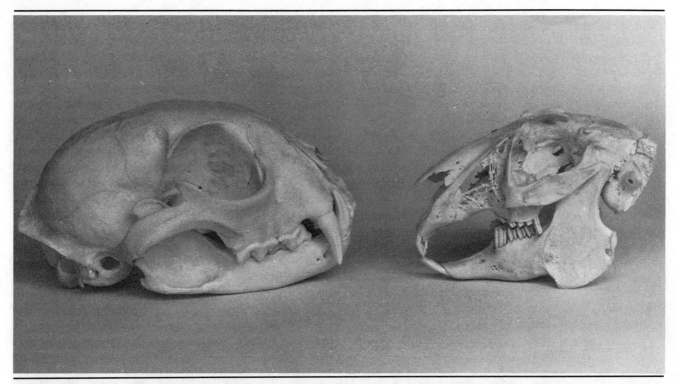

An interesting comparison between the predator and the prey—a lynx skull on the left and a northern hare on the right. Differences in size and strength are obvious.

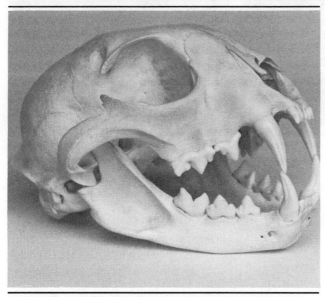

This skull shows the short, compact, yet powerful nature of the bobcat's eating tools. Few prey are match for this muscular predator whose jaws hold 28 intimidating teeth.

row slit; in the dark of night, it opens to fill nearly all of the eye's iris. This allows most of the available light to enter the eye.

The cats' eyes are well outfitted with rods and cone cells. These are the highly specialized light-sensitive receptor cells that translate light wavelengths into neural impulses, which are then transferred to the brain, sorted and sent out as sight. Cats have more rods than other predators, making their eyes more responsive to low light levels and giving the animal tremendous nocturnal seeing ability. Thus, the cats are able to hunt at night with vision that nearly approaches that of the daytime.

What also contributes to their optical superiority is good depth perception, due to both the location of the eyes in the head and their ample size. This means that felines can more readily distinguish the foreground and background features of the landscape. For the hunter, it means greater care must be taken, both in the use of camouflage and in the amount of movement during calling.

The wildcats' eyes are outfitted with highly specialized, light-sensitive receptor cells that equip the animals with vision second to no other predators. Don't be fooled by the pussycat appearance; bobcats and lynx make poor house pets.

Evidence suggests that the cat relies on this excellent sense of sight to sort out danger. Many hunters have had cats spook at some distance when the hunter moved, although he was well hidden in bush and trees. Others have had cats approach from the downwind side when they should have been able to smell the hunter, suggesting that perhaps they were not relying on their sense of smell, but rather on sight. The eyes can pick out the slightest movement and can do this easily and quickly. Once visual contact is made, the animal wastes little time in quitting country.

Breeding Habits. Unlike the coyotes, the wildcats do not mate for life or spend much time together. The only time the two sexes come together is during the short winter breeding season, and if a male can find them, he'll breed several females. Sometimes bobcats will remain together with the young from one litter, forming a family group, but this is uncommon.

Breeding is a typical cat affair with much growling, caterwauling and hissing. The animals rub one another or some nearby vegetation just like a domestic cat prior to breeding. Most females breed at two years of age, although under poor food conditions, this may be delayed. The sex ratio favors the males slightly, so it is possible that not all sexually mature males will breed in any given year. Breeding takes place during February in most parts of the range, but it may continue into early summer. This, in turn, means that the young are born at various times of the year. It is not unusual for a hunter to see very young cats responding to a call in the fall of the year.

The young are born in dens that may be in any type of rough habitat. Gestation is 60 days and the litter may range from one to seven, with the average being one or two. The female will bring meat to the den site. Sometimes she will bring half-live mice and rodents for the young to practice on. Other times, she will drag whole carcasses for miles to the mouth of the den for the young to feed on. Interestingly, at birth a baby lynx may weigh as little as eight ounces, but by fall may weigh 10 pounds or slightly more.

The male of both species will kill the young of the year if they can be found. This is a bizarre habit that biologists have not really fully explained and

Both cats hunt by stealth, using their exceptional sight and hearing to locate prey. They will stalk closely, especially rabbits, then pounce quickly.

one for which no biologically sensible answer seems to exist.

The post-lactation period is very crucial for bobcats and lynx. A failure in the food supply at this time of year means the young cats will starve to death.

One myth surrounding wildcats is that young kittens make good pets. Although friendly at first, kittens taken from their mother may become as wild and unpredictable as their adult counterparts. Friends who have tried to domesticate these animals say that the cats become aloof and unfriendly after the age of six months. Impossible to discipline, the cats become household nuisances and have to be returned to the wild.

Feline Life-styles

The life-styles of the bobcat and lynx are remarkably similar. Both are powerful hunters that will eat a wide range of meat items. Diets are therefore slightly more restrictive than those of the coyote or the fox, but may include many of the same species. In the summer months, birds and especially eggs and young nestlings are favored foods. Both of these wildcats will consume carrion when necessary, but both prefer live meat.

Both cats hunt by stealth, using their exceptional sight and hearing to help locate prey. They will stalk closely, especially rabbits, and make a quick pounce. If a chase is needed, either cat is capable of topping 30 miles per hour over a short stretch. Usually, a few quick powerful bounds will capture the prey. The cats' excellent protective coloration helps in the stalking procedure also.

Unlike coyotes and foxes, male and female cats do not hunt together. Solitary hunting habits are the norm. A favored hunting technique is to wait in ambush by climbing a tree and pouncing on passing deer or other smaller prey. A cat can hunt for days in this manner and expend very little energy in the effort.

As mentioned, the cats hunt at night, although hunger can send the animals out at any time of the day. This is especially true in the winter when little daylight and long nights make hunting unrelated to the time of day. These felines are very secretive and capable of living next to man, unnoticed, for years. In the boreal forests of the north where the lynx is king, hunting times are determined by hunger, rather than avoidance of man and dogs.

The animals show considerable caution in just what they hunt and the conditions under which the different prey are taken. Porcupines are avoided, since the quills can penetrate deeply, sometimes killing a young cat by damaging internal organs. Skunks, too, are largely bypassed, although they are easy prey.

Wildcats rarely dig out rodents. In the south, the bobcat will scratch after pack rats, but this usually does not involve moving much earth. Unlike the canids, the cats have retractile claws, which make them inefficient diggers; so most rodents that make the den entrance are safe from further pursuit.

Any game animal, however, especially the young of the year or the infirm, is usually an easy target for the quick-moving cats. In the north, moose calves may fall prey to hunting lynx, and in the

Bobcats and lynx are both solitary hunters that show considerable caution in what and under what conditions they stalk. Once killed, a carcass is returned to until the bones are licked clean.

Predator specialist Ed Sceery holds a bobcat he called in with calls made of his own design. The animal had staked out a territory that included regular visits to this boulder-strewn part of the range.

Hunting wildcats requires great patience and hunter acumen. Dennis Seline used a hound to track down this bobcat near Effie, Minnesota.

south, a bobcat is a successful predator of antelope and deer fawns. When times are tough, either cat may shift to a diet of carrion and waste. Cattlemen who own calving yards within areas of bobcat habitat may find cats developing a taste for veal. Ranches and farms farther north are also routinely checked by resident lynx on the lookout for any easy meal. During long, cold winters, either cat will rob traps baited for other species, especially ermine. Miscellaneous foods may include fish carrion, insects, and green grass that provides bulk and a source of vitamins.

In the far north, just south of the extreme northern edge of the boreal forest, the lynx lives largely on snowshoe hare during the winter. An interesting balance exists where forestry operations occur and create a thriving habitat for mice, voles and other ground-living foragers. These are the areas that become preferred habitat for the lynx, and are also superb calling sites for hunters intent on col-

lecting the desirable lynx furs.

There is a widely held belief among hunters and naturalists that the cats will not return to eat on freshly killed animals. This is true in only the most extreme cases of game abundance. Usually, a cat will return to a carcass and feed daily until the bones are licked clean. Many will continue to visit such sites, rolling in the remains and gnawing on bones and scraps of hide for months to come. Carcasses often become territorial markers.

Another means used to mark out territories and home ranges is to leave scrapes, which all the cats do. Claw marks are also found on rotted stumps and logs. An anal exudate is used to mark more serious territorial boundaries, as is urine and scrapes that have been rolled and fussed over. Scats will often be found that are partly covered with scratch marks and vegetation surrounding these sites is disturbed. Hair, especially in the late winter, may also mark out a boundary.

Territories vary. Lynx, for example, may set out 50 or 60 square miles of habitat as a private hunting area. Within that zone, several hunting routes would be preferred, but the entire territory would be routinely covered in the span of a fortnight. Bobcats, on well-outfitted summer ranges, will meet all their needs in as little as one square mile. Winter territories will expand until the food requirement is met. In rough country, hunters should watch for prey species, such as rabbits and various game birds. Compared to the coyote, territories are far more rigidly delineated, and intrusion is not tolerated. The strictly carnivorous existence of these animals has meant that territories must fulfill very special needs. While the size of the ranges may vary, they are generally much larger than those required by the coyote or fox.

Compared to the bobcat, the demands of habitat and territory are slightly greater for the lynx. It is considered to be the less flexible in its food habits and behavior patterns of the two cats. Fortunately, the lynx has learned to live in the remote reaches of northern Canada and Alaska where the influence of man, while present, is still minimal compared to that experienced by the coyote in the southern regions.

Both wildcats are susceptible to various types of accidents. One scientific study suggested that accident is indeed a major population regulator in these animals. Some pitfalls include breaking through the ice during the early part of winter, broken limbs that might occur when leaping onto prey from high places, or damage from porcupine quills picked up from scavenged animals.

The bobcat and lynx have few enemies. Dogs do not give these animals any problem. The same applies to coyotes. Wolves will challenge the young where the ranges overlap, but few references are present in the natural history literature indicating that this happens with any frequency. Bears will take the young, but this again would have to be incidental to other hunting on the part of the bear.

Bounties have existed on the bobcat since 1727, although none are known for the lynx. However, population levels for both wildcats are probably better today than at any other time. The lynx has been pushed back from some of its traditional haunts, such as Indiana and Pennsylvania. This has been balanced off with increases throughout the Yukon and other parts of northern Canada; also Idaho, Washington and parts of Oregon. There may be some in the Upper Peninsula area of Michigan and Wyoming is home to a few now, too.

Bobcat populations are doing well. While the wildcat species do not show the population resiliency of the canids, one source indicates that there are probably as many bobcats today as when the Pilgrims arrived. Bobcat numbers may be down in local areas, but in general the species has not yet retreated from the largest part of its native ranges. Several thousand are harvested every year. In some areas, in fact, the animals have been given game species status.

Notes to Hunters

Hunting bobcat and lynx requires great patience on the part of the hunter. Regardless of the area hunted or the technique used, both cats make special demands on the hunter's skill and knowledge.

The cats are so secretive that they are only rarely encountered in the open. Indeed, northern bushmen still measure the skill of fellow woodsmen by the number of bobcats they have seen.

Many hunters believe the bobcat or lynx does not use the sense of smell. It is perhaps not as well developed as in the coyote or fox, but the animal can sniff out rodents and mice that hide in the grasses. Both cats will react strongly to crossing a human scent trail. They will also circle, attempting to approach anything suspicious from a face-into-the-wind position. While the cats may not rely on the sense of smell to the same degree as the canids, it is still well developed and very useful in their day-to-day survival. A hunter should not discount the sense of smell.

One deeply interesting aspect of behavior that is important to the hide hunter is the cat's love of catnip. Catnip is derived from a plant (*Nepeta cataria*), which is common in Europe and Asia and has invaded North America. Early circus workers found that any member of the cat family fed pastes made with catnip became more manageable and friendly. All noticed that the animals were attracted to the odor of this plant. It wasn't until 1923 that the oil of catnip was derived from the wild plants. Hunters, especially those interested in

Wildcats are so secretive that northern bushmen still measure the skill of fellow woodsmen by the number of bobcats they have seen. Tony Garnier (right) took this prime bobcat with the aid of guide and hide man Joe Orth.

calling. Territories are large, especially in the north, and a cat's food supply will take in a lot of country during the prime winter season. Sign is difficult to find during most of the year, but winter will let the hunter plainly see any well-traveled trails the animal has forged. Trails are particularly important to the bobcat and the lynx, as both animals will routinely stick to such paths throughout the winter. This is especially true if the hunting has been rewarding and there is little need to extend the hunting range.

When calling from either a blind or a well-located stand, more time should be given to the calling effort and a sharp eye kept to catch a glimpse of the approaching animal. Cats have little to fear in their natural environment, and will use all the time necessary to approach the sound of wounded prey. Few other animals will beat them to the distress call, so they take their time. Sometimes calling for as much as twice what is recommended for the other predators is needed. Cats approach a call very slowly and cautiously, just like a barnyard cat making a stalk on a mouse, or a house cat playing with a ball of paper. More on calling in Chapter 9.

If a cat is not hungry, it might approach the call in an unorthodox manner. Sometimes a cat will stop and roll around in the snow 60 or 70 yards from the caller. Others will growl or hiss, oftentimes giving the hunter a scare that gets adrenalin flowing and stands the hair up along the back of the neck. With cats, expect the unexpected and plan for it to take some time to occur.

Hide Quality

The fur of the bobcat and lynx are similar in many respects. Currently, color is important and, as with all furs, the handling must be excellent to realize high prices.

Comparatively speaking, the lynx has traditionally been more valuable than the bobcat. Because of its northern existence, the fur is, of course, thicker, more luxurious, and features longer guard hairs. The bobcat of the northern ranges, however, does compare favorably with the lynx. For many, including experienced fur buyers, it would be difficult to differentiate two well-prepared specimens.

The winter pelage of the lynx bears soft, thick

predator control in the wool-growing west, were some of the first to use the oil as a lure.

Catnip seems to excite the cats sexually. It also tends to sedate the animals somewhat and the odor is sought out by them. Catnip oil can be used to lure an animal into an area or be put into bait that is set out to attract a cat.

A hunter can make his own catnip by acquiring the plant and boiling the leaves. When the leaves are rendered to a pulpy paste, it is ready to use. Some hunters grow a few plants of catnip in their home gardens and follow this recipe. This provides a cheap, available source of supply for the winter months. The actual oil of catnip is perhaps better than the homemade paste, but leaves plucked during the summer and placed in plastic bags, stored until winter, and rendered by boiling are sufficient for most practical purposes. Catnip in a manufactured form is available in most pet stores.

Wildcat country must be well scouted prior to

fur, with hairs as much as four to five inches long. The colors range from light shades of gray sprinkled with brown spots to almost a lavender tint. Sometimes many pastel colors are seen. A blue hued mutation is also evidenced in one out of every 2,000 or so furs. It is much more gray than a normal skin and may have black portions in the fur. Lynx is a highly prized fur used for trimming coats or in stoles. At one time, it was considered fashionable "après ski" wear by the ritzy European ski crowd.

Bobcat fur can also show much local variation. Color may vary from a dark gray in the forest regions of the U.S. and Canada to pale, clear-colored furs in the west. In all areas experiencing cold winters, the fur is slightly more gray than in the summer and features fewer spots and more bars. Black or melanistic cats have also been reported in the

In grading the fur of bobcat or lynx, the belly fur is a good indicator of the state of the back. It must be thick and long, and clear-colored without reddish or brownish tones. In addition, it should have good fur flow.

scientific literature. It is a beautiful fur and in many areas considered a valuable hunting prize. It will often be seen adorning the walls of hunting cabins and lodges throughout the country.

Southern bobcats became valuable during the early 1970s when trade in leopard and other cats was stopped by the successful lobbying of the antitrapping, antihunting factions of the day. The spotted back of the bobcat and the lynx were eagerly sought after and were the reason for some of the higher bidding at the international auctions. Buyers were also trying to signal all types of fur takers to bring in such furs and this pushed prices at northern auctions to $300 and $400 when only a year before a third that amount would have been considered good. This interest in the bobcat has continued.

In grading the cats, condition of the belly fur is important. It must be thick and long, and clear colored without reddish or brown, dog-like tones. The condition of the belly is usually a good guide to the state of the back.

Top money goes to the fur that has what graders or buyers call good fur flow. This is determined by passing the hands over the belly, then over the back. A high-quality fur will have hair that bounces back as the hand is passed over. It will be thick and silvery.

Rubbing is obvious to see in these pelts. It is the long, silky part of the hair that is rubbed off easily and, as a result, both lynx and bobcat may lose their prime condition very quickly. The skin part of the hide may also crackle when moved and this will indicate weakness to the fur.

The wildcats are interesting animals. Their secretive habits and great fear of man have restricted their species to the last wild habitats in North America. For the hunter, either cat is a tremendous trophy and a valuable addition to the hide pole. They can be particularly lucrative species, and in some years astounding takes can be made from relatively small areas.

Chapter 5

Locating Long-Hairs

Looking for long-hairs, the actual seeking out of the animals, harbors no deep secrets or mystery. All that is really needed is knowledge of the animals, their habits, the territory and the pluck to put it all together. Any hunter worth his salt knows that scouting, or the physical looking for the animal, is a necessary task for the hunt to be successful. Looking for long-hairs can be done at any time, either before the season, during the season, or while actively hunting. In short, the long-hairs are present, the hunter need only to look.

Long-hairs have spread throughout North America. For example, coyotes originally moved into the wilder areas of the continent around the turn of the century. In the far north, they eventually out-competed the wolf in all but the most fierce and remote habitats. As well, the animals spread east of the Mississippi River as settlement pushed westward. Other fur bearers could not take the unrelenting pressure of life next to man, but the coyote actually prospered; today's coyotes are even found throughout the New England states.

The coyote spread because of a genetic flexibility that few other animals possess. There is little doubt in the minds of biologists who study the matter that the coyote we shoot at today in no way resembles the animal of the past century. Man has honed the animal's cunning, improved his ability to live in the scavenge of western society and, somehow, has trained the animal to realize when man is dangerous and when he is innocuous.

Other factors have contributed. One is the actual reduction of the rural population in western farming country. At one time, when large families farmed every other quarter section of land and the price of hides was high, the coyote lived under great stress. Pressure arose because those large families shot the rabbits that were a major food source for the coyote. For many years and even now, farm families have been on a decline with fewer active farmyards every year. Farms are now larger, and human contact with wild animals is reduced. This has allowed the coyote to creep back into its former haunts. Better economic times have also removed the rabbit as table fare for most rural families. Food species for the coyote, especially the rabbit, have entered a more stable stage in their population cycle. The result of the interaction of these factors is that coyotes have returned in ever greater numbers, surviving with a new cunning and greater adaptability to the ways of man.

Foxes have followed a similar pattern, but this species has an edge, having evolved next to man for eons of time. With four, separate, free-living species, the fox has occupied any combination of habitat with man that North America has had to offer.

In the far north, where there were few men, the arctic fox has thrived next to generations of hunting Eskimos and hard-living northern Indians. The dry south developed its own fleet-footed version called the kit fox, and the gray fox made its home in the comfortable eastern woods. The red fox has become the most cosmopolitan.

The red fox has survived in much the same manner as the coyote. Using its centuries-old cunning, the red fox is an opportunist that can transform almost anything into a nutritious meal. The animal will adapt to a wide variety of diets from insects and

Be sure to check all types of country. Most predators will space themselves out across the available range and will hunt every area within their home range.

Predators continually pass through the different parts of their range, checking for food and expanding their hunting territory. Prominent areas should be checked for any sign. Include regular stops at such places during your hunting activity.

berries in season to rabbits and carrion in winter. This has made it natural to follow man westward in his drive for settlement.

Fox hides were in demand well before coyote skins were popular. Their durable, yet soft and dense fur was wanted for ladies' stoles, jackets and short coats. In 1929, just before the stock market crash, an average fox hide sold for 50 dollars. In Europe the fox was relentlessly pursued both for its skin and for sport. The fox has always been in demand wherever man existed and, in short, the animal has survived a longer, more heavily hunted and harried existence next to man than its cousin, the coyote.

It is probably because of this long relationship that foxes continue to work the cultivated fields next to our major cities for their daily ration of mice

or other rodents. They have learned to cope with man and his activities in a modern-day environment. This adaptability has allowed the fox to disperse over most of the country and permitted the many species to find their ecological niches next to the super predator.

It is this spread of fox and coyote that makes today's hide hunting possible. Previously, fluctuating population numbers due to any number of reasons, including the sporadic occurrence of adverse environmental conditions, prevented large concentrations of the animals. Now that populations are well established, hide hunting has become viable as a sport and for the serious pursuit of long-haired pelts for profit. A plentiful supply of animals of all the long-haired species ensures this type of hunting.

The Territorial Imperative

Predatory species are strongly territorial in their intra-specific behavior. This means that each animal of the species sets out a piece of real estate that belongs to it alone. An animal sets out a territory to meet certain specific needs: food, shelter, water and, at the correct time of year, a mate to reproduce the species. Needs change as the seasons change. Larger feeding territories are required during the winter simply to survive. Behavior may change. The territories may be more weakly defended or food shared. Hunting may also be shared. However, no matter what the situation, all predators establish territories. Biologists call this the territorial imperative.

Knowing that the predators have a natural tendency to space themselves out across the available country is of great help to a hunter. It means that each territory houses an individual. As such, individual traits learned through various experiences of the animal will influence how the animal ultimately behaves. How it hunts, how it responds to sight, smell, and noise stimuli, and where it goes can reveal incredible individual variation.

For this reason, a detailed knowledge of the countryside is mandatory for predator hunting. Territories must include the things an animal needs. River banks, highways, railroads and other features of the landscape will many times set the edges of territories. A river may be used to drink from, at least at very specific places, or a highway may yield a good return of carrion through road kills and garbage; railroad bed grades may produce more mice than a nearby summer-fallowed field. An animal living by its wits knows these things.

Territorial Boundaries. Check out the possible boundaries of territories by looking for tracks along the river bank or edge of the road. Soft, dusty, little-traveled back country roads will often yield a few tracks along their margins. Begin by checking these, and note where the tracks veer and the country that lies beyond. In the west, this will most often be a coulee or a draw. In bush country, tracks will usually turn in toward paths or travel runways through briars and tangles.

All predators spend hours patrolling or searching the boundaries of their territories, forever attempting to pick up new scents. They will regularly pass through areas where some new attractant has caught its attention in the recent past. Note, too, that predators will continue to return to a kill site long after any remains of a meal have been cleaned up. Checking or testing their own boundaries also provides a way in which a territory can be expanded. Many coyotes and foxes display incredible curiosity. Bobcats are extremely curious, too. These animals will frequently check such things as culverts, irrigation structures, abandoned vehicles or farm machinery. Old farm garbage dumps and abandoned yard sites are excellent points to begin looking for these animals.

Fence-lines and hedge rows are also good places to comb. Hedge rows, stone walls and old-style wooden snow fences along railway right of ways provide homes for numerous mice and rabbits. As these are preferred foods, both coyote and fox will actively hunt along these structures. Check for hair, tracks and loafing spots.

In some areas, hay bales will inadvertently be left out in the fields. As winter approaches, the bales trap snow and become warm niches for mice and voles. Coyote families will move into such areas, incorporating these fields into parts of the home range. Many adult male coyotes will use bales as marker posts, outlining the boundaries of the territory or the winter home range. Calling near such areas or hunting around such places will produce long-hairs on many occasions.

Proverbial Sign Posts. Game biologists always look for the presence of the animal's scat. The condition of the scat, whether fresh or old, will give a good indication of when the animal was in the area. The quantity of the stuff will also give some idea of how frequently the site is visited. A significant amount of scat heaped into a little pile or with several scratch marks in the soil usually indicates that this is a territorial marker. In such cases, it will be only a matter of time before the animal will return to check the sign post.

Locating two or three sign posts will always help find the animals. Some places to look for these clues include hay bales or forage stacks left out in the field or any other place where fresh-cut hay is stored in the open. Small rock piles along the edges of farm fields and the corners of adjoining fields are also likely places for this kind of sign. These are homes for mice in both winter and summer, so these will be hunted by all the predators in the course of checking or expanding a territory.

Throughout the East, stone walls and split rail fences abound. While many of these are being removed and replaced with more practical fencing, these structures provide excellent game habitat and shelter for foxes and coyotes. Nearly always there is a tangle of vegetation and shrub in and around these walls. Rabbits love the briar and tangle. Foxes and coyotes will den in these areas or loaf in shade or the warmth of these areas at all times of the year. It is also from these bases that foxes will stage raids on the nearest chicken coops.

Throughout the dry west, knowing the location of watering sites, such as dugouts, stock watering tanks, windmills and their water troughs will help any long-hair hunter. These are often incorporated into the predator's territory and he often hunts around them. In the summer, dead insects on the surface of the water serve as an easy source of protein. Foxes and coyotes will readily water at these sites. Many more will loaf near these or sit in the shade of the troughs. On particularly hot days, an individual animal may lay on the cooler mud shore of a dugout or water hole. Nearly all predators are on the lookout for the young of the dozens of shore birds that live around such places. Always check any soft spots for tracks, and look for recent signs of a kill.

Irrigation ditches are patrolled by bobcats, coyotes and foxes. High country reservoirs that feed the irrigation lands below are frequently used by the bobcat as a single water source. Once the ditches are dry following the completion of the year's irrigation, foxes will routinely check the bottom for voles and mice. Rabbits will make homes in the edges or banks of the ditch and any irrigated hay field is sure to have an abundance of prey spe-

Fence-lines are excellent places to check for long-haired animals because they often provide homes for mice and other rodents. Coyotes and foxes will actively hunt these structures, so check for hair, tracks and loafing spots.

Be sure to comb snow-choked fence-lines during the winter for tracks and evidence of predators. Many predators routinely patrol fence-lines throughout their home ranges.

During the winter, predators will move to include special areas in their territories. This open grain pile is home to dozens of mice and was visited daily by a half-dozen different animals. The warm grain and easy hunting were no doubt attractions.

cies spread throughout. Always check these areas for sign of recent predation and tracks.

Crop lands can also be useful for the fox and coyote. The edges of fields or the headlands, as they are called, will hold fox and coyote sign. Most fur seasons occur after a crop has been taken from such fields. Grain spills or crop missed in harvesting at the corners or edges of the field become home for numerous mice. Coyotes will check these spots. Foxes will often bed right down in the spilled grain or a missed swath. They will also use the straw left behind for bedding sites, sometimes staying in a given field for days if the hunting is going good and the weather favorable.

Predator Movement

Once a hunter understands territoriality in the predator and how it relates to the specific environment, it is easy to understand the how and why of predator movements. The fact that animals move in fairly predictable ways is the reason hide hunting is successful. Animals are committed to movement. They must move to hunt, to find shelter, to find mates and to escape danger. The well-developed capability to move is characteristic of the predator.

Predators have very strict travel lanes or corridors. Some of these routes are used frequently, others only during escape. Hunters can successfully determine how an animal will move given a certain situation, and if familiar enough with the country, to where the animal is most likely headed.

Travel lanes are usually associated with the roughest spots in the habitat. A coyote will follow the edge of a coulee for miles at a time, watching the upland and the lowland while moving. Foxes frequently cling to the edge of cultivated fields and will rarely expose themselves in the open. Bobcats will hang to the roughest and most severe habitat an area has to offer.

In areas where winter wheat and fall rye are common crops, the tracks left by the disker, or whatever seeding implement was used, will become travel lanes for all the long-haired species. Snowmobile tracks that become hard-packed are used by all predators. Some will follow these routes right into towns and farmyards. These are factors to keep in mind during the hunting process.

Movements will vary with the seasons. In the prime fox and coyote country where I hunted, winter movements were far less frequent and yet of greater duration than those at other times of the year. For the animal this saved energy, but for the hunter it meant more patient calling and closer watching of the countryside. In the summer, it was possible to see one of the predators standing at the

Stock watering tanks are important watering sites for all predators. In the late fall when cold nights lightly freeze the water surface, predators shift their drinking times to late afternoon after the warm sun has melted the ice.

edge of a field. However, by January a hunter would almost have to step on a coyote to get the animal to move out of its chosen bed.

By now, every hunter knows that animals move more at different times of the day. Mornings, especially in the warm season, are preferred. Evenings are likewise favored. However, in the winter, most predators will delay movement if the weather is bad. Peak activity on a cold Saskatchewan morn-

ing is more toward mid-morning than at daybreak, for example.

Movements are, in part, determined by the countryside. Rivers are barriers, while highways may improve the travel opportunities for an animal.

Movements are also influenced by the condition of the territory. Any field that has been hayed will have mice that are busy building nests throughout the fall and early winter. Hay fields will have more mice than cultivated fields. Predators will move to include such areas in their fall and early winter home ranges. Mice construct their wintering nest from lost hay and vegetative debris. The long-hairs will spend hours searching through the snow in such fields, only too willing to dig out the wintering occupant and have a quick meal.

High-Yield Garbage Dumps. One area that is nearly always included in the circuits made by the long-haired species is the garbage dump. Foxes and coyotes will scavenge such areas with an abiding interest that will seem fascinating, not to mention productive, for the hunter.

Many dumps are located in rough country or waste areas in an out-of-the-way part of the farm. Sometimes a slough will be nearby, or at least a coulee and some trees. Nearly every farm in North America has a special spot that has been used to dump the family refuse. Many of them have been in use for generations. Coyotes will visit these, and in many instances den near such places. Foxes will also frequent them. Any bobcat that becomes a visitor to such sites invariably becomes a pest problem. Strange as it may seem, these wild animals are fascinated by shiny tin cans and discarded bits of non-degradable plastic. The natural history literature is replete with references to predators seen playing with such garbage.

Part of the advantage of hunting farm waste sites is that few are visited frequently. A farmer, unlike his city cousin, takes garbage out to the dump only a few times a year. Compare this activity with an urban dump site and it is little wonder that coyotes and foxes will readily include a visit to back country dumps on a routine basis.

One hunter of my acquaintance plotted the farm

Travel lanes that are habitually coursed will usually be associated with the roughest part of the habitat.

A typical farmyard garbage site. Note the old cow bones in the foreground. These bones were visited throughout the winter by a dozen different coyotes.

garbage dumps on a topographical map of his area. Since the farms were small, averaging about 200 acres, he had pinpointed dozens of sites. Each morning he would visit selected spots that showed recent activity and try his luck. His success, especially during the coldest part of the winter, was nothing short of phenomenal.

In many places, he was able to set up permanent stands from which he either called or perused the area. He had access routes to the dumps all thought out, and was able to approach from existing cover or with favorable winds. His mixed bag of foxes and coyotes was taken strictly on his terms and often under near ideal shooting conditions.

Many big game seasons offer a microcosm of the farm garbage dump in the form of field dressing remains. Deer, moose and caribou innards are sought-after food during the fall and winter big game seasons. For the predators, it is much easier eating than rooting out fat field mice from under snow or dead vegetation. Some hunters claim that the predators will not each such carrion, because the smell of man pervades the area around the gut pile. This has not been my experience or the findings of hunting friends. It is true that on some occasions big game innards remain untouched for days, but more often than not, it is because the animals have not yet found the gut pile, or there are simply no predators within the immediate vicinity. During the winter months when food is in scarce supply, coyotes and foxes waste no time in locating such table fare and converting it to much needed energy.

Following the close of a short five-day pronghorn antelope hunting season, I was out hunting coyotes. Snow covered the ground, and it was very easy to see where dozens of hunters had driven the fields searching for the elusive pronghorn. Following many of these vehicle tracks, I located about a dozen gut piles. Nearly every one had been visited by predators, as evidenced by the tracks and scats that surrounded the sites. Those not visited were closer to a highway. Calling anywhere within a mile of these areas was productive.

I am certain that the heavy concentration of coyotes was due to the presence of the antelope gut piles. All had been put there by man and much human scent must have pervaded the area. Some hunters had obviously lit fires while they field dressed their game. Others had dropped cigarette packages, and many had left behind blood-stained rags and paper towels. None of this deterred the coyote from feeding on the remains—with gusto. By the end of the month following the season, all such sites were completely cleaned up.

Around the farmyard type of garbage pile, the scene of man is so prevalent that most resident canids become accustomed to it and pay it little heed. Many times, even when the wind is blowing the wrong way, an approaching hunter can get strangely close to a coyote or fox that is intently checking out the latest kitchen garbage. Head down and gnawing on an old dish towel or discarded milk carton, any fox or coyote is a quick target. This type of familiarity on the part of the animal occurs only in these isolated situations. Most times, the mere whiff of man sends the animal into high gear.

Outright scouting of the countryside for the long-haired species can be productive in areas with good populations. Basically, a hunter must drive and look. In the west, the hide hunter can drive the back trails and fireguards that criss-cross the open range country. Many such trails lead to stock watering sites, dams, corrals, small cultivated fields or hay meadows. Roads that lead to irrigation projects or fields of winter wheat are also good possibilities. Other trails lead to salting sites for cattle, windmills, or little-used line shacks or cattle corrals. By driving such areas and keeping close track of aerial photos or maps, a hunter will often put up the odd animal and get a good feel for the area.

A wise hunter should divide his hunting area into allotments or sectors. He should then divide his time so that the more productive scouting areas receive the largest share of the hunting time.

When checking for fur species, use your binoculars extensively. A good rule of thumb is to spend as much time glassing the countryside as is spent driving. However, do not expect to see the long-haired species in the same manner as in hunting big game. Most predators seen in this type of hunting will be moving. A particularly observant hunter may catch the odd coyote or fox in the act of hunting, totally unaware of the hunter's presence. Spotting from a vehicle may also put the animals in flight. In these cases, it is best to decide where the animal is going and try to set up a calling site.

A wise hunter divides his hunting area into sectors, then devotes the largest share of his hunting time to the more productive scouting areas.

More Prey, More Predators?

Beginners should remember that a coyote or fox cannot be found behind every hill or stone pile. Predator populations respond emphatically to food supplies. No sign, yet an ample supply of prey species, such as rabbits and mice, may indicate that few predators are in the immediate area. The opposite may also hold true. A lot of prey may mean that there is an active and large predator supply whittling down the available prey and the hunter has just not yet found the sign.

Interpreting the findings may be difficult, but fundamental to the presence of a predator species is an abundant prey supply. It is not necessarily true, however, that abundant prey means abundant predators.

Most long-haired species respond to an increase in food supply by increasing their populations in very specific ways. Coyotes and foxes begin to breed at younger ages and the number of young surviving in any one litter increases dramatically. There is also increased movement by the young of the population to occupy new habitats or to search out areas of reduced competition for food.

These basic biological observations will become very plain to any hunter who takes 200 or 300 long-hairs within a given area. Such things as more young in the hide take and the presence of well-aged individuals showing good body condition, as told from well-supplied back fat or heavy omental fat, will be apparent. These factors show that the population is living well and expanding in number. Another observation might be the finding of long-haired species in areas where they have previously been absent or infrequently seen.

A hide take consisting of a large number of young will indicate a growing population of predators, with a ratio of more young, usually about three to four, per adult. A stable population will show about two to three young for every adult. However, a declining situation, one which tells the hide hunter to move on to new territory, will reveal more old in the take than young. While the foregoing greatly simplifies the dynamics of a predator population, a hunter will still be able to observe these relationships and make decisions on where to continue hunting predators.

Any time a discussion of predator populations begins, the topic of cycles and their influence on the population will come up. Cycles are essentially oscillations—ups and downs—in the population levels. Cycles are great topics of conversation among hide hunters and area farmers.

Cycles in an animal population are a biological curiosity that nobody can really explain. There are two main schools of thought on the subject. One contends that predators eat themselves out of house and home and end up on a starvation course. The other school feels that the whole phenomenon of cycles is one big accident and that fluctuations in any animal population are random and indeed have no cause in nature. As in any other debate, the opponents have set their positions and have given evidence to support those positions.

Food shortages have been the explanation in vogue for the longest time. As rodents and prey species increase in numbers due to food abundance, perhaps brought on by good growing conditions over one or two seasons, predators likewise begin to increase. The high rodent population eats out its food supply and rapidly declines. This puts great

The author calls from within an area that offered good animal sign. For best results, call in areas that show positive evidence of predator activity.

pressure on the predators that must now switch to other food sources, since their main supply is declining. Because there is now a large supply of predators, food competition increases greatly and the predators must move on, looking for a more stable food source. The unfortunate starve. The result is a great swing downward in the number of predators.

The second school of thought says that, since the environment is so diverse and capable of depleting any population living in it, a great population crash is only an expression of these environmental factors at work. There are many instances where this would certainly seem to apply.

It is not the purpose of this book to enter into the debate on cycles. Suffice it to say that as a practicing hide hunter there will be many instances when you feel that the food-predator theory is certainly operating. Then, too, there will be enough environmental variation over the course of two or three winters that a hunter might consider the other argument as valid.

For the hunter, it will become clear that wide and erratic swings in population levels do occur. Many times these will seem to have little relationship to anything in particular. An area that enjoyed great hunting one year may become a total bust the following year. In the end, some will blame the moon and, who knows, they may be right.

Cycles do seem to be well established in the far north, where environments are more harsh and the results more easily observed. Less influence by man is also the rule. The snowshoe hare and the population levels of the lynx have been closely related to lagging peaks and depressions since records were kept by the Hudson's Bay trading company dating back to 1735. The ruffed grouse, likewise, shows such a cycle, since the lynx supposedly shifts to these birds when snowshoe hare decrease in supply.

In the settled portions of North America, little evidence supports the cycle theory in foxes and coyotes. The influence of man has probably been responsible for this. There is enough refuse produced and sufficient habitat created for mice and other species in agricultural America that conditions never reach cycle-creating proportions.

I, personally, have my doubts that the seemingly well-established cycles in the north are actually at

The Model 100 Winchester in .284 and a pair of showshoes lean against a log that blocks the trail along one of the author's favorite calling spots.

work. The data used in the studies to conclude that a lynx-snowshoe hare cycle existed were faulty. The information was supplied by the Hudson's Bay Company based on hide purchases made at their far northern posts. These types of records are unreliable, since trapping effort in any one year is not comparable.

In addition, the company was notorious for holding hides off the market for years at a time, waiting for higher prices. Trappers and hunters, especially those who lived and worked in the far north, would be aware of this kind of hold-over. Naturally, they would not pursue hides that were not being turned over by the company, since the company paid little for them. Thus, the cycle observed is more likely the result of individual effort related to the actual market conditions that existed at the time. It has little to do with the actual animal populations.

Again, I stress this as my own opinion.

Finding good areas with above-average populations of any long-haired species is still a large part of the hide hunting game. Combing the countryside and checking in unique places are the first steps in finding animals. In addition, talking with knowledgeable people familiar with the area and the outdoors is often useful in locating predators.

Sometimes contacting key personnel in the local or state game department may prove worthwhile. The game department can usually direct the beginning hunter to valuable state-published information on predators. A few states maintain counts on the long-hairs, but many more do not. However, the U.S. Fish and Wildlife Service operates a coyote index program throughout parts of the western U.S. This type of information can be useful in directing a hunter to areas where the animals will be found with some frequency. Other publications will at least pinpoint where specific studies may have been done and the people who have done

them. Visits to such areas or contacting the authors of such information may prove helpful.

Keep in mind that few states and provinces operate programs directly related to the long-haired species. Coyotes and foxes have long been regarded as predators and, therefore, pests in most cases. These species have not benefited from the kinds of scientific studies done on big game such as white-tailed deer. In fact, it is only recently that many jurisdictions required small game or trapping licenses for taking fox or coyote.

In all this, a great degree of patience is required. Careful study of habits, the country, techniques used in hunting and the development of winning skills all take time and effort. Patience in searching for productive areas and applying the techniques of hide hunting will require time. Remember, too, that mistakes will be made along the way. Missed shots, spooked animals, and stuck vehicles will all challenge your interest. Patience is a watchword in this type of hunting.

Chapter 6

Learning About The Territory

Getting to know the hunting area is the single most important task every hide hunter faces. Familiarity is the key to making your time in the field pay off—by reducing the amount you spend traveling, and increasing the time devoted to actual hunting—with the result being a good take of furs.

Gaining the kind of knowledge that pays dividends is often difficult. It requires a lot of time either to walk or to drive an area with the purpose of finding animal sign, getting to know the landowners, and actually spotting predators. A commitment of time and effort must be made or the hide hunting will suffer.

The predators already know the countryside. They were born there and have lived there every minute of their lives. Their intimate knowledge of the terrain, the travel routes, the little visited places and safe hideouts are part of their survival repertoire. For a coyote, no mental gymnastics are required in deciding when danger is present. It can leave an area by a different route every day.

A hunter will probably never know the countryside as well as the average predator. Nature has decided that. However, the average hunter could absorb a great deal of this knowledge by doing a few things to gain mastery over his chosen area.

Next to good eyesight, it is important for a predator hunter to become intimately familiar with the fine points of the territory in which that eyesight will be used. In other words, knowing the background against which you will be looking and spotting will go a long way in helping to distinguish animal from countryside. Knowledge of what is where will prove useful in finding animals, learning where the animals will move, and the areas that are generally avoided. Familiarity is the element that a client pays for in a guide. However, in hide hunting the same type of familiarity must be developed by the hunter himself.

Becoming intimate with a stretch of territory is a major undertaking. Often it is difficult to find that necessary time to learn all the back roads and trails that still exist in even well-populated parts of the country. The urban fringe, as the town planners call it, is home to more foxes and coyotes than ever before and the benefits of knowing these areas will enhance a hunter's take in any one year.

Aerial photographs are one means of allowing a hunter to become more familiar with the territory without physically covering the country on foot or with a vehicle. Maps are another way to let the hunter look at an area without actually being there. Both methods, when combined with ground trips, will help the hunter learn about the geographical things he needs to put hides on the yard pole and money in his pocket.

Photomap
of
Twp 32 Rge 10 W3rdM

Aerial photos are an excellent way for a hunter to learn about his area. Familiarity and knowledge of an area are two of the hunter's most important tools in taking long-hairs on a consistent basis.

Using Aerial Photographs

Aerial photographs are one of the best available sources of information on any kind of countryside. Aerial photos can be so useful to a long-hair hunter that he should study them and become skillful in using them. They provide a way of exploring a broad area quickly and accurately without a long, exhausting journey over the terrain, and provide a fast, efficient means of discerning the likely habitats of long-hairs. Marshes, lakes, streams, tree cover, field edges, and the relationships of these topographical features are all obvious from the photo.

Important for the hide hunter, an aerial shows where farm buildings are located. Things like water sites, dams and windmills are also visible and these are often included in the territories of coyotes and foxes. Knowing the locations of these features allows the hunter to check quickly for sign or use these as calling sites.

Besides the obvious advantages, the aerial photo

can also be used as a map. Topographical maps do not always include the many little back trails that course through the countryside, but these show up extremely well on aerials. This type of information can be helpful in checking for access to remote areas, for selecting routes used to look for more furs, and for locating alternate roads for use in poor weather or emergencies. They are also useful in determining the boundaries of areas within which a hunter has been given permission to hunt. The aerial photograph lets the hunter plan where he wants to be and how he can best get there. This saves time and gas money.

Sources of Photos. The best source of aerial photos is the U.S. Geological Survey. This agency handles thousands of photos from which they produce excellent topographical maps. Should you want to order an aerial from them, send a description to the nearest office and request the most recent price list for the areas involved. This may take some time, but the wait will be worth the effort. If you live near one of the state capitals, you can visit what the U.S.G.S. calls browse files, which are catalogs of available photos. A review of these will often turn up a useful photo.

Hunters should also avail themselves of other sources of photos as well. Oil exploration companies, common throughout the West, are regular users of such photos. Contact these companies, especially if there is an exploration unit or large field office in the area. They will always have photos of the immediate vicinity, and many companies will allow a hungry-looking coyote hunter to have a look at their supply for free.

Another source is the local library. Many of the bigger or better-run libraries will order a set of photos that can be loaned out to an interested party.

The local district agrologist will also often have a good set of aerial photos on hand. Sometimes he can be persuaded to loan these out or at least permit a hunter a peek at the photos. Irrigation companies are good places to try. Another excellent source is the Bureau of Land Management. It uses aerials of all its range lands to set stocking rates and to locate fence and water sites. Many offices will have several sets, dating back several years. An interested hunter could probably borrow some of these with a few well-chosen words to the local range managers.

If you hunt in a forested area, the company holding the timber rights for the area will usually have a complete set of photos. Many hunters already work on large forest reserves and will oftentimes know the local forestry representative. Also, the Forest Service will have aerials of the area within their jurisdiction and sometimes these can be garnered for a few days viewing. If you live in a semi-rural area where a lot of land development is underway, the developer, as well as the town office, will invariably have photos of their respective areas. Often, too, the county or other rural jurisdiction will have aerial photos for use in land assessment and taxation. These can often be seen by any member of the public.

How To Arrange and Use Mosaics. Once a hunter has assembled a quantity of photos, it will be necessary to arrange them so they can be conveniently read and studied. Photo specialists call their arrangement a mosaic.

Basically, there are two kind of mosaics—controlled and uncontrolled. A controlled mosaic is one in which the photos have been corrected for the tilt of the airplane and brought to a common scale. An uncontrolled type is merely one in which the photos are not all to the same scale.

In making your own mosaic, photos of the controlled type are the best. However, when this is not possible, a mosaic made up from any set of photos of varying scale may be used.

The kinds of photos available to most hunters are vertical photographs, or those taken at a right angle to the earth's surface. Vertical photographs are usually shot in lengthwise strips across the area being covered. Photo workers refer to these as flight lines and some maps are designated by the flight line. Along the course of each flight line, the photos will usually overlap a certain amount on both sides. This is called side lap and normally runs about 15 to 20 percent of the adjacent flight time.

At the top and bottom of the photo is end lap. This is just the overlap of the previous photo along the same flight line. End lap may be as much as 50 percent, though. All this is worth knowing before purchasing aerial photos for your own work. A good amount of lap is necessary so that similar points may be joined when making your mosaic.

Collecting the photos and cutting them to make

a mosaic may sound like a lot of unwarranted work; but the mosaic provides such a compendium of information that it saves time in the long run by aiding your planning and making travel in fur country much easier. Remember, too, that with a little knowledge of the area, your confusion in the field is reduced, thereby allowing you to spend more time hunting for predators and less deciding where you are. After all, how much trouble can you really get into when you know the type of habitat that is around the next bend?

I usually carry a photo mosaic of the area I am hunting. Right in the truck with me on the seat, it is an essential part of my gear any time I trek into new territory. The photos allow me to find routes that are off the beaten path and that would otherwise take hours of driving or specific directions to find.

Once you are in an area, find a prominent landmark or building and let the photo start working for you from that point. Bush or treed areas show up very distinctly on good-quality, black-and-white

Janet Pyle studies an aerial mosaic of the area her husband will be hunting. This is also a safety precaution, since the author's wife knows exactly where he will be hunting and, should some emergency arise, the jump-off point is known in advance.

Any type of aerial is useful in predator hunting. This one, taken from the window of a small plane, clearly shows the relationship between a nearby river and some pasture and cultivated land.

air photos. It is possible to find hidden clearings within the bush cover and then check the areas within for sign or as a potential calling site. Orientating from landmarks will prevent you from getting lost or "turned around" even in country that has winding roads and trails. Interpret any vegetative information, however, with some caution. Trees and shrubs can expand rapidly under the right circumstances and, likewise, disappear. Most aerials do not accurately outline the vegetation changes in an area from season to season.

Using Maps to Advantage

Maps offer an inexpensive way to study the countryside from the comfort of home. They are also considered a compact tool that can—and should—be carried in the field. As a condensed version of the world expressed in a series of symbols and signs, a map will greatly help you in choosing where to hunt or scout next.

For the user, a map provides four basics: direction, distance, position and identification. Direc-

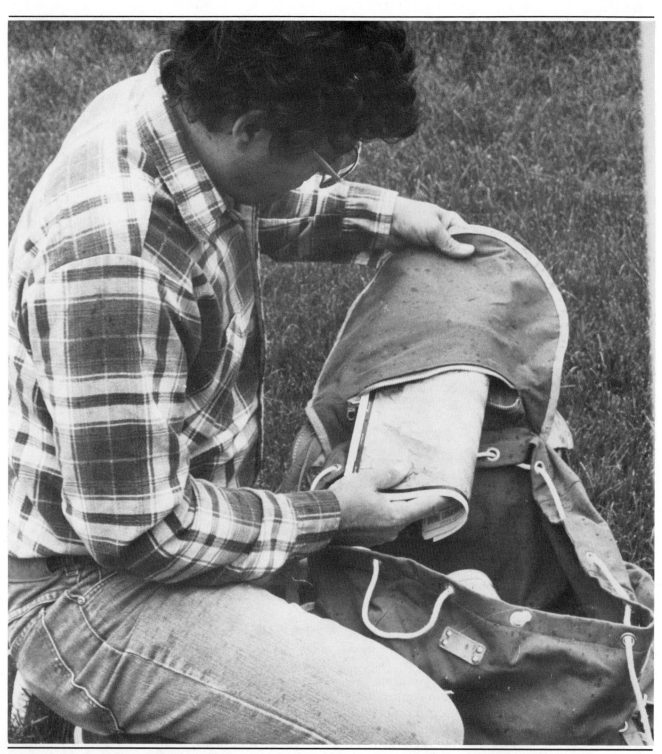

Carry your aerial photos with you when you hunt. This provides an excellent method of determining what lies around the bend without really having to look, and lets the hunter check the most potentially productive country first.

tion is the reference point, usually the top of the map, which represents north. Distance is established by a scale and is usually stated as one map unit equals X land units; for example, one inch equals four miles. Position in map reading is the physical location of the observer in relation to some item on the map. Identification is the language of the map and tells the user through symbols what lies ahead. Distance and identification are explained in the "legend," usually in a key place near the "live" part of the map.

State Highway Maps. A hunter new to an area would do well to acquire three types of maps. A standard state highway map should first be consulted. This is the kind of map that is available at the local gas station or restaurant and will show the major roadways into an area. This map will give the hunter a route to his chosen area, showing towns and cities in the vicinity.

County, Municipal and Land District Maps. The second map should be one that shows the boundaries and subdivisions within the hunting area. County, municipal or land district maps will fill the bill. These maps are usually used for taxation purposes and are available at municipal or county offices. Some types will show the landowners within the jurisdiction and the secondary road system. Others will show how the land is laid out or surveyed. In the eastern states, this is done on a county system. In the west, the country is set off in a series of grids that begin at 24 mile intervals and reduce to six square mile squares and finish off at one square mile divisions called sections. Some maps show the sections broken down into their respective quarters.

The city-bred hunter should pay close attention to the county or municipal map. Area residents and local farmers will very often refer to their land holdings by legal location. Thus, a farmer might say to an inquiring hunter that he has cattle on the S.E. 4 Township 6 Range 12 West of the Third and would prefer to restrict hunting in that area. A quick check of the local map would show that the townships are the divisions that run north-south on the map, while the ranges are the east-west delineation. A given township or range is divided into 36 square sections or miles. Each section is further subdivided into four quarters, namely the northeast, northwest, southeast and southwest, with

each quarter corresponding to the compass point. Each section is numbered from 1 to 36. In the U.S., these section numbers begin with number one in the extreme northeast corner of the township, while section numbers in Canada begin with number one in the lower southeast corner. Putting it all together, a hunter can find very specific locations in the area and always know his own position. In the vast seas of grass found in the wide-open West, knowledge of this survey system will give any hide hunter the advantage in becoming familiar with the countryside, gaining permission to hunt, locating areas that he has been directed to or simply finding his way with competence and confidence.

Many times a county or similar map will have to be consulted to ascertain legal hunting areas. All the states and provinces are divided into game management districts or zones. In some cases, the game department will have areas closed to predator hunting, while other parts of the state will be wide open. Trapping seasons may also interfere with areas in which rifle hunting for long-hairs may be conducted. Specific knowledge of these zones may be gained by using any of the maps that show the townships and ranges. Some zones will even be defined by township and range and this makes proficiency in map reading mandatory.

It also brings up the need for the hunter to be familiar with the *game districts* or *zones* available for hunting. Game departments regularly publish a synopsis or guide to hunting areas and regulations within their states. Many of these are in the form of maps or bulletins. Any hunter should equip himself with such a guide and use the rough maps presented within to sort out where to hunt legally. This guide should be used in conjunction with the three types of maps reviewed here, especially the county or municipal maps.

Topographical Maps. The final type of map, and perhaps the most important, is the topographical map. The topographical map derives its name from the symbolizing of the elevations and contours of an area. No other map offers this detail and accuracy of scale.

Now nearly every square foot of North America has been mapped and plotted onto topographical maps. In the United States, the U.S. Geological Survey is the main producer of such maps. The U.S.G.S. prints maps in scales of 1:24,000,

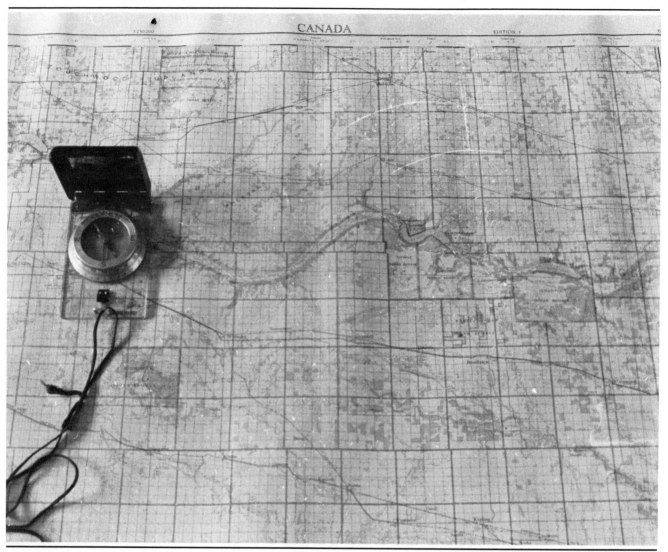

Up-to-date maps are a good way to gain knowledge of an area without actually setting foot in it. Topographical maps, in particular, show the elevations and contours of a region with detail and accuracy provided by no other type of map.

1:62,500, 1:100,000 and the 1:250,000 series. Each covers a large land area, but the hide hunter should begin with a 1:250,000 map for his area. This will cover from just under 5,000 square miles to about 8,000 square miles, depending on the exact region. Once a few specific hunting spots have been selected, a larger scale map can be purchased. For example, the 1:24,000 series will run from 50 to 70 square miles of coverage, or about a dozen coyote home ranges. The scales available may be

chosen to fit your need.

A topographical map carries two distinct advantages. By showing the surface features in relief, it first shows the lay of the land translated into elevation readings or contours; and, second, it transcends property lines by giving an unencumbered view of the countryside. In short, it shows land in much the same way an animal might discern the surroundings. Land can be seen as bands or strips of habitat and the relationship of these may be studied. Drainage patterns and the influence of water movement become obvious also. Both are important factors in finding predatory animals.

Topographical maps show the countryside in a series of symbols or representations. A hunter wanting to take hides should become familiar with these, as they provide the means of translating the map into meaningful land information. A detailed description of all the dozens of symbols currently used in modern-day cartography is beyond the scope of this book. Study of any map will show the symbols and their meaning, and all topographical maps printed by the U.S.G.S. include legends that describe the map symbols and their interpretation. In general, man-made features are delineated in black—farmyards, old buildings, roads and bridges. Water features are marked out in blue; this runs the gamut of rivers, creeks, ponds, and streams. Vegetation characteristics are colored green. Red is used for major roads. The important contour or elevation lines are shown in brown.

The thin brown lines called contours plainly show the slopes on the landscape or the lay of the land across the area. In effect, a contour line is an imaginary line drawn along the field joining every point of the same height above sea level. Contour lines are really a description of the ups and downs, the valleys and the draws that an area has to offer.

The space or distance between each contour line is the contour interval. It is the distance in height between one contour line and the next, and its dimension may vary from one type of map to the next. On most topographical maps, the distance is 20 feet. Maps obtained from the Geological Survey will have the contour interval printed in the lower margin.

For hunting purposes, the closer together these contour lines are, the steeper will be the slope; the farther apart, the gentler the slope. The lines become V-shaped for valleys and U-shaped for spurs or hogbacks. Contour lines along rivers or water drainages will often run beside each other for miles.

In short, a study of contour lines will indicate the rougher terrain. These areas are often the reservoirs for predator species, and the adjacent uplands or lowlands will make for productive calling or searching for sign. A map used to pull these features together will save the hunter miles of driving

and fruitless scouting.

When studying the contours, note the shape, steepness and height of the area. Study the distribution or spatial relationships between such features and plan where to be or where the most effective hunting may be achieved.

As noted previously, pay close attention to the way the land is drained. Check for the location of streams, creeks and rivers, as crossings may be possible only in certain places. Look particularly for intermittent stream beds. Observe the water runs, as these topographical features may exist well within cultivated fields. While the waste areas that surround them are rarely frequented by man, foxes and coyotes will often loaf in such places. Watch for lakes and especially swamps, bogs or long, narrow-shaped marshes; these are often home to prey species and actively hunted by predators. Water runs, drainage courses and slopes influence where plants will grow and therefore influence cover characteristics of your hunting area. Topographical maps show all this clearly.

Topographical maps also show the hunter the location of landmarks or reference points. This helps keep a hunter oriented in strange country. More importantly, it allows the active hunter to divide his hunting area into sectors. He is then able to comb the most likely habitats more methodically and discover unvisited chunks of country.

Landmarks may take many forms and each part of the country will offer some unique examples. The most obvious are roads and rivers, but fire lookout towers in forested areas, abandoned buildings on the prairie, clumps of trees in the parklands, rocky outcrops in the foothill regions and distinctive vegetation will all help the hunter parcel his hunting territory and make his effort more efficient.

The hunter after furs must study a topographical map to determine where the most edge effect prevails. "Edge effect" is an ecological term familiar to most hunters, used to describe the borders or edges where different types of habitat meet. It has long been an observation that the best habitat for a wide range of predators and their prey exists where there is mixed countryside or where one kind of habitat borders on another. Another, more sophisticated term for the same phenomenon is "habitat juxtaposition," or the side-by-side existence of habitat. Thus, a fence-line with an open field on one side and a small adjacent wood lot on the other is vastly more productive than one large, open cultivated field. Topographical maps, because of the symbols used in overlaying the contours and vegetation, provide an excellent source of locating hunting territory with good edge effect.

One of the major criticisms of topographical maps is that some of the information may be out of date. New roads may have been constructed, buildings removed, vegetation cleared, or creeks and rivers diverted or dried up. The topographic series is produced from aerial photos and a limited amount of ground checking. The length of time required to bring a map into being and the passage of time after it is printed make it difficult to keep current.

For the hide hunter, however, this may not be such a problem. For example, maps showing out-of-date information are actually historical records of the way things once were. Roads that have become abandoned may now be good hunting territory. Dried-up river beds become available habitat, and any land clearing of large trees or forestry operations create their own hunting opportunities. The map is still useful to the hide hunter, and may reveal new opportunities by its being out of date.

Vegetative features also receive some criticism. Many times the vegetation is not present. Many more times vegetation is growing where the map shows none. Also the extent of the coloration may not be accurate in all circumstances. In the parkland areas where I hunted and spent much of my youth, clumps of popular trees several acres in size were never printed on the various editions of topographical maps. It is my experience that where the contour lines are sharp and the accompanying vegetation is colored green, the areas so delineated will be accurately portrayed. The greatest inaccuracies occur in the parkland areas and the treed draws of the west, where small clumps of trees are not recorded.

A shading system is used on the U.S.G.S. maps that shows heavily forested countryside as dark green and two lighter shades of green depicting sparse tree cover or shrub. For almost all predator hunting, this coloring system will suffice. After all, the map is only a guide to where vegetation exists; it is not designed to direct the hunter to the very tree he should begin calling from.

One final point should be made about the value of the topographic series. As mentioned, this series largely ignores the geopolitical arrangements that cover nearly all of the land in North America today. This means the map can be studied without interference from the boundaries of municipalities or counties. Vegetation, drainage and habitat relationships are plain to see as are the extent or size of the habitat. The value of an area to predators can be gleaned from these maps. Very early in the study of maps the hunter will find that the country is divided by drainages and borders that are largely man-made. Remember, too, that the coyote, the fox and the bobcat do not recognize man's self-imposed boundaries, and wander back and forth across them daily. The most important point about topographical maps is that they put the hunter on more equal terms with the predators.

Gaining Access to Productive Areas

A big part of being familiar with your hunting area is knowing where you can hunt. Sounds simple, but every year would-be hide hunters take to the field and drive thousands of miles looking for somewhere to hunt rather than actually hunting. For most, knowing where to hunt translates into being allowed to hunt.

Searching for open hunting country has really become a major preoccupation for all types of hunters. Farmers, concerned with trespassing over freshly planted crops, and ranchers, worried about losing cattle, are closing thousands of acres every year. Authorities from police to game wardens, flooded with complaints, are recommending land be barred to hunting.

Seeking permission to hunt is the only way access to these closed lands will be gained. Hide hunters who work near large towns or cities will invariably face much posted land. In the more open west of the U.S. and Canada, the problem is not as severe, but is constantly growing. Every hunter at some point will have to deal with the thorny issue of permission to hunt.

The best advice is to begin requesting permission long before the prime hunting season. It is my observation that much of the best hunting country, especially near cities, is already closed to any

Reading a map under field conditions will help the hunter learn how to use the map as well as show him what lies ahead.

type of activity. Many farmers who live near urban centers are perpetually bothered by nighttime party goers, motor or trail bikers, fishermen, picnickers and bird watchers. They will be tough nuts to crack and may require good public relations effort.

I emphasize the small areas close to towns and cities, because many hunters are denied access to these places and, yet, with appropriate permission, a good take of hides is possible. One time I had received permission to hunt land on a nearby estate. It had a small coulee running through it and the lay of the land was considerably higher than the nearby town. From my position hunkered down at the top of the coulee, I could make out my home in town. In fact, I worked out a system with my wife that at exactly 8:30 in the morning she would go to the kitchen window and look toward the coulee. On bright mornings, I would flash a signal mirror indicating that I was about to pack up my gear and would be home directly. It would be her signal to have the coffee ready and perhaps a late morning

Intimate knowledge acquired from both field reconnaissance trips and intense map and aerial photo study will put fine hides on the yard pole every time.

breakfast. That aside, my expenses in taking a half dozen or so foxes over the course of a winter were considerably lower than those of other forays. The money in my pocket was due to having that special permission.

How To Get Permission? Just Ask. The best way to obtain permission is simply to ask. A polite call on the area farmer or rancher and an explanation of just what is wanted and when you wish to do it most often will allow you access to hundreds of acres of posted land. Much of this land has been unhunted for years and could prove very productive. It has been for me.

Many farmers *will* give permission to hunt on already posted land. This may seem contradictory; however, once you introduce yourself and talk over your style of hunting and show that you're not a reckless urban stereotype, permission is usually granted. Indeed, it seems that the presence of a vehicle is oftentimes the really bothersome point for the landowner; if he knows your vehicle and what you are doing, there is little real need for concern.

During the season, it's a good practice to recheck with the farmer contact to make sure the permission is still intact. This is especially wise if the hunter has not worked the area for several weeks. Situations can change and the landowner may have actually forgotten he talked with you. Sometimes he may just change his mind.

Combine Your Hunting With a Service to the Owner. Farmers who keep chickens or sheep still generally harbor an intense dislike for coyotes and foxes. Because of this, a sheepman will give a coyote hunter virtual "carte blanche" to hunt his lands whenever the season permits. Many years ago I compiled a list of the sheepmen in my immediate vicinity. I contacted each one personally and was able to secure hunting on just over 500,000 acres of good coyote and fox country. They were happy to have me and I was essentially given a free hand to call and hunt with very little public relations effort.

Few farms today have chickens; for some reason the economics of this practice just does not pay. But some smaller farmers still keep a few hens for the eggs and the odd chicken dinner. As covered in folklore, the red fox finds chicken an irresistible treat and one that is fairly easy to take. Consider becoming friends with several farmers who continue to have fox and chicken problems. Your take

in furs from out behind the chicken house may far exceed the cash value of the chickens. For me, my farmer friends and perhaps the chicken and the fox, a true symbiotic relationship has often evolved in these situations.

Badgers are disliked for their habit of digging holes to root out gophers and other small ground-dwelling species. The holes or dens for the badger are large enough to give a mounted rider a tumble or an old cow a jolt. On cultivated land, the front wheel of the tractor or other machinery has been known to drop into the hole, giving the operator a scare and sometimes breaking the equipment. I have had no trouble securing permission when I let it be known that I'd shoot every one of these critters whenever I saw one. Few badgers mean fewer holes and this is appreciated. Just as an aside, badger hides can also bring a decent dollar during the prime season as well. It is wise to capitalize on these dislikes and promote your hunting pursuits as a worthwhile service to the farmer.

While coyotes have come in closer contact with man over the past decade or so, it is really the fox that has learned to live best with man. Foxes are common on the urban fringes of even large centers. Securing permission to hunt these areas will require considerable tact, and it will help to know the landowner and attempt to meet some specific need he might have. For example, I was once given permission to hunt a large estate in exchange for checking the buildings to comply with an insurance agreement the owner had entered into. On another occasion, I traded some photographs of the buildings and yard site with one owner for permission to hunt a strip of land he owned.

Establish Contacts With Rural People. Having contact with rural people is a good way to get invited out to hunt or to develop the necessary contacts to gain hunting privileges. A friend worked as a farm machinery mechanic. His contacts became so good that when winter arrived and the repair work declined, he simply went out coyote and fox hunting on a full-time basis, calling in the invitations he had built up over the summer. Over the years, he had invitations that he could never get around to and was nice enough to pass several of these contacts on to me.

Likewise, a carpenter friend had similar success. He did odd jobs throughout the country in the

The hide hunter should try to secure permission to hunt areas closed to other hunters. This sometimes requires more than one public relations trip, but the effort may be worthwhile if you are the only hunter working the area.

summer and fall and, when the prime season struck, he merely put down his hammer and picked up his rifle. He would hunt in the mornings and work the afternoons and evenings. Many times the farmers and ranchers he worked for would tell him when the prime season began. He would use this as his signal to begin full-time hunting.

A lawyer friend who handled a lot of rural business had a grand opportunity to gain permission to hunt. He used his contacts to outfit himself and

his wife with long winter coats made of coyotes he had taken himself. He was especially proud of his results and his clients felt they had played a big part in bringing his pet project to completion.

Much time can be exhausted working areas that are open to others, but short on long-haired species. The serious hide hunter must open up land closed to others, because more often than not these animals choose "the road not taken," where the best results will be obtained. In recent years, wildlife associations and some game departments have devoted some effort to the opening up of posted lands, with most of that effort being directed toward the big game hunter. However, many times areas free to all hunters become overhunted. In reality, these programs are marginally effective, making for great press releases and doing little for the actual hunting.

Hunting on previously posted lands versus hunting public areas means few hunters. This translates into less disturbance to resident predator populations and also to the hunter. While it is true that most of our predators are now at home living next to man, even these adaptable creatures will move on if man becomes too much of a nuisance.

Asking permission to hunt and following up on calls often produces good relations between the farmer and the hunter. Many times long-lasting friendships develop from these initial contacts. For the hide hunter intent on making money at his hide hunting effort, these friendships are invaluable. Good friends will always keep the hunter alerted to where animals may have been seen or any new activity in the area. Some landowners will only allow friends to hunt their lands.

This type of friendship really helps to reduce hunter competition. Let's face it, if I am the only hunter allowed in a 50 square mile area, the odds of me taking the resident long-hairs are greatly increased. In addition, opportunities improve if there are fewer vehicles, fewer shots fired, less scent of man near feeding and loafing sites, and generally less travel in the area. This is a real advantage.

Building a good reputation as a hide hunter is also wise. This means respecting the property on which you hunt, as well as always heeding landowner requests on such things as closing gates, not driving across seeded fields, and not hunting in fields where cattle graze. Roaring down roads with a four-wheel drive all decked out for a safari is not smart, either. The number of things that can offend people is probably endless. A good reputation can be established by using common sense.

Being attentive to the wants of the landowner and being his friend can pay other dividends. Adjacent landowners may extend permission to hunt on their land. Farmers will mention to their neighbors in the course of a friendly conversation that they have given a certain hunter permission to hunt. The neighbor, hearing favorable comments, may invite you to hunt or be ready to allow you to hunt should you call seeking similar permission. A sort of domino effect occurs and it is possible for a single hide hunter to tie up hunting rights to large areas just by dint of many friendships.

Letting residents know you are hunting an area has other advantages. Throughout the west, the growth of range patrols has made it a good practice to let these people know you are working a particular area. Suspicious headlights along some back road early in the morning or late at night may cause some concern to these patrols. Indeed, initial contact under these conditions may not be friendly, especially if some cattle rustling has recently occurred.

Once you are known in an area, most people will leave you alone to pursue your hunting. Being known often means ready recognition of your vehicle, so it is wise to use only one vehicle for hunting purposes rather than show up in a different vehicle every two weeks. Try to arrange to leave your jeep in the farmer's yard and walk to any nearby hunting areas. This lets the farmer know you are about and does offer some protection for the vehicle. Good relations in the field and quiet pursuit are the cornerstones of this type of hunting.

One of the greatest advantages of being known is that others will tell you where they have seen animals. School bus drivers, by the nature of their occupation, are often out on the back roads early in the morning. They will invariably see coyotes and foxes, and a particularly observant driver might even spot the odd bobcat.

It only stands to reason that the wider your intelligence-gathering operation, the greater the odds of finding animals. The more sets of eyes working, the better. Any truck driver who works the country roads early in the morning is a good source to be tapped. Bulk-milk truck drivers, rural postmen, linemen, railway workers, road maintenance crews or fuel truck drivers are only too glad to share their observations with an interested hunter.

Try and solicit information from these sources at every opportunity. A visit to the local tavern may bring in some reports, but by far the best way is to try the local coffee shop around the time of the morning coffee break. A day that is particularly stormy will find many people bent over a warm mug of coffee. Any workers who have been out early that morning will have their observations fresh in mind and most will be literally bursting to tell someone what they have seen. On a stormy or rainy day they will also have the time to relate incident after incident to a listening passer-by. A friendly conversation may turn up some interesting possibilities.

This method is so reliable that a personal incident in northern Montana serves as a good example. I was traveling through and happened to stop at one of the local coffee hot spots. Sitting next to me was a county lineman, and it was not difficult to start up a conversation about the weather. As is my nature, I worked in the topic of coyotes. This wind-burnt fellow wasted no time giving me specific directions to where he had seen a big coyote only two hours before. The story is almost anticli-

Badgers are disliked because of the holes they dig to root out small rodents. When asking permission, let it be known that you will shoot badgers as a service to the landowner.

mactic. Since the directions seemed reliable and I was generally heading in the same direction, I gave the critter a try. I shot the coyote in what I am sure was the area described by my coffee drinking friend. The whole effort took less than an hour and I pocketed $45.00. I have always felt a little guilty about that since I really should have picked up the coffee tab that day.

Once permission is in place and a hunter is making a good effort in the area, many farmers will report fox and coyote sightings. In my single most successful year of cat hunting back in the 1970s, I had a rancher friend phone me on mornings he spotted bobcat sign around his wintering cattle. Adult bobcat had been taking the odd calf from this hard-working man, and he didn't like it one bit. What had obviously happened was that local bobcats were cleaning up on the postpartum remains following a calf birth. It took no time for them to extend this taste to the live and kicking version of young veal. My friend had lost two newborn calves when he finally gave me a call. I took a cat that day and on four following occasions. His contact by phone simply gave me five excellent opportunities that I would not otherwise have had.

Good contacts help in another way. It is a fact of agricultural life that animals routinely die or reach a point where they have to be destroyed. Some animals routinely die or reach a point where they have to be destroyed. Some animals are accident victims, some succumb to disease, and still others are killed by freak storms. The carcasses of such animals provide choice bait for all the long-haired species. Baiting, in the strictest sense of the word, is illegal in many jurisdictions, but the idea is to use the carcass to lure animals into an area. Calling from a blind or near the carcass is all that is required. In the winter months, when territories of all the long-haired species are large and poorly established, it is likely that several coyotes or foxes and individual bobcats may remain near the area for an easy meal.

The key is to have your farmer friend haul the carcass out to good habitat or place it in such a way that a hunter can check activity from a nearby bush or established blind. Some of my farmer friends will do this automatically and call when the carcass has been visited. Over the course of a winter, several strategically placed carcasses will pro-

Areas that have travel restrictions may be good predator haunts. Check these closely for sign, or talk to area residents who may know the local conditions.

duce good returns.

One of my rancher contacts lost an adult cow around the beginning of the prime season. It was the third year I had been hunting his ranch and, when he half-jokingly suggested we haul the carrion down to a nearby bush with his front-end loader, I jumped at the opportunity. Being a familiar visitor to his ranch proved valuable.

Bait stations are worthwhile for the serious hide hunter. Carrion is visited repeatedly by any of the predators. If the visits and the availability of the material coincide with the prime part of the season, a dramatic take in high-quality hides may result. A hunter would, of course, regularly include bait stations in his scouting and either visually check or call near such places during the season.

Be sure to check with your local game department regarding the legality of hunting predators near dead carrion. In most jurisdictions, it is legal when hunting fox and coyotes. However, in the odd place, it can be construed as game baiting, which is of course illegal in many areas.

I have been lucky enough to have some farmers call me when they place out such carcasses. Others have gone ahead and placed the remains in well-known predator areas or spots they know I routinely hunt. The cooperation I have received from several ranchers and farmers has been tremendous. One winter it enabled me to do most of my hunting in and around areas where carcasses had been placed. These contacts should be developed, as they will put dollars in the pocket of any hide man.

To Pay or Not To Pay. One final aspect of contacts and permission must be addressed. Many landowners and farmers consider the game they raise to be a cash crop not unlike their pigs and chickens. This has led some to request an access fee or trespass charge. While this is perhaps more common in big game hunting, it is not entirely unheard of in long-hair hunting. It could be something a hunter might have to deal with. I share the view of the majority of hunters. I would dislike to pay for the privilege of hunting. Having said that, however, I am businessman enough to know that if I were getting exclusive or near-exclusive hunting rights to a significant chunk of real estate with good long-hair potential, I would pay for the opportunity to hunt. I would view the cost as a legitimate business expense, much like the gasoline for my four-wheel drive or cartridges for my rifle.

In many areas, especially in the West where there is much open public land, many feel that hunting should be free. On the other hand, states like Texas have pioneered fee hunting and turned it into a reputable business endeavor. Yet, in the East, thousands of acres of posted land and the densely populated countryside have almost eliminated any opportunity to hunt. In the final analysis, if fee hunting means that sport hunting can survive, then most of us must reluctantly give our support to this system.

Chapter 7

Honing Your Tracking Skills

Being able to read tracks and interpret animal sign will no doubt help any hunter locate long-hairs. Indeed, some sort of sign, usually a track, will be the first indication an animal is present. Where I live in Canada, cougars are rarely seen, but whenever a track is found, a report appears in the newspaper and a photographer is dispatched to record the event. It makes great news, and the local farmer gets his picture in the paper, but actual observations of the cougar are rare.

Having stated that tracks are important, I want to make one disclaimer. Much has been written about reading tracks and gleaning information about the animal's behavior, sex, age, destination, or other circumstances from them. Frankly, much of this is pure speculation on the part of the authors. Tracks serve only to tell that an animal was present sometime in the past. Finding a good set of tracks and taking them at face value can be useful. I have tracked bobcats from fresh kill sites when the tracks were only a few hours old and the snow conditions were right. I made no further deductions or played Sherlock Holmes. The tracks led me to the animals that made them.

Predators are difficult to track. The tracks are small and the weight of the animal does not leave much of an imprint on grassed-over soil. Essentially, all canids walk on their toes and therefore have little bearing surface touching the ground. Then, too, the prime fur season rarely coincides with good tracking weather. In addition, predators follow erratic travel routes, stopping frequently to investigate any oddity within their sight or smell range. So, while it is possible to track down a lone buck whitetail, it is infinitely more difficult to track a predator—and connect.

Tracks deteriorate quickly and, since they are on the ground, they are often shaded by vegetation or plant debris. Many soils, especially in the agricultural areas, are of such a powdery nature that the tracks will disappear almost as quickly as they are made. In the north, the spongy, soft muskeg country is inadequate for recording any kind of track. Bear, moose and caribou leave holes, not well-defined tracks, in the soft ground. Rocky or mountainous country shows little sign of an animal's presence. Even snow is not a good tracking medium when winds and warm sun are at work.

Fresh tracks are the ones to look for. "Fresh" means only a few hours old, say, five at the most. They will be well defined and sharp, even if they are only holes in the mud or snow. Probability will be high that the animal is still in the immediate vicinity, and further searching will be productive within a short time.

Old tracks merely signify that animals were pres-

This rabbit trail offers good evidence of active prey species in the immediate vicinity.

Tracking success depends entirely upon the environmental conditions at the time—and they can change dramatically within hours. Fresh, light, early-season snow is the best a hunter can hope for.

ent at some point in the past. They tell you no more. As an old deer hunting friend, Reubin Mills, often quotes to me during deer season, "If only you could fry tracks." The same could be said about predator hunting, "If only I could sell tracks." All things considered, however, an area with old tracks is a better place to start calling or hunting from than a territory that has none.

A mixture of old and new tracks tells the hunter that the area is frequently visited by predators, which means the hunter should likewise scout the vicinity, either by actual on-foot hunting or by calling from surrounding cover.

Reading tracks is often little more than common sense, practice, and a nominal ability to observe. Outdoor literature is full of tales of expert trackers and their success under near-impossible circumstances. The serious hide hunter will rarely have time to track down any predator unless he's working from fresh sign or tracking a wounded preda-

tor. Following a set of cold tracks is an inefficient way to hunt, and certainly not rewarding.

As a youngster, with my head full of tracking stories from the likes of Edgar Rice Burroughs and James Fenimore Cooper, I made numerous attempts to track down dozens of foxes and coyotes that coursed through our prairie farm. It didn't take me long to discover that most trails or spoor, as the Englishmen call them, simply disappeared in the snow or became so mixed with other trails from cattle or horses that sorting out which way an animal went ended in total frustration. The odd time I would actually put up a coyote or fox I naturally attributed to my increasing skill as tracker and scout.

Identifying Tracks

Recognizing the tracks left by hide-bearing animals in your area is paramount to any appreciation of tracking and sign reading. It is important to be able to distinguish fox, coyote and bobcat tracks from those of domestic dogs and cats. Many times in the search for tracks, a novice will be fooled by sign left by feral species. Their tracks are almost indistinguishable from those of their free-living cousins. Anyone who has lived in a rural area will know that many domestic cats are quite able of living rugged existences on the edge of civilization without any contact with man. These cats can grow to as large as 20 or 30 pounds and behave much like any wild bobcat or lynx. It is not uncommon to have a feral feline respond to your calling. By the way, since these animals become nuisances to the local farmers, it's not a bad idea to shoot them.

The same applies to dogs. Many farming regions are home to stray dogs, either ones that have been deliberately left behind by misguided city folks, or animals that have actually chosen a life of little contact with man. While wild dogs have never yet responded to my calling, their presence in any backwoods area is the source of countless tracks and other sign. Most sheepmen and many farmers will shoot these dogs on sight. Just in passing, the predators waste no time in killing such foundlings, either. Indeed, one of the signs that bobcats have entered a farming area is the disappearance of the farmyard tomcat, not just from one or two farms

Tracks such as these are good places to begin checking for predators. Calling in an appropriate site near here could prove worthwhile.

but from farms for miles around. Coyotes will routinely kill any canine that dares to cross the fine line between domesticity and a wild existence.

Coyote Tracks. Coyote tracks are very similar to those made by any large domestic canine. They can be anywhere from two to four inches in size. If you compared adult tracks, they'd usually appear larger than those of a domestic dog, but there is so much variation that a hard and fast rule is not possible; there are some very large domestic dogs. Coyote tracks are certainly larger than those made by fox, however, and claw marks are always discerni-

ble in good fresh samples. The hind foot has pads that are slightly larger than the pads on the front foot.

Most coyote tracks appear as holes in the snow. If the coyote is walking, the tracks will touch. The hind foot will always be placed nearly upon the spot where the front foot has broken the snow. If running, coyote tracks will be separated, repesenting where the coyote landed and moved into the next leap. A trotting coyote will leave a pattern similar to that made when walking, except that about two or three inches will separate the front and rear marks.

Expect some variation, though, such as could be found when deep snow or wet ground are encountered.

A coyote follows an ambling route that really seems to go nowhere and often cuts back to points previously visited. It seems that the animal plays as much as it hunts. It is not uncommon to see where a coyote rolled in the snow, rubbed his jaw against some dead and dried shrub, or simply stopped and sat down for a few minutes.

Another sign that should be mentioned is the coyote's habit of laying scent markers. As mentioned, these are invaluable hunting aids. Most trails will end with a visit to a prominent marker. These can be any trail crossing, bale stack, exposed rock or just a high point in the land—any point in the countryside where the animal can advertise its presence to others of its species.

Fox Tracks. The tracks of the various fox species are very similar. More dainty than those of any coyote or feral dog, they would not be more than two and a quarter inches long. Compared to those of a coyote, the pads on the feet are widely spaced and much smaller. In the summer months, the pads are distinct, but during the harsh winters, much additional hair grows between the pads. Many times the pads will not be clearly distinguishable due to this wintery growth of hair. As is the case with the coyote, the hind feet are nearly superimposed on the track made by the front feet when walking.

A fox will generally walk in a straight line, frequently stopping to sniff around one thing or another. It will often leave a tail mark in the snow, where the bottom of the tail has bumped the snow in passing. Sometimes coyotes do this, but it is less common. Coyotes will often drag their feet, while the fox leaves a more distinct trail.

Foxes also leave sign posts. Scratch marks will be seen more often than dung piles. Foxes love to scrape down to the dead grasses below the snow and make a temporary bed. Many times the animal urinates in these beds prior to leaving. A bed with no fresh urine stains may mean that the hunter has put the animal up and it has not bothered to stretch or perform the usual. It has merely taken off.

Sometimes when a fox is stalking prey, the hind feet will actually step into the very same track made by the front foot. Many times skid marks will be evident in the snow, indicating that either a fox or coyote has chased up a rabbit. In the heat of the chase, the predator has momentarily lost control as the rabbit turned too sharply and the predator couldn't match the turn.

Bobcat and Lynx Tracks. The bobcat has very

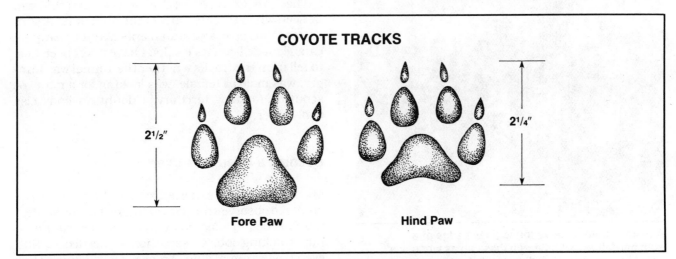

COYOTE TRACKS

2¹/₂"

Fore Paw

2¹/₄"

Hind Paw

Coyote tracks can be anywhere from 2 to 4 inches in size, with clearly discernible claw marks in fresh samples. When walking in snow, the hind foot will always be placed nearly upon the spot where the front paw has broken through the surface. Distance between paw prints ranges from 12 to 14 inches.

A well-defined coyote track in hard soil such as this will last for months. Even so, all that tracks tell the hunter is that animals were once in the area.

A plain coyote track as found on the edge of a summer-fallow field. Search these areas whenever checking for sign. Soft dirt quickly loses tracks and the presence of any sign means that the animal has only recently passed.

complicated-looking tracks. In the wet seasons, a clear track can be found, but usually by the time the prime hunting season rolls around, fur has thickened on the lower leg and only a hole in the snow is apparent. Tracks are about three inches in size and the animal spaces them out about seven or so inches when walking. A well-grown feral house cat would show a two-inch paw mark spread about six inches apart. The feral cat does not have fur on its feet. The bobcat will grow some hair, but only the lynx grows hair between its foot pads.

Cat tracks follow a pattern similar to the canids. The hind foot is placed in the spot made by the front foot. Cats actually do this more characteristically than do the dog species. Remember, too, that all cats have retractile, or retractable, claws, so these will not usually be seen in the footprint. In general, a bobcat track is more rounded than a fox or coyote.

Other bobcat sign include scats and loafing sites. As with all cats, the bobcat will bury its wastes. However, this is usually done in a halfhearted manner, and the scats, as well as the scratched ground, are valuable signs of the animal's presence. The bobcat also has the habit of scratching trees, ostensibly to sharpen its claws or as part of its loafing habit. The scats may vary from small pellets to constricted-looking segments; all will contain hair.

These are examples of the kinds of sign that can be seen when tracking any of the predators. Again, I stress that no grand statements about the animal can be made from its tracks. I have never been able to tell from the tracks whether the animal was hungry, was male or female, was looking for a mate, or scouting for new territory. I doubt anybody else can, either.

Become a Keen Observer

My own youthful experiences taught me that the ability to observe and an avid interest in the subject were needed to succeed at even the most rudimentary tracking job. Observation is needed to find even basic animal sign. Tracks, scats, loafing sites and scent posts all can be found with a little patience, perseverance and observations.

Part of the problem today is that many hunters never get the opportunity to hone their abilities in the field. Many hunters, by far the majority, are now coming from the cities, where familiarity with the animals and even the rural way of life is difficult experience to obtain. Most hunters lack the ability to observe or have never tried to learn observation skills that could be applied to hunting.

Developing the powers of observation is important to contemporary hide hunters. A hunter from a rural environment should have an easier time, but even the city-born kid who has seen country no more rugged than a downtown park can develop the necessary ability to observe and observe well.

One of the most successful techniques used to develop or hone the powers of observation is the ancient English military game dodge called Kim's Game. In its simplest form, 25 or 30 small articles are laid out on a table and covered with a cloth. The observer, having never seen the articles before, is allowed a few seconds, say 20 to 30, to look at the articles. The cloth is then replaced and the observer told to record his observations.

At first, a reasonably good observer would be able to recall about 20 percent of the items. With practice, the percentage will climb and it is not impossible to name all the articles within a very short period of time. However, the benefit of the game is not so much the number of items recalled. It is that the game causes the observer to focus attention on detail. The real gain is that the game forces us to stop and really look at what is there. This is exactly the technique needed to track and follow animal sign.

You can develop Kim's Game to the point that it is mandatory to describe in detail all the objects under the cloth. In tracking and trail craft, it is this ability to perceive the fine points, coupled with a deep knowledge of animal habits, that leads expert trackers to the grand imputations I talked about earlier. While I may scoff at some of these tales, it is possible to become a credible tracker and be able to say with some authority that one set of tracks is larger than another, that the animal was in a hurry; or to make other such common-sense observations using the available sign as a starting point. Practice, experience with the animals, and the ability to observe are what is required.

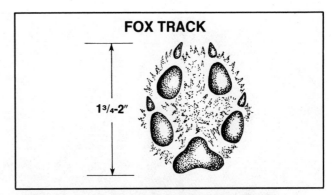

FOX TRACK

1³/₄-2″

Compared to the coyote, the fox track is smaller, with wider spaces between the pads. In the winter, additional hair growth makes the pads less distinguishable. The fox walks like the coyote with prints about 11 inches apart.

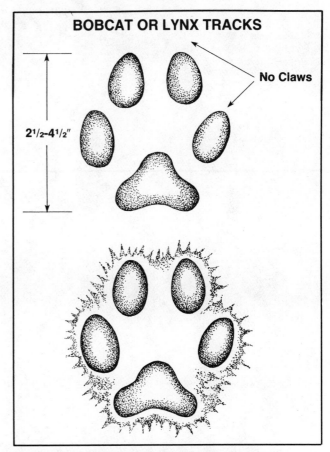

BOBCAT OR LYNX TRACKS

No Claws

2¹/₂-4¹/₂″

Bobcat and lynx tracks appear similar. The lynx's will be larger with considerable hair growth between the pads. In wet conditions, clear tracks may be apparent, but during prime hunting season, expect only a hole in the snow.

The author and his brother, Ron, almost stepped on the fox who belonged to these tracks, so they are fresh. The fox barely broke the crust layer on the worked soil. Note how small and delicate the prints are and the extreme variation in size and shape all made by the same animal.

Coyote scats are very telling. This one contains nearly 100 percent rabbit hair—clear evidence that this animal's diet included all the rabbit it could eat.

Other Tracking Basics

In addition to becoming eagle-eyed, here are a few other basics that should help you sharpen your tracking skills.

We know there will be times when finding tracks is difficult. At these times, cast your eyes slowly over the ground. This will turn up tracks and scats far more readily than quick glances or rapid checks that fail to focus completely on the ground. Move slowly, examining for disturbed stones, broken leaves or twigs, or displaced soil.

Take into account the light conditions for they will greatly influence success at finding sign. Bright, overcast days are the best. On these days, less light is being reflected back to the eyes by the surrounding soil and ground cover. As well, shadows are nearly absent. In the winter, the sharp angle of the sun in the northern parts of the range will make tracks look fresh when they are actually days old.

Like any other kinds of tracking effort, fresh snow is about the best medium the lucky hunter can have. Clay is difficult to find any sort of sign in and sandy soils don't retain evidence for long. Vegetation that is broken or disturbed will only be useful as sign while it is fresh. Warm days, even in the fall, soon dry out any of this type of sign and the same applies to the organic litter found along the forest floor. On the prairies, most vegetation is so dry and coarse that any disturbance by animal or man must be fairly substantial before any mark is left. Wet slough bottoms are good for recording sign, but the sign here may look fresh for days. The litter-covered shore lines of such places are so spongy that few tracks will remain. Faint depressions in the vegetation that were once tracks are difficult to discern, and the species that made the tracks may be anything from a nearby dog to a male coyote.

Always be alert for the animal to spring into view from behind nearby vegetation, or from under fences or hedge rows. It is not uncommon to have a coyote take off from under some sagebrush within only a few yards of the hunter. The same applies to a fox that might be holed up under some root pile until the hunter almost steps on its tail. This is especially true during the winter months when deep snows and cold temperatures make a predator—or any animal for that matter—reluctant to leave a warm, comfortable bedding site.

While tracking, frequently glance ahead along

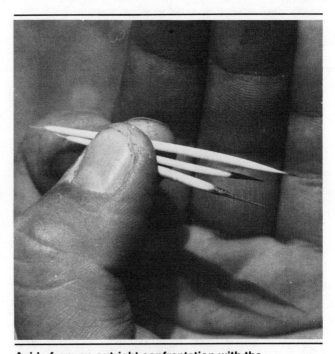

Aside from an outright confrontation with the porcupine itself, predators may pick up quills from abandoned dens or from carcasses of road-killed quill pigs. Look for these quills as possible clues to predator whereabouts.

Freshly disturbed ground where a fox searched for feeding mice. Sign such as this is usually found along the edges of cultivated fields.

last sign will usually help discover new clues to the animal's route.

In my experience, the trail goes cold when the animal has made a quick change in direction by zigzagging through the vegetation and across the country. From the eye level of the predator stand-

Become a keen observer. Take advantage of high points to become familiar with the countryside or to spot animals moving across openings or along water drainages.

the possible route an animal may have taken. Keep in mind the direction of the wind and the amount of cover. In general, an animal will want to remain under cover, circle upwind, and go high for a look over its back trail to see what might be following. Remember, too, that a fox or coyote can hear a tracker coming for yards before the hunter comes into sight. A predator will slip out from protective cover unseen in those circumstances. If the animal should cross a hill that provides a view of the trailing hunter, it will often stop, thereby according the hunter an excellent opportunity to shoot.

Many times the sign runs out within a short distance of where the animal was first spotted. It is then important to concentrate on the available sign, casting the eyes foward and looking for the next clue. Sometimes the sign will just stop cold. It will appear as if the animal was plucked from the air by some ancient god who looks after such things. Although many hunters will quit when this happens, walking in ever-widening circles from the

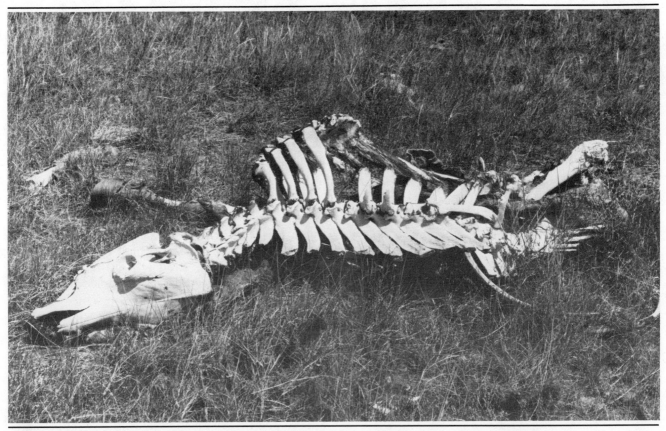

A winter-killed cow carcass—and all that remains is the bones. A site like this is always visited by predators, and sign will usually abound. It's a good starting point for the beginner to check for animal sign and an excellent place from which to try calling.

ing some eight to 12 inches above the ground, the trail and terrain will look very different compared to the six foot high vista of the hunter. Routes will vary, depending on the animal's purpose in traveling. Finding a mate or fleeing from the rapport of the hunter's rifle will cause different changes in direction. The route that looks logical to the hunter is not always the one chosen by the predator.

It is important to mark the location of the last observed sign. Try using a hat or bandana, then circle forward, always keeping your marker in sight and closely watching the ground for any kind of sign. Use the marker to deter yourself from straying all over the countryside.

Also, guard against spending too much time trying to relocate lost spoor. As a rule of thumb, don't spend much beyond half an hour searching

for sign. Many times, once sign becomes difficult to find, the next piece of sign or part of the trail is even harder to locate. The result is a lot of time wasted looking for tracks or broken vegetation and little real trailing of the animal. After a half hour of luckless searching, chalk it up as one for the animal and get on with other hunting.

An exception to this rule would be when you thought you had wounded an animal. In this case, take all the time necessary to make sure you have not inflicted injury or that a prime fox lay only 200 or 300 yards from where the trail stopped. Search diligently for any trace of sign and check areas where you think it likely the animal would go.

No two wounded long-hairs behave alike. Circumstances all vary. In deer hunting, it is a sage bet that a big buck hit in the heart-lungs area will

Marking the location where an animal was last seen or where the last evidence of a hit was seen is a smart practice.

several miles. Whatever, it is usually done very quickly. Signs are often several yards apart. On the other hand, I have seen wounded foxes take cover in whatever habitat is available. When the hunter approached, the animal would make a dash for further cover. It is under these kinds of circumstances that it behooves the hunter to search hard and do all he can to locate the animal. At no time should hide hunters show disregard for the predators they seek.

In conclusion, reading sign is a difficult art. It requires knowledge of the animal and well-developed skills of scrutiny on the part of the hunter. There is a lot of lore written on the subject and any hunter new to hide hunting is warned to take much of this information with the proverbial "grain of salt."

Important in this kind of hunting is having a good mental image of what the track or sign of the particular predator looks like. The would-be hunter should continually compare what his field experience tells him with what he has read and heard from other hunters. Remember that soil conditions, the time of year, and the weather conditions will greatly influence what a hunter sees.

The perfect tracks? They probably don't exist. But it is possible to develop a repertoire of what a set of good tracks looks like under various conditions. Study the tracks or sign of freshly taken animals and watch how that sign deteriorates with time. From this, much will be learned and absorbed, ready to be recalled when similar circumstances present themselves.

go down within 100 yards. A coyote or fox similarly hit could go to the 200 yard mark. But a poorly placed shot would send the animal scurrying, covering great amounts of country in very short order. The distance could be anything from a few yards to

Chapter 8

The Sounds Of the Caller

While standard hunting techniques—tracking and glassing the countryside—will give you some success, the real key to successful predator hunting is to master the art of calling. It is difficult to say when predator calling first began. The Plains Indians routinely lured predators, especially wolves, into bow range by making a sound using the lips and fingers. As a sport in America, calling came into its own only within recent times. The late Bert Popowski was probably the first to write much on the subject of calling, and he principally concerned himself with crow calling. Throughout the outdoor literature, predator calling does appear on a regular basis, but many of the articles pursue the varmint rather than the hide aspects of this type of hunting.

Morton Burnham is often credited with first attracting North American attention to calling. He hunted to reduce the pest populations around his home in central Texas. His sons, Winston and Murray, have carried on the traditions of predator calling and are known worldwide as experts and manufacturers of high-quality calls.

Basically two types of calls are on the market today: the newer electronic models and the traditional mouth-blown hand calls. As in anything else, each kind has its pluses and minuses. Although there are only two basic types, a staggering variety of new models and modifications are introduced by manufacturers each year. This may lead to some confusion when purchasing one, but personal preference and special hunting conditions will largely influence which call to use.

Electronic Calls

The term "electronic call" is really a misnomer, because an electronic call is actually a battery-powered cassette or tape player. Some models are designed specifically for hunting, but any battery-powered tape outfit will suffice for most predator hunting. Most everybody has or has seen a "Walkman" tape player or some other closely related model.

Advantages. There are some real advantages to using an electronic tape player. The most obvious one is that no previous experience is required. You can buy one in the morning and be calling by afternoon. You simply turn it on and the calling begins.

A second benefit lies in where you can position the machine. Many times it is advantageous to place the tape player some distance from the shooter. Since most predators focus on the sound, there is a good chance the animal will spot the shooter using a hand-held call. With an electronic call, the hunter can stay off to the side and thereby reduce the incidence of runoffs.

Electronic calls produce very uniform sounds. There is now a grand selection of tapes from which to choose, ranging from dying cottontails, jack rabbits and bird calls to sounds of the young. Any of these, popped into the player, can give good results in short order. The sounds are well done, technically correct and uniform. This kind of uniformity is not possible without a good bit of experience on the part of the caller using a mouth-blown call.

Disadvantages. There are, on the other hand, a number of disadvantages to the so-called electronic calls. Perhaps the worst of all is the need for bat-teries to operate the player. Most machines literally seem to eat batteries. Poor-quality batteries are no doubt part of the problem, but the power demanded to operate the recording must also be a factor. The cold conditions that the dry cells must work under also do nothing for their longevity. More recently, rechargeable battery packs have come on the market and to a certain extent reduce the problem. However, they create additional problems, as they have to be recharged frequently and more equipment has to be lugged and set up each time. In addition, the life of a rechargeable is also reduced by the cold. In short, the standard-sized battery is an abomination left over from a bygone

A Johnny Stewart electronic caller complete with carrying strap and amplifier.

An electronic predator caller can be easily transported into the fields. The big advantage of this type of caller is that it can be used immediately upon purchase. No practice is necessary and the sounds produced are excellent.

era, and something that this highly technical world should have replaced long ago.

Perhaps the next most important disadvantage is the delicate nature of the tape machines themselves. Any rough handling will leave most models inoperative. Then there is the problem of getting the things repaired. Models become obsolete, few dealers stock parts, and the plastic and light metal construction sometimes seems designed for breakage. However, where rough usage is held to a minimum, reliable service can be expected from those machines designed specifically for predator calling.

Another area of complaint is the time needed to set up an electronic call. A mouth-blown type requires no setup time. You simply pop the call into

your mouth and start blowing. However, with the electronic device, the entire system must be unpacked, tape rewound, cords untangled, batteries checked and the assemblage put in place. Added to this are problems such as forgetting the extra batteries, leaving the tape in your other hunting jacket, or being all set up and having to run back to the truck for some forgotten item.

I know of one outdoorsman who left his stand to trail a wounded coyote. He switched off his tape just after he shot and ran after the humped-up coyote. He was able to track the coyote down, but was unable to relocate his calling setup. Believe it or not, he made three or four trips back to the area in a span of a few months looking for his electronic caller. He finally found it, no worse for being weather beaten, but of course the batteries were dead. With a hand-held model that would have been with the caller, the whole situation would never have come to pass.

During the recent citizen's band rage that swept the country, a good friend had an externally mounted speaker placed on his truck. He could be called over the C.B. and hear it outside the vehicle if he was within hearing distance. We soon figured out how to hook a tape player to the external speaker.

That year we were hunting in a parkland area where clumps of trees were interspersed with much prairie. Trails wound through many of these bushes, so it was easy to hide the vehicle by leaving it right on the trail to operate the call. We would spread ourselves out from the truck, usually about 50 or 100 yards apart, along the edge of a bush overlooking the open grassland. Since the grass was well razed off, a coyote could be seen from a great distance out on the prairie.

We never had any trouble with batteries using this technique, and never once ran the vehicle battery to the point that the truck would not start. It was about the slickest system I have ever seen, but in reality could only be used within the unique habitat we found ourselves hunting that year.

Hand-held Calls

Based on their construction, hand-held calls can be divided into five categories. They are the enclosed reed, the exposed reed type, the semi-closed type, the kind where the reed is fixed at both ends, and the bellows call. There is a sixth, called a mouth diaphragm type, which is treated separately.

Advantages. Hand-held calls offer many advantages. Right off the top, they are nearly foolproof. Only occasionally will one ever break, and when they do, the reeds can usually be replaced easily and inexpensively. They are portable and can be worn on a lanyard or string around the neck, or stuffed in a pocket. There is, of course, a plethora of models from which to choose, and the average call costs less than a box of cartridges. In addition, they are virtually maintenance-free.

The professional callers claim the single greatest advantage of a hand-held call lies in its versatility of sounds. Using the lips, tongue, hands, and changing the angle at which the call is held, the tone, strength or length of calling sound can all be varied. Loud, strong, bellowing calls can be made at will, or soft, death-rattling cries that will drive a

Adam Lynn Lindsey with the results of a day's hunt in central Texas. Lindsey was one of the first to produce predator calls for the American hunting public.

Here is an example of the enclosed-reed, hand-held type—an original Pied Piper. This was one of the first calls ever manufactured and regularly advertised in the United States.

meat-hungry predator in at full tilt. All these can be had from a single call.

Disadvantages. The only disadvantage is that it requires a little practice to become proficient in using a hand-held or mouth-blown call. Otherwise, the advantages far outweigh that drawback.

The *enclosed reed* type of call is the most common. As the name says, the reed is completely enveloped in either wood or metal. This type of call is easy to master, since one need only blow into the mouthpiece and an appropriate sound will come out. Some calling purists believe that this kind of call lacks a certain amount of versatility. It is their opinion that not enough variation in the sounds can be produced. That concern aside, this type of call works very well.

There are many makes of the enclosed-reed predator call. The Pied Piper was one of the first on the market, designed and sold by Adam Lynn Lindsey and Wayne Weems. Later both men developed and marketed their own brands of calls, although the Pied Piper is still available today. Another popular enclosed-type is the series made by Ed Sceery, a well-known predator control expert and animal scientist. These calls have excellent tonal qualities and are great for beginners concerned about making the right sounds. Lohman of Nesho, Missouri, produces calls in cottontail, jack rabbit, and medium or close-in versions, and offers the largest selection of predator calls available. The old call company, Faulks of Lake Charles, Louisiana, manufactures a nice walnut-finished distress call that imitates an adult cottontail. Scotch, a well-known manufacturer of duck calls, offers several enclosed-reed predator calls, one of which features a high-volume design.

The *exposed-reed* call is made with a larger reed than the enclosed kind. The vibrations of the reed are controlled by the positioning of the lips and this

Ed Sceery, well-known predator control expert, designed his own line of predator calls. They are very well made and produce terrific sounds. The reed sections are interchangeable, offering a wide range of sounds for the hunter. Anyone new to predator hunting should try these.

The Crit'R Call by Major L. Boddicker is an example of a totally exposed-reed call. Only a single call, it is capable of producing 40 different sounds.

gives great variation to the sounds made. Foremost among these is the Crit'R Call, designed by Major L. Boddicker of La Porte, Colorado.

The *semi-enclosed* kind of call features a reed that is fixed between two pieces of plastic extending back from the main body of the call. These extended portions are called voice channels. The caller bites down on the channels to control the vibration of the reed. This, in turn, will yield varying sounds. This type of call is really a combination of the enclosed- and exposed-reed calls. Examples of this type are the Johnny Steward PC-3 and the Scotch 1533.

The fourth kind consists of a *reed fixed at both ends* and the lips pass air over the length of the reed. Sound is changed by biting down on the housing to shorten the length of the reed. These calls are good for short-range work, but do not develop the volume necessary for most average calling situations. One model in my collection consists of a plastic reed sandwiched between two other pieces

of hard plastic, while another uses a similar principle but employs wood to hold the reed. These types of calls are most often advertised as "close-in" predator calls.

The *bellows call* is typified by the well-established Scotch call that has been on the market for years. A long rubber bellows is placed over the end of a wide-mouth predator call. When the bellows is pulled and released, air is forced into the mouth of the call and the sound is produced. This type of call is easy to operate, and fairly accurate sounds can be produced by pulling the bellows to the same distance with each call. It can also be tied to a tree and a cord run to the hunter's position, thus placing some distance between the hunter and the calling sound. While the bellows call is easy to use, it does have the disadvantage of needing both hands to operate.

The *diaphragm squealer* qualifies as more of a mouth-held call than a hand call, because the user pops the call right into his mouth. This call is positioned with the horseshoe end forward and the call body resting against the roof of the mouth. The tongue is placed tight against the call. Air is then forced between the tongue and the rubber membrane of the call. Currently, Lohman makes a model solely for predator use, which reproduces with incredible realism the scream of a wounded rabbit. However, this is a fairly difficult call to master. The major advantage over other calls is that the

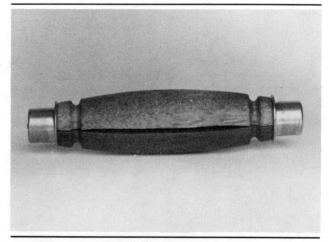

Here is a compact close-in predator call from Lohman, a company that offers one of the largest selections of predator calls available.

Three excellent examples of semi-enclosed, reed-type predator calls: (1) by Pied Piper; (2) by Johnny Stewart; and (3) by Scotch. The remaining calls are close-in type: (4) the Sceery Varmint Getter; (5) the Scotch 1563; (6) by Pied Piper; and (7) the Faulks PCR-61 Cottontail Call. A hide hunter should have one of these as well as a regular long-range type call as part of his kit.

hunter can place both hands on the rifle while continuing to call at the same time.

Selecting the Right Call

The number of predator calls available today is incredible. This gives the hunter a great selection of manufacturers and a variety of shapes and sizes from which to choose. There is also a difference in the sounds produced. What may work well in one area may turn out to be a disaster in another; it is probably for this reason that calls are often local in manufacture and distribution. Calls made in a hunter's home area are probably more attuned to local conditions, but it can also work the other way, with the predators always hearing one brand of call. They become wise to this and picking another call can prove helpful. Anyway, this wide choice is appreciated by the practicing hunter.

In addition, hunters are always trying new or different tricks to call coyotes. One hunter pursued coyotes with a horn and reed combination that somehow imitated the howls of a female coyote. Howling for coyotes is not the same as using a predator call, however. The coyote is howling to be heard and does not always seek out the other howling member of the species. Predator calling brings the predator to you because he thinks there is an easy meal waiting. In essence, the game hunts you. When a coyote howls, he is not necessarily answering anybody or attempting to give his location away. Howling like a coyote will not give the results that squeaking like a dying rabbit will produce.

There is probably no such thing as the perfect predator call. The professionals continue to argue amongst themselves and current thought in call design seems to be emphasizing the need for variable-pitch ability. This, it is said, will allow the hunter to produce the pup-type squeaks, mid-

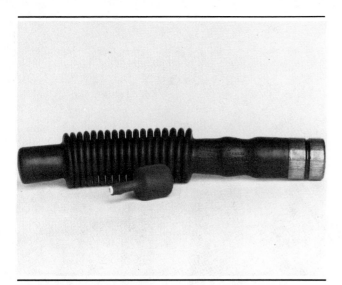

Two examples of bellows-type calls—Model 1509 for predators, and the close-in mouse squeaker call sold by many calling firms.

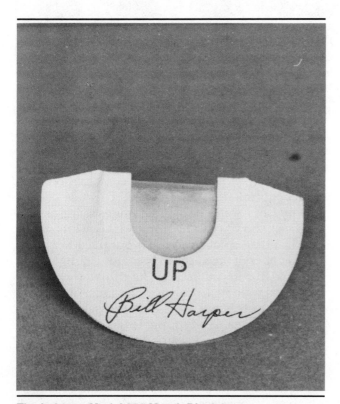

The Lohman Model 250 Mouth Diaphragm Predator Call. This call is very lightweight, produces good sound for close-in work, and leaves the hunter's hands free to use the rifle.

range squeals, and the louder, long-range calling sounds. In the minds of the professionals, this kind of versatility is needed both because one call can serve so many functions and the same call can be varied to produce unique sounds that will still attract predators in areas that are heavily called in by hunters using the traditional single-pitch type calls.

For the beginner, the wise choice would be to buy several calls of different manufacture. Three or four would be a good start, depending on the availability of the different types in your area. The enclosed-reed type that produces a uniform sound would be best. Also, the bellows type, as produced by Scotch, would be a good beginning, since it is an easy call to practice with and the hunter can quickly learn the sound.

A variable-pitch type call can be bought later. Currently, Johnny Stewart offers a variable-pitch call that combines the traditional call design with an innovative rubber bubble that can be bitten down on to change the pitch. It is easy to use once you know what you want your calls to do.

Another variation on the standard call is the old Faulks adjustable call. It is really an average enclosed-reed call that has a rubber washer placed over the shaft of the reed. By moving the rubber band about one-sixteenth of an inch forward, the pitch is altered to produce a higher note. This can be done until the band is at its furthest forward position and it produces the faint, close-in squeaker sound used by some callers. The call is particularly good for beginners since it comes factory set to produce an average jack rabbit death squawk. Once your calling ability improves, it is possible to make the kinds of adjustments that give the versatility demanded by professional callers.

Care of Calls

Whichever type or combination of calls you purchase, they should be cared for as any other type of outdoor equipment. Accidents do in more calls than any other cause. I have stepped on them as I got out of the truck too hastily. I have left them in coat pockets that were later sat on. And I had one small call disappear down the defroster slot under the windshield of my Dodge truck. Many more get

AUTHOR'S FAVORITE CALLS

Manufacturer	Models	Sounds Produced/Comments
Ed Sceery E.J. Sceery Company 1949 Osage Lane Santa Fe, NM 87501	Varmint Getter 1 Varmint Getter 2 Varmint Getter 3	Rodent distress Cottontail Jack rabbit Excellent sounds for all calling environments; highly recommended. Calls show excellent workmanship.
A.L. Lindsey Pied Piper Calls Box 80921 Midland, TX 79703	Long range Woodsman	Variable; crow-to-mouse distress Wailing jack rabbit, a foolproof call for beginners, giving good volume and sound
Major L. Boddicker Rocky Mountain Wildlife Products 4620 Moccasin Circle La Porte, CO 80535	Crit'R Call	Produces 40 different calls An excellent choice for the more experienced caller who wants only one call.
Faulks Game Calls 616 18th Street Lake Charles, LA 70601	P-60 PCR-61 P60-A	General-purpose distress call Cottontail sounds Top-quality adjustable call; precision made to imitate jack rabbits, cottontails and distressed mice
Scotch Game Calls 6619 Oak Orchard Road Elba, NY 14058	1523 1533 1563	Rabbit; a high-volume call that generates a lot of noise A semi-enclosed reed call that gives a broad range of tones from ear-piercing squawks to squeals A high-pitched rabbit squealer
Lohman Manufacturing Co. 320 East Spring Box 220 Nesho, MO 64850	210 220 230 211 250	Jack rabbit distress Cottontail voice Squeaker call Variable tone; excellent quality High-pitched-cottontail Lohman produces a very comprehensive line of calls with a pleasing finish.
P.S. Olt Box 550 Pekin, IL 61554	T-20 22 33 CP-21	An all-purpose distress sound A dual-range call that produces very clear sounds; well made Intermediate-range rabbit distress call Close-in call that produces a fine, high-pitched noise
Johnny Stewart Game Calls 5100 Fort Avenue Box 7594 Waco, TX 76710	PC-1 PC-3	Variable-pitch animal call that covers jack rabbits, cottontails, both long and short ranges A semi-enclosed reed call that produces an ear-shattering squawk

Scotch call Model 1523. The largest predator call on the market, it is capable of producing an incredible volume of sound.

Three variable-pitch predator calls: the famous Faulks P-60A, the unique rubber-bulbed Johnny Stewart PC-1, and the new Lohman Triple-Tone Varmint Call. These are excellent choices for the advanced predator hunter.

misplaced in rucksacks, lunch bags and tool boxes. Few have ever worn out. Indeed, I have noticed that vehicle cleaning time is most dangerous for hand-held calls left on the dash or seat.

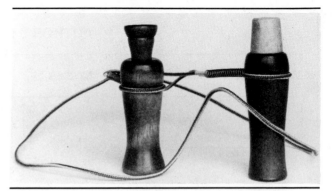

A lanyard is a sound, inexpensive investment for the active hunter. It keeps a call handy and reduces the chance of loss or breakage.

All of this argues very favorably for a lanyard, a little device many of the call makers try to sell us. Some companies make a type that will allow two calls to be fastened to the same string. It is a great invention, even though it is little more than a piece of string or leather that has a hook that fastens to the call. Most companies make a lanyard that fits their particular models. However, anyone can find a leather shoelace and make one of his own. Anything will work, and I currently have one made from a piece of nylon baler twine. A lanyard will go a long way in helping the hunter keep track of his call, not to mention keeping it handy when needed.

Although most hand-held calls are virtually maintenance free, in cold weather moisture builds up in most models. A rap on the knee or quick dismantling and cleaning usually will correct the situation and keep your call in good working order.

The reeds of almost any type of call can, though seldom will, wear out. But when they do, you'll know. It will seem as if they are no longer producing the right kind of sound. In most cases, this only occurs after very much calling and is due to the metal fatiguing, or just becoming soft after so many vibrations. In fact, it usually happens to the call that you have done most of your at-home practicing on. Most reeds will outlast the caller, so it is not a serious problem and I only point it out to show that it is possible, though unlikely. Should a call break or malfunction, however, replacement is an inexpensive proposition, because of the low cost of the call.

Chapter 9

How To Call Predators Effectively

Calling predators is a skill with a few simple basics that can be learned by anyone interested in the technique and willing to practice. Calling saves the hide hunter valuable travel time and allows the countryside to be worked in a much more methodical manner. The art of calling and hide hunting are made for one another.

The four-footed predators respond well to calling. Coyotes, red foxes and bobcat will all come when called. Coyotes and red foxes will usually run directly to the sound. Gray foxes will come in through the cover and bobcats will come in slowly. Even badgers will react to the dying rabbit sounds of the average predator call. Indeed, the broad spectrum of reactions from the predators clearly shows how important dying animal sounds are to these meat eaters in their daily lives.

Results of predator calling can be dramatic. I well recall the first time I tried calling. As luck would have it, I was in the prime coyote country of southeast Alberta's short grass prairie. Here you can see for miles in any direction, yet the land has a distinct roll to it that makes things look closer than they really are. I was driving down a back road and spotted a coyote standing in the prairie to my left. In one swift motion I stopped the truck, rolled down the window, and had my rifle on the animal. The shot, hastily made, only sent the coyote farther

out into the prairie. I sat there watching the coyote disappear into the morning sun, feeling somewhat down in the mouth for being so slipshod in my technique. I picked up my recently acquired predator call and began making a few amateurish squawks and toots out of the window of the truck. Three coyotes loped out from behind one of the rolls in the prairie and started heading toward the truck. I perked right up and, despite my amazement, was able to down one animal. Needless to say, I was a confirmed predator caller from that day forward.

Too much fuss has been made about the sound needed to draw predators into range. With any good-quality call, a sound can be produced that is sufficient to attract the predator's attention, and this is really the caller's objective. He is not attempting to speak the coyote's language. Any predator will respond to the sound in some way. The animal will use its other senses, especially smell and knowledge of the territory, to sort out the sounds and determine if a meal really lies just beyond the next ridge.

The most common and effective call for all hide hunters is the dying rabbit sound. If there are jack rabbits in your area, be sure to purchase a call that will reproduce that sound. On the other hand, if you hunt in an area where the little bush rabbit

An adult coyote comes toward the calling sound. The coyote can be fooled into rifle range, but the hunter must overcome the coyote's natural survival instincts.

predominates, be sure to use the call that imitates that sound.

Avoid using any of the dying bird sounds. Very few birds are around during the prime fur season in most areas. Upland game birds are not a major food source for most predators in the temperate areas of North America, and calling on this basis would not be productive. In most of the settled regions, a predator will live successfully being a scavenger long before it will shift to a diet based on a few remaining upland game birds.

Beginners should not try to overcomplicate the call. Remember, in nature the source of a dying rabbit call will also vary. Not all rabbits are the same. This means that any fox or coyote will already be familiar with a broad range of calls. As well, these calls will have come to the predator with a great variety of pitch, amplitude and rhythms.

Having said that, it is still important to know how to blow the call correctly. Let's face it, a predator survives on its ability to sort out danger and locate food. A radical change in the sound due to a mistake in technique will send most predators high-tailing it for the hills. These animals have survived by stealth and using their smarts, and a strange sound only signals danger to them.

Controlling the Variables

Although certain calls produce specific sounds, there are variables that the caller can control. The volume, the length of pauses between calls, the pitch, the cadence or rhythm and the arrangement of the calls are all easily controllable with the proper technique. Many factors will influence how far the sounds will be heard, including the volume of the call, the type of terrain and the local weather conditions. Sound is obviously interfered with by any kind of wind. It also carries better out on the open plains than in the dense bush of the north.

Volume. Using a recording or tape to start out is an excellent way to determine the correct volume used by the professional. It will also give good guidance on overall technique.

Keeping a steady stream of good volume requires that the caller have a reasonable set of lungs. While blowing your heart out is not what is being recommended here, it is necessary to blow hard and

constantly. There are many sounds in nature, not to mention many more created by man, that assail the predators ears all day long. Volume is needed both to compete with these sounds as well as to draw the predators attention and keep it from being diverted by dozens of other environmental noises.

A snowmobile or chain saw being operated in the nearby bush will almost always obliterate your calling sounds. This holds true even on quiet, cool fall mornings that are free of wind. Predators are particularly wary of loud snowmobile or chain saw noises. They sound very similar, and generally the predators will move away from this kind of disturbance. Coyotes and foxes are not bothered by the sound of moving vehicles. However, I have seen foxes actually fall flat in stubble fields when a vehicle stopped. The moving vehicle seemed not to bother them. The same applies to coyotes.

For beginners, a loud, high-pitched "waa-waa" is the best call to start with. If an animal comes to the call, do not switch volume or the way you are calling. Why tamper with success? Later, as you develop better skills and become more familiar with the important aspects of predator hunting, you can try a high-pitched close-in call.

Cadence of the Calls. The cadence or pace at which the calling is done is important. Measured movements that rise and fall seem to be more effective than a straight blurt of sound. A series of sounds that are at first fast, then slowed seem to keep the predator interested in the possibility of a meal. Short bursts and long, drawn-out "waas" that are almost wailful also work.

Some callers achieve that bleating crescendo of cries by opening and closing their hands over the end of the call. However, this ties up both hands and causes scrambling to retrieve the rifle at the first sight of the predator. Naturally, the risk of the animal spotting such movement is far greater than it seeing a still, hidden figure. You'll never recapture a lost moment, so keep calling with both hands on the rifle, ready to shoot at the first clear opportunity.

Pauses and Patterns. Most of my calling has been done by first beginning with a series of long, wailful blasts. This is followed by a brief pause, and then a series of quick, short calls. I use a long pause after this and then repeat the entire sequence. The

Outdoor writer and hunter Jerome Knap demonstrates good calling technique. The hunter places himself in the shade and against a vegetative background.

Brendan Pyle shows how to use the Johnny Stewart close-in predator call, which emits a close copy of the sounds of a dying rabbit.

theory is that the loud, long, beginning calls will at least get the predator's attention. If the animal is on the move toward the sound, the short, high-pitched squawks will focus his attention and provide for a lot of opportunity to watch for the animal's approach. Also, listen very intently, trying to hear the animal passing through bushes or crossing stubble fields.

Some North American hide-producing areas have become overhunted. As a result, they are the same areas that have suffered from overcalling. Here predators are wise to the mechanical squawking of either hand-held calls or the fancier electronic models. Under these circumstances, only the most skillful of callers will have good luck, because it will be necessary to vary the calling repertoire. Using quick, short bursts of sound alternated with slow, almost melancholic sounds may be successful. Various situations will dictate when different combinations of calls and techniques will be necessary.

One theory of predator hunting says a coyote can be pinpointed by its howling. As a hunter moves toward the sound, a predator call can be used to draw the animal into rifle range. This part of the theory may seem plausible at first glance.

The theory goes on to say that a coyote can be enticed into howling by using a siren. While a coyote often does howl to get a response from another coyote, any coyote worth his reproductive salt can certainly discern a siren from the replies of a young bitch in heat. It is my belief that any coyote older than a pup will not respond to these tactics. If anything, the animals will be put to flight and the en-

Brad Pyle demonstrates the Johnny Stewart Fox Tinney. This is a squeaking predator call that is primarily used to draw an animal into view once it is known to be in an area.

tire effort counterproductive to good efficient hide hunting.

Driving the countryside with a siren blaring in the prairie morning would most likely arouse a visit from the local police. No doubt, too, it would do little for a hunter's public relations in an area; he would probably end up being dubbed as some idiot from the city. The techniques and methods a hunter uses in taking his furs are closely watched by the rural public; it behooves all of us to use care and practicality in our techniques.

On the subject of howling, coyotes will call between themselves. Howling is usually done by sexually active animals, and frequently when one dominant male crosses into the territory of another. Young coyotes practice howling daily. They howl when they find food, when they see one another or, as any old sheepman will tell you, because of the moon.

Let's leave it this way. If you are not getting predators to respond to your calling something is wrong—not the least of which may be simply poor predator density in the area. The actual sound made is not nearly as important as several other factors. Calling still works best in areas with good to above-average predator populations and with few callers to arouse animal suspicions.

When To Call

Some say that calling is influenced by the moon. Others claim that local weather conditions affect the results. However, in reality there is probably no perfect time of day or weather in which to call.

It is true that weather conditions will produce changes in animal behavior. A snow storm will usually cause foxes and coyotes to lie up somewhere for the duration of the storm. Following the storm, especially a long one, the canids come out hunting in force. This is probably one of the best times in which to call.

Many outdoorsmen will also tell you that the few hours before a storm, especially a rain storm, are good calling times. Experience seems to bear this out, and there is little doubt that animals do alter their movements and hunting patterns before and after storms.

In areas with good predator populations, the an-

In overhunted areas, only the most skillful callers will succeed—and with a varied calling repertoire. Here Ellen Elman calls from the shade of a haystack.

imals can be called in at almost any time of day. Early morning and just before sunset are proven to be the most productive, but results can also be had at three o'clock in the afternoon.

A beginner should try to do his calling during the early part of the morning. The period of an hour or two just after sunrise should be most favorable. At this time, the wind is calm, the air seems clear and the sound of calling travels the farthest.

Wind is the caller's greatest enemy. Aside from the fact that the calling sound will not carry well, the animals will refuse to move. Wind seems to disturb their senses and foxes and coyotes are unwilling to travel for all but the easiest meal. Wind also betrays the hunter's position.

Hunting seasons for other game, especially big game animals, are important to the hide hunter. The big game seasons in most jurisdictions begin before the hide hunting and often overlap with it. Indeed, hunters often hold licenses for both.

Many big game hunters are not adverse to popping off the odd fox or coyote. On the positive side, they can pay for their trip with hides taken while big game hunting. Although many of the hides are a tad too early, the majority will still bring in needed dollars to pay for the gas or lodging in distant places. It also adds another dimension to the big game hunt.

On the negative side, it means that many hides are harvested before they are really ready for market. This is unfortunate. In addition, it is not the time to be afield calling predators. They will be moving far too much and too cautiously for the results to be fruitful. Coupled with this is the need to wear bright-colored fluorescent outer clothing in most states and provinces to comply with the big game season regulations, and the difficulty only increases.

Perhaps worst of all is the disturbance to the fur bearers themselves. It takes nearly a month following the close of the big game season for the predator population to settle down and respond in a normal fashion. The animals are incredibly wary, especially in jurisdictions where short, big game hunting seasons exist and large numbers of hunters participate. In my opinion, this is one of the reasons long-hairs are difficult to call at the beginning of the fur season.

Sometimes there will be no cover from which to call. Try and position yourself in a water run that affords some cover and keeps the hunter from silhouetting against the sky.

Winter offers the most opportunities for hide hunting. When calling on bright, sunny days, it is crucial to sit in the shade of any cover. This will reduce the chances of light reflecting from equipment such as rifle barrels and eyeglasses.

It also drives home the importance of gaining permission on areas that have been closed to big game hunting. Here fur-bearing populations will not be as disturbed, and some evidence supports the theory that foxes, and especially coyotes, will move into these unhunted areas for a few weeks at a time. From a strictly biological point of view, few animals ever permanently move out of their territories. However, there is little doubt that some resorting of territories does occur when several animals are removed from the population during the big game season. This, then, is a good time to be out with permission in hand on areas that were unhunted and visited by displaced predators.

One of the biggest advantages of hide hunting is that it can be done almost anytime during the open fur season. Certain problems aside, hide hunting can be neatly combined with a full-time job. I hunted coyotes for years just on Saturdays. Many times it turned out that it did not matter what time of day I called. The long-hairs in my district did not eat only at morning, noon and dusk; they would take an easy meal anytime.

Most calling will be done during the prime season. This will vary with the area in which you live, but in general it occurs in late fall or early winter. The animals will have grown into their winter coats in preparation for the coldest part of the season. After this time, the fur begins to lose its primeness.

Winter, of course, offers the most opportunities. Fewer people are around, farm operations are finished for the year, and the animals are actively seeking food to generate energy for the long, cold prairie nights. Sign is easier to locate and the an-

Calling under tough winter conditions poses special problems. A cushion is recommended for sitting on during winter calling sessions. A rucksack, old feed sack or, in this case, an extra winter jacket can be used. Some padding is needed to insulate the hunter from the snow below.

imals can be seen at greater distances when approaching a call. Foxes will be found closer to farmyards and outbuildings. Coyotes will individually be covering more ground in search of rabbits and sleeping field mice. It is easier to get around in the country, providing snow conditions are not excessive. And, finally, if you can hunt during the week, you'll have fewer people to contend with or disturb your hunting activities.

Where To Call From

Choosing the place from which to call is one of the most important elements of hide hunting. When calling technique is rough, a good stand will help make up for this.

Right off the top, a good calling site will be in an area that has plenty of predator sign. Preferably, you have scouted the immediate area and found tracks and scats, and perhaps an old kill site, so you are reasonably confident that foxes or coyotes are around. The sign has, of course, been fresh enough to keep your interest up. Perhaps you have seen a coyote on occasion standing in a nearby field.

Calling in an area where there are no animals is probably the biggest mistake beginners make. Time spent checking for sign is time well spent, and an area with really good sign can be used for calling several times in one week or over the course of a month. This means less driving time and more actual hunting time.

It is important to take a position that overlooks

a good part of the country. This is often difficult to achieve, but if you can get about 50 yards of visibility around your position, you'll be in good shape.

One of the best positions from which to call is up on the side of a valley. I have a special knoll located next to an old granary that sits beside a cultivated field. It overlooks a wooded valley some two miles across and dozens of miles long. With my back to the granary and my calls cascading down the valley wall, I can spot a coyote coming from 200 yards. I have made some long shots from this vantage point and it continues to be one of my favorite calling spots.

Another excellent location is along a treed fence-line. With my back to the fence and calling sounds spitting out across the cultivated field, I have had tremendous luck. Foxes and coyotes will routinely hunt along such fence-lines and have little fear of the call. To them, it is just another dying rabbit in their neighborhood, something they live with daily.

During the winter, fence-lines blow in with snow, which makes for excellent calling vantage. The drift gives the shooter some height to overlook the surrounding area, and digging into the snow will also help conceal your position.

Try calling near out-structures that may be found in far-off fields. These include irrigation works, old wells, abandoned buildings and corrals. Such areas as this used corral always harbor small rodents during the summer and predators seem to remember taking meals there.

In parkland areas, the edges of the woods offer good calling positions. One of the better locations is to find a slough bottom surrounded by trees and willows. Cattails and other emergent vegetation may be present, although much of this will be packed down with snow. Any such place that provides cover in the woods or vegetation and overlooks an open area will fill the needs of a calling site.

The ends of trails, old logging roads, abandoned back roads, pathways cut off by new road building or little-used, intermittent farm trails are ideal places from which to attempt calling. All predators patrol such areas and, if the sign is running right, these will be productive.

An irrigation head ditch is also good. In the winter, the ditches will blow nearly full of snow. Since the ditches are higher than the surrounding irrigated land, a good position can be had in the vegetation and snow that is present. A coyote can be seen as far away as a half mile under these circumstances.

Another zone that has proven productive over the years are the railway right of ways. Where I live there are lots of rail lines with few trains. Many go unused for months at a time, especially in the winter. Most right of ways are poorly maintained, and surrounded by a lot of shrubs and briars. Some have good stands of poplar growing on the more moist northern sides. This makes great rabbit habitat and can lead to productive calling. A position against a railway fence or in some of the larger trees will work very well.

Previously, I mentioned farm nuisance grounds. These should, of course, be called from at every opportunity. I have had calling results from stands that were only a couple of hundred yards from the farmyard. Never overlook such sites.

Farms that have cattle will put up some hay with which to over-winter the herd. Foxes frequent these hay yards in search of mice or rabbits, and also use a straw stack as a lookout point while basking in the morning sun. Calling near such hay or stack yards, as they are called, will regularly yield foxes.

Field corners make worthwhile calling sites. Sometimes there will be a rock pile, or a scrap of bush or shrub has grown up where the machines cannot reach when turning. Sitting in the shade of a rock pile or some of this shrub can be productive when overlooking larger fields.

In an area north of where I often hunt, a lot of land improvement is under way. Bush has been broken down and pushed into long piles called windrows. In time, the windrows will be burned and the land broken and brought into grain production. These bush piles become great habitat for bush rabbits. Jumping on the loose sticks and vegetative debris that comprise the pile will often send a bush rabbit scurrying for cover. Coyotes and foxes will habitually hunt these areas with zeal. It is easy to hide within these piles and call almost unseen by the predator. So sure are they that a meal is present that many coyotes will almost dig the caller out of the sticks and stumps he is using for cover.

In the west, coyotes will prey on the prairie dog and a ubiquitous burrowing rodent known variously as a gopher, picket pin or ground squirrel. These animals go below ground well before the prime fur season, although on the odd occasion, prairie dogs will remain above ground until the first snow. For some reason coyotes will continue to hang around these large colonies long after the ground squirrels and prairie dogs have gone into hibernation. I have had good success calling near these colonies. Perhaps the predator recalls easier pickings from earlier in the season.

Coyotes and foxes can be taken from the same calling site. Many times, especially in the Midwest, fox and coyote share the same range. These animals are virtual competitors and, given any opportunity, a coyote will attempt to kill a fox. However, the coyote is rarely successful, for his lighter and more agile cousin knows all the escape tricks, too.

In areas where cultivated farmlands blend into extensive pasture or ranch land, both species will be found along the margins of this combination of habitats. Successful calling can induce both species to respond to the call.

Setting Up. Getting into a calling site has to be done with some caution if the calling effort is to be successful. Leave your vehicle hidden some distance from the actual site. In the open prairie, leave your car or truck between two rolls in the prairie, then follow the lower ground until you reach your targeted position.

It is important not to waste time getting into place. Winds change quickly, especially out on the

When hunting along fence-lines, bush edges or meadows, dig yourself into the snow. This will help hide the hunter as well as give some protection from the weather.

prairie, and the scent stream can be blown in several directions within only a few minutes.

Sometimes there will be no cover from which to call. This most often occurs out on the open plains or large cultivated fields. In these cases, try to find the edge of a water run, lie down on your side and call, using whatever vegetation is present for cover. Also, use any existing fence and sit with your back against a post. This will somewhat break up your silhouette and provide a good calling site. In stub-

ble fields, lying down in the tracks left by the combine or grain truck will provide some cover.

When calling, it is crucial to sit in the shade of any cover. Rifle barrels, scopes, belt buckles and other hunting gear reflect light very easily, and this gleam will alert any predator for miles around. Eyeglasses are one of the worst offenders. Shade will markedly reduce the chances of any reflection.

In the winter this is especially important, because little vegetation is left to offer cover. As well, the snow reflects bright winter light up to the hunter and off his spectacles and other equipment. At this time of year, dig into the snow to help camouflage yourself.

Wherever you happen to be, try to sit with your back against some type of rest—a tree, a stone pile, some broken bush, an old log or a fence post. A back support will make it easier for you to scan the terrain in front of you and will help steady your shooting when the time comes.

Putting It All Together

Once a hunter has picked his stand and set up comfortably, it is best to begin calling right away. There does not seem to be any advantage to or reason for waiting. Your approach to the stand will have scared off most animals in the immediate vicinity, and predators rarely return once they have been put to flight. This is true unless a food cache or old carcass is about and, then, depending on the time of year, the odd animal will be very hesitant about quitting country. Start calling quickly.

However, not all predators are scared off from the more intermediate ranges. For this reason, calling should begin at a reduced volume for the first two or three minutes. A fox asleep under a log some 200 yards away may not have heard your approach and could easily be brought in by this low-level calling.

Increase the volume of calling until you are working at your maximum for effective calling. Overzealous blowing on any predator call will sound out of place. Avoid those high-pitched, uncontrolled squawks that are the result of too much air. Practice calling at various volumes beforehand. Once at your loudest, continue to use a series of calls or an arrangement of short and long calls with a pause in between.

Even though fur bearers will respond differently, calling should generally be conducted for no more than 20 minutes from one site. On a day with favorable weather conditions I might extend this time to 25 or so minutes, but rarely more. If your calling is covering an area of one or two square miles, it would take a coyote only that long to cover the distance. If the animal were closer, less time would be required to respond to the call. Ultimately, all forms of predator calling are directed to

animals in the immediate vicinity, and most predators will react to a call within the 20-minute span.

If you are in an area where you have a good field of view and you can see an animal approaching the sound from some distance, it is often wise to continue calling longer than prescribed, especially if you lose sight of the animal. However, if it does not appear, your scent or some other factor has probably alerted the fur bearer to some sort of danger.

Most hunters will stop calling if an animal responds within five or 10 minutes of the initial series of calls. I prefer to keep on calling and have my hands ready on my rifle. I use my mouth to hold the call and keep blowing my standard series of calls until something develops. If nothing happens within the time frame, I might try one of those high-pitched squeaker calls or shift my Faulks to a high-pitched tone. Once I have called about five or so minutes with the squeaker—and still no results—I pack up my kit and move elsewhere.

Remember, too, that other factors can foil your calling success. The classic is to have the animal respond to the call, and then be scared off by some noise or extraneous event. When calling in heavily populated rural environments, do not be surprised if your coyote turns tail because a vehicle stopped near an adjacent field. Also, some unusual activity associated with man will send the responding coyote heading for cover, like a snowplow operating on a rural back road. The din is just too much for a fox or coyote.

On one occasion after sending out a series of calls, I heard a vehicle stop on the road, followed by a flurry of voices, then a volley of gunfire. Obviously someone had spotted the fox I was calling and wasted no time trying to take the hide for himself. Be alert for these kinds of interferences, and stop calling if one of them occurs.

If an animal starts to leave, do some follow-up calling. This could be a quick change in the cadence or series used in your calling. Usually, the animal is leaving because it has become suspicious. Sometimes a rapid bleating set of calls will cause the animal to reconsider just briefly enough for a quick shot.

Remember, too, that in nature a wounded or dying rabbit does not call out for very long. It is rare that an animal would cry for 20 minutes. A coyote or fox has evolved with this condition and the animal's instincts tell it that only a limited amount of time is available in which to find the dying rabbit. Discovery by another predator, or death, could overcome the prey animal. Thus, a long, drawn-out calling session is simply not natural.

Predator Response. It is difficult to give absolutes but, in general, most fur bearers will respond to calling within the first 10 minutes. A surprising number will show up within two or three minutes, especially in areas with good predator populations. Foxes seem to arrive on the scene quicker than coyotes. Bobcats take much longer and will invariably take toward the 20-minute mark.

The above times will vary with the terrain. Wooded areas are the most difficult to call in, and results will appear to be much more variable. Wind will also alter the results.

Wooded or brushy areas with a good leaf and twig or humus cover will usually tip off the approach of a coyote or sometimes even a fox. A snapped twig or the crushing of dried leaves are sure signals to be alert. Snow rarely gives any clues, but sometimes a sort of swishing sound can be heard as an animal approaches. In areas with a lot of sagebrush, movement of the twigs can be seen before the animal comes into view.

However, on many occasions the animals will seem to appear out of nowhere. That is quite a statement considering the intenseness of observation and the dedicated attention being paid to the countryside. For my money, coyotes and foxes arrive on the scene like ghosts. They materialize out of nowhere and can disappear just as abruptly.

Until fairly recently the fact that predators could be called to within a few yards of a hunter was relatively unknown. However, where areas have become overcalled, the population of predators have also become wise to the situation. Most either learn quickly or become the take of hide hunters or varminters.

In all parts of the range, and with each long-haired species, it will be the young of the year that are most anxious to respond to the call in the early part of the season. As the season progresses, these untrained pups are either killed off, or smarten up.

Part of good fur-harvesting technique is to take these younger, usually smaller, animals as early in the season as possible. The main prime season then is open for the wiser, larger adults. This is kind of a trash harvesting program, but the young hides still bring good prices in top fur years.

Calling with your back against a tree or other structure helps both to hide the hunter and to provide him with some support.

Using Electronic Callers

Using electronic calling equipment in rugged country may prove difficult. The only electronic call I have ever used that was specifically designed for outdoor use was the Model 1200 Game and Bird Caller by Johnny Stewart. This call, in various forms and models, has been around since the early 1960s. It is now vastly improved and a worthwhile investment for the serious hunter or photographer.

The cord on the Model 1200 is just over 24 feet long and has to be unwound and parceled out everytime you set up calling in a new place. In addition, the speaker has to be handled carefully. You can drill holes into the base so you can run a wire through and tie the unit to a tree, or you can carry a long spike and push it into the ground to hold the speaker upright. Indeed, a factory improvement

An electronic predator caller in use. The hunter has a good view of the surrounding opening. In addition, he is ready for any predator that may appear.

would be to place one or two holes in the base of the speaker so that it could be handled in the manner described.

My Model 1200 takes eight size D batteries and this becomes an ongoing expense over the course of a winter. Some callers place an insulated pad below the calling unit to help ward off the cold and prolong battery life. Others usually carry the batteries in an inside jacket pocket and place the warm batteries in the unit just before use.

One trick that works well in extreme cold is to place a pocket hand warmer inside the tape unit next to the batteries. Be sure your hand warmer is in good operating condition, though, and does not get too hot. Mine is an old Jonie that must have been one of the first ever made. Two of them were once used inside pockets sewn over the kidney area of my eider down jacket. Although this is a trick that has long gone out of fashion, the heaters kept my back warm for hours during duck hunting season. Anyway, the little hand warmer made famous by this company and others now comes in very handy for my kind of predator hunting, and greatly prolongs battery life.

The latest Johnny Stewart model can be operated from an exterior rechargeable power supply. This reduces the need for such a large number of batteries as well as reducing the need to make frequent battery purchases. There is also a power cord that allows the unit to be operated from a cigarette lighter. This is handy, but only in limited situations.

Other hunters build a second, larger, more insulated box and carry this to the calling site. It means added weight to carry into some of the more remote calling sites, which expends a lot of precious energy.

Although extra time is involved, it is necessary to check for correct operation of the electronic unit. Weak batteries have already been mentioned. Shorts in the wiring due to rough handling or indiscriminant jarring can cause problems in the field. Loose wiring, especially where the operator fits the cable into the jack, may also bring trouble. And since the machine is basically little more than a tape recorder, it may be necessary to clean the tape heads. Most teenagers know how to clean a

tape head these days, so if you have trouble, ask one of your kids.

A hunter can develop certain efficiencies when using one of these calls. For example, be sure the tape is rewound and at the beginning of play. Also, place the tape into the machine before arriving at your calling site. As a matter of habit, be sure to check that your volume switch is turned off.

The actual technique in using an electronic caller is very similar to that of the hand-held, mouth-blown type of call. Begin with a very low volume in case a fox is sleeping just down the trail. On the Johnny Stewart call, this is the number one setting. Then, if nothing has arrived, turn the volume to about setting number three for five or six seconds. Return the volume to number one and remain there for the rest of the calling session.

Under windy conditions you'll need to increase the volume. The same applies if you're calling in dense bush country or coniferous forests. However, it is fair to warn that the most common mistake of beginners is to have the volume too high. It is better to begin low and work up in accordance to the weather and terrain conditions.

Chapter 10

The Careful, Concealed Hunter

The fur-bearing predators you are calling use their senses for survival—to acquire food, seek shelter and protect themselves against danger. And, while faulty calling technique may reduce your chances, odors that are carried on the wind, threatening noises and careless movements contribute far greater to hunting failure.

It is important to avoid noises such as slamming the car door when getting out of your vehicle or pushing a clip into a rifle with great force. These noises can be heard for great distances and may alert a fox or coyote to your presence.

Remaining out of sight is also important. In reasonable predator country that shows good sign, odds are that the animal may be only a few yards away and could easily spot a careless approach to the calling site. The caller would never notice the animal leave by some back route, never to return.

Keeping out of sight is easier to do in bushy country. However, the rustle of passing through shrubs, especially in winter, can alert nearby animals. Crunching snow is a terrible noisemaker and is an alarm to virtually all game in the vicinity. On a cold, crisp, winter morning the combination of breaking snow and shrubs rubbing against the pant legs will almost ensure poor calling success Select routes to calling sites with these considerations in mind.

Once in position, make sure your rifle is ready for use. Check to be sure it is loaded. Fill the magazine with cartridges just after leaving the truck, then slowly and quietly chamber a cartridge. If you are using reloads, make sure they will all work through the action properly while you are still at home. Leave the safety off, since a hunter must be ready in an instant and flicking with a noisy safety only creates more problems.

Check your scope carefully. In the winter, this is very important. Snow and condensation have a way of showing up on either lens. Always carry a small, soft cotton or terry cloth towel that can be used to wipe the lenses. Sitting in the shade of trees or shrubs reduces the worry of light reflecting from the objective lens. Most scope sunshades are now big enough that this is no problem. Routinely check to be sure your scope is still tightly mounted by giving the scope a wiggle with your hand.

Most of my rifles are outfitted with slings. The sling is useful, both for carrying the rifle to and from the calling site, and as an aid in shooting. Some sling swivels will squeak minutely and you can eliminate this problem by oiling the swivel part at least once a year. Many models are detachable and, when working in close quarters, removing the sling can be helpful. But it does cause more movement, more equipment to look after, and can be a

The careful hunter tries to anticipate everything. Using a sling, for example, helps in carrying a rifle to the calling site, and also to steady the weapon while shooting.

bother when a hunter wants to get on with calling.

A moving sling can also be seen by an animal. It can signal your position from yards away. Wind can blow a light, loosely strung sling and it can catch on low shrubs that then move when the rifle is pulled to the shoulder. In short, a sling can be a pain, but I still like to use one and would recommend it to other hunters.

Most species of game, except perhaps the wildcats, use their noses far more than their ears or eyes for detecting food and danger. Prairie country and any farmland that features an up-and-down rolling terrain is subject to thermal breezes. Twice each day the hunter can expect light breezes to blow his scent across the country. These are winds that are caused by differential heating of the rolling slopes. When the sun rises in the morning, it heats the eastward facing slopes cooled by the night before. As the sun sets, the westward facing slopes are warmed up. Both of these events cause winds, as warm air rises from the warmed slope and is replaced by cool air from the opposite slope. On the prairie, this type of wind movement is most easily noticed just after suppertime. However, the air movement around coffee time in the morning is probably more significant to the hide hunter.

These winds can betray a well-chosen site and should be taken into account when calling.

In the winter, wind is also a problem. Dark, vegetation-covered slopes absorb more heat and create the same kind of thermal air shift or wind. The winter itself is characterized by brisk winds that blow out of the north or far Arctic. Foxes or coyotes out snoozing on the snowbanks can pick up this scent blown hundreds of yards away.

Minimizing the chance of being scented by predators is a crucial concern when selecting a stand. Keen noses react to small molecules of scent in the air. A male coyote can smell a bitch in heat at over a mile. Man, too, can react to as little as .24 mg. of peppermint per liter of air.

Foxes, coyotes and bobcats all will circle a calling hunter, attempting to get a downwind sniff of just what is making that enticing sound. Any of these predators crossing a human spoor will quit country at once. Bobcats will cry a typical cat scream, foxes often bark, and coyotes simply depart with such haste that it is common to hear breaking twigs or crashing vegetation. Once wise, the animals will rarely respond to calling again.

One time, while calling bobcats in Saskatchewan's Skull Creek country, I had to snowshoe into my area over a two-mile winding course. It was prime wildcat country. Several farmers had lost their barnyard tomcat to the highly territorial predator. The long course into my calling site was my undoing. About 10 minutes into my calling scenario, I heard a bobcat scream. Further calling netted nothing, so I began to follow my trail out. About 200 yards back along my trail was a picture-perfect set of bobcat tracks that led off into their own trail almost parallel to my own. For me, the story was clear. The cat had picked up my scent, but continued coming into the call. After having done a bit more thinking about the setup, the cat screamed once and departed.

Coyotes will also circle, attempting to get downwind so they can use their excellent sense of smell to help check out the calling sound. Many times it will be a hunter's undoing, and he will never see the coyotes that have successfully sniffed out his position and given up on the call. Foxes will often lie down and bark just out of sight in some vegetation. I saw one fox roll about on the ground when he caught my scent.

At the risk of being somewhat anthropomorphic, imagine the frustration that a fox or coyote must feel at these times. The sound is so convincing, but the scent trail spells danger. It is little wonder the animals seem baffled and confused by the conflicting readings their senses are giving them. However, these animals live by their instincts and they will make the right choice most of the time. Aside from sounding good, a dying rabbit simply must smell right.

Using Masking Scents

In recent years, many varmint callers and hide hunters have begun to use scents to mask their own odors. In reality this is difficult to do because, being human, they emit scent all the time. Gasoline, tobacco, soap, toothpaste, deodorant, lotions, hair tonic, and dozens of other man-made substances instantly reveal human presence.

Using scents to disguise the human scent will work, but it is not foolproof. Remember, even though there may be a camouflaged scent present, the human odor will still come through. Scent, however, does provide a type of deception that helps man's effort to take more furs. The idea of the scent is to make the animal feel secure as it approaches the calling sound. The more familiar the scent, the less cautious the animal will be.

This is part of the reason that calling in some localities will pay off better than in others, like the farm garbage dump. Everything from old, sweaty farm clothes to baby diapers can be found in some of these areas, and the scent of man must be everywhere. The predators apparently accept this odor as part and parcel of the area, yet they are bold in checking out the scavenge that might be available. The predator becomes used to, or unafraid of, the odor of man, and is much less likely to react to a whiff of man.

I believe, too, that a predator will become familiar and therefore unafraid of other scents. One good example is the feed yard on most farms. Foxes, coyotes and the odd bobcat will visit these with regularity, and yet these areas will hold the odor of cattle almost all year round. This little bit of knowledge can be put to use by simply walking through the feed yard on your way to call. Enough cattle scent will be picked up on your boots and pant legs that it will hide the human odor for two or three calling sessions. The predator will smell the cattle odor and be much less suspicious as he approaches the stand. For the predator, there is no danger associated with the smell of an old cow. In fact, the old cow could be the meal at the end of the trail.

With most predators, the most effective scents are those of their own species. Urine taken from a female coyote will distract a male coyote from a human scent. The scent of another male coyote will accomplish the same thing, and sometimes seems to give the oncoming coyote the idea another coyote has found the meal first. The same applies to foxes.

Much of the success of scents hinges on the sensitive noses of the predators. The animals are really responding to pheromones. These are unique chemical compounds produced by an animal and designed to have an effect on or to communicate with another animal of the same species. They were called social hormones by the scientists who first described their existence in the early 1960s.

All predators are very sensitive to pheromones, as these chemicals are used for marking out territories, attracting the opposite sex, and in some animals as warning substances or markers indicating food. Also, the animal may be sensitive to some of these, such as sexual attractiveness, at only specific times of the year.

Pheromones are produced by certain glands. Specialized glands exist in between the toes of foxes and coyotes that allow an individual trail to be produced by the animal. There are also glands around the anus and at the base of the tail that are used in marking out territories. Pheromones are carried in the urine of these animals.

Scents and lures, as we'll see shortly, use this biological information to influence the animal. The coyote and fox are already programmed to respond to these substances, so placing and using them under the right conditions can produce dramatic effects on the animal.

Popular Masking Scents. The most popular cover scent is skunk. Unlike most everybody else in the world, I cannot smell skunk, so I have no trouble using it. Indeed, just as an aside, the only way I can tell if skunk odor is present is when my eyes tear. Ask my wife about the skunk I took from un-

der the front step of our house, with the idea of making masking scent. The smell of the whole operation drove her crazy and annoyed the neighbors, but I didn't smell a thing.

Since others are sensitive to skunk, I am very careful about how I use the potion. One of the best methods is to use a pipe cleaner to carry the scent. Simply dip the pipe cleaner into the bottle of scent and attach the wire end of the cleaner through your boot laces. Other hunters wear the cleaner in their hat band. One cleaner on each boot works well at masking the trail. At the end of the day, you can throw the reeking pipe cleaners away and not have the scent of skunk on you. Or, if you use the same calling spot on a number of occasions, leave the pipe cleaners twisted around some nearby vegetation or just lying on the ground. Sometimes coyotes will return and check these out.

Other odors are also used as masking scents. Some are pleasant, while others are less so. Some of the oldest include things like oil of catnip, anise, peppermint, honey, lemon or orange, or even greasy old bacon fat. Many of these ingredients are mixed with mineral oil or glycerine and carried in small bottles.

Some hunters use buck lures left over from the deer hunting season. These at least work to disguise the human scent enough so that the predator diverts his mind to deer rather than man. For most predators, the odor of whitetailed deer would be commonplace and nothing to generate fear. In fact, it might also suggest some scavenge to a winter hungry coyote or fox anticipating a gut pile or a fallen buck.

Other hide hunters go to elaborate lengths to locate scent around their calling sites. Some place them downwind so that a circling predator will pick up the masking scent before the human scent. This might work, but I don't advocate it, for two reasons. First, it means a lot more movement as you go away from your stand and place the scent. This exposes you and uses up time. Second, it is difficult to place the scent so that the wind will carry it in the right direction. In most places, the wind shifts direction frequently and in wooded areas wind eddies come down from over the trees, so it really means that the scent will get blown around in every direction. With that happening, it is just as well to keep the scent with you on your

The objective in using lures is to attract animals into the area you are hunting. This works particularly well if you are trying to bring animals from areas where access has been denied into areas that are open to hunt.

stand where at least it will be blown in the same direction as your human odor.

Choose Appropriate Scents. One final point about scents—be sure to pick a masking scent that is practical for your area. One of the finest masking odors on the market is the scent of rotting apples. However, in my part of the country, apples simply don't grow in any numbers, and a predator will never have smelled a rotting apple anywhere, other than perhaps at one of those farm nuisance grounds. Another scent smells a lot like grape. It might work well in the grape-growing portion of California, but out on the plains? Worthless.

Luring Predators With Scents

Since olfaction is the major sense used by long-hairs, a predator that picks up a good scent trail is capable of following it to its source. Hide hunters can use lures to attract animals into an area, and then, once the animal's presence is established, call the animal into view.

A wise hide hunter would place lures in strategic places within his area. For example, a good fox lure could be placed in the opening of a meadow and a calling site chosen in the surrounding woods. Using animal lures with calling is a little like making your own garbage dump in the woods. An animal will eventually find the site and may include trips through the area as part of its travels. Lures can be concocted for the particular species being attracted. Most are based on food, but many other recipes represent a kind of sexual attractant or simply draw the animal's natural inquisitiveness. The whole point of lures in hide hunting is to entice the animals to visit the area and have them remain there.

Weather will effect the success of either a scent or a lure. Strong winds will, of course, make it difficult for a predator to detect your scent or follow a scent trail to a lure. Also, it will disperse enough odor that the animal could pick up the scent or lure at a far greater distance away. Moist or wet weather will cause odors to remain nearer to the ground. This will place the smell right in the scent plane of a traveling predator.

During the winter, odors seem to carry better

Attention to detail pays off. Ron Pyle and the author hold a skinned coyote taken from an area that was lured and then called. Some effective lures consist of organic matter taken from the same species of animal being hunted.

than at other times of the year. There are fewer competing odors and the air is clear. Both man and prey species travel less, so there is less conflicting spoor in the air. Snowfalls will obliterate most odors in the air and snowcover will cloak the source of odors, such as trails, dung piles or territorial markers.

Types of Lures. Foxes are attracted to a mixture of meat scraps and lard. Sometimes a few eggs can be mixed in with this, and if the area you hunt in has a chicken farmer, ask for a few spoiled or undersized eggs that can be added to the mash. This mixture should be spread over two or three trees about two feet up off the ground. The odor will last for several days, depending on the weather conditions.

The meat scraps should be shredded or cut fairly fine. If not, magpies or other birds in season will pick up the scraps in as little as two or three days. The more decomposed the mixture, the more liquid it will become. This will make it ideal for spreading and leave a powerful food attractant.

Some hunters will bury this concoction in the ground for several days to allow some decomposition to occur. Another way is simply to put the mixture in a jar and let it sit out in the sun for a couple of days; the results are just as good. Store it in an out-of-the-way place until hide hunting season.

Another lure that has proven workable in a number of situations over the years is the use of fish. The odor of fish is strong and most predators find it difficult to resist. The remains of carp, trout and jack fish placed in a jar and allowed to decompose for a few days will draw predators from miles around. Use a screw-top jar and simply take the lid off when you want to use the bait. In doing this, you don't have to mess with the stuff and can leave the jar out for days at a time. In fly season, I simply poke a few holes in the lid. Leaving the concoction in the jar makes it very easy to handle and travel with.

Beaver castor has been used as the basis for several lures for a long time. However, most hunters of long-hairs will have little opportunity to come in contact with or obtain this oily, strong-smelling substance of beaver sexual glands. In addition, as I write this, the price of well-dried whole beaver castors is $59.00 per pound, so how could anyone really recommend that they be used as lure mate-

---

EFFECTIVE PREDATOR LURES

Foxes and coyotes are attracted to:
1. Mixture of meat scraps and lard, sometimes with the addition of spoiled or undersized eggs.
2. Fish—any kind.
3. Beaver castoreum.
4. Urine or animal droppings.
5. Parts of animal's food canal, lymph tissue or glands surrounding anus; liver is particularly effective.

Bobcats and lynx can be lured with:
1. Mixture of catnip and vaseline (*See also* page 45).

---

rial? Incidentally, beaver castoreum is also used in the perfume industry.

A lure that has been effective for bobcats is a mixture of catnip and vaseline. This is smeared on the vegetation in an area and almost assures the presence of cat sign within a few days. This is an easy lure to use and can be mixed on the spot with little of the mess and special effort needed for other lures.

Foxes and coyotes respond especially well to the urine of their species. As previously mentioned, urine carries a good supply of pheromones and these are tough for any long-haired predator to resist. A hide hunter should collect urine from the animals he takes. Once bottled, it can be used both as a lure and a masking scent.

Collecting urine from these carcasses is not difficult. Following skinning, simply open the body cavity and locate the bladder and associated ducts. Remove the entire bladder and use it as part of the lure mixture, placing it in a jar for use when needed. Often the shock of being taken with a modern high-power rifle will cause the bladder to be evacuated. However, the bladder itself can be used as a lure.

Keep the female and male urine and bladder samples of any species separate. If possible, store them individually. Use a male urine and/or bladder sample from a different area each time you hunt. This is really trying to tell the resident predator that a

Lure can be placed along fence-lines or field edges. These are the kinds of places predators travel in their search for food or to establish territory.

stranger has entered his territory; the result may be that the animal will react with much less caution. Use female urine in areas where the hunting has been slow, but you know there is a good population of animals. It will often bring in animals that have otherwise been overly cautious and perhaps a bit wise to calling or hunting.

Urine can be used to cover human scent. Use it with the pipe cleaner technique mentioned earlier, sprinkle it around the calling site, or leave the bottle open for the entire calling session.

If you are going to make your own lures, become familiar with the anatomy of the animal and where the major scent glands are located. On all of the dog species, there are glands that surround the anus. This area could be excised and used to make scent concoctions. The same applies to the alimentary canal. Food-based lures could be made from the partly digested remains found within the canals of the taken animals. Parts of the liver have been used in some recipes; lymph material from around the jaw is also useful.

Blending and mixing of ingredients is best done with warm material. This usually means fresh, although frozen or dried parts can be mixed with warmed urine or water and mineral oil. Parts of the food canal, lymph tissue from around the mouth, or any other part the hunter feels might work can be dried in a modern-day microwave oven. (Secure your mate's permission before starting!) The parts can be broken into a rough powder by working with a mortar and pestle. This powder can then be blended with glycerine, mineral oil, urine or any of the naturally occurring scents, such as peppermint or clove, to custom-make the lure or scent desired.

Animal droppings also make effective lures. The lower bowel of the predator will usually contain fresh feces. These can be collected and saved in plastic bags. Feces placed at a known territorial marker of another animal of the same species will invariably bring the predator into the area for scrutiny.

One of my favorite lures is fresh coyote liver placed in an area of other known coyotes. In the winter, with most predatory birds having flown south, only magpies exist to bother the bait. Within hours it freezes solid and will become a fascination to area coyotes for most of the winter. The

animals will never eat the lure, and it is indeed rare that a coyote will eat part of another dead member of its species. However, the animals will examine the bait as is indicated by the number of tracks in the immediate area. Usually calling within 200 yards of this point will put up a fine coyote or fox.

Some hunters put out a trail of lure across one or two miles. The hope is that any traveling predator will hit on the lure trail and take up residence nearby. This can be successful in areas where there are trails or old roads. Lure placed along these will usually be found by predators on the move.

Frequent checking of the lures and the vicinity around the lure is required if the hunter is to obtain maximum benefit from any luring attempts. If there is evidence in the form of tracks, scratchings or defecation, the lure should be replenished and calling taken up a few yards upwind.

The dog family is known for its natural curiosity. This is well demonstrated in the outdoor literature. Coyotes and foxes have been seen playing with tin cans, old rags and paper plates. I have observed foxes playing with discarded fast food chicken boxes for quite some time. Stomach analysis of nearly any predator will turn up paper, plastic and bits of metal from aluminum cans and tin foil wrapping. These are the results of the canids' natural inquisitiveness. Some natural history buffs claim this is the way the predators adapted so successfully to life next to man. Natural curiosity simply gave certain animal races the opportunity to experiment with things in their own environment. If the trial and error paid off in a full-stomach and enhanced reproduction, then this was the line or strain that continued to develop and repopulate. If not, the line fell by the wayside in the evolutionary scheme of things. Perhaps innate curiosity has given these animals some type of survival edge over others. It is enough for our purposes to identify that all of our long-haired North American predators have a tremendous sense of interest in their environments. Hide hunters should use this to advantage.

While all predators have a learned or ingrained fear of man, they are still curious of man and his activities in the country. Bert Popowski once told me of climbing a tree and watching a coyote follow his trail until the animal was right under the tree. Popowski said that the coyote was obviously confused by this ruse and tried in vain to relocate the large white man's trail. The coyote happened to glance up and see the amused hunter sitting some 20 feet up in the tree. He then decided to quit country, but Popowski's .22 caliber handgun caught the critter behind the ear. The hide went on to pay for mortar needed in the Popowski cabin. Anyway, Bert suspected it was plain curiosity that caused this ki-dog to take up a human scent trail.

Foam rubber padding, for some reason, intrigues foxes and coyotes. A piece soaked in one of the lure recipes given previously and placed in predator country will invariably be visited by one of the animals. Fish and foam rubber are ultimate favorites. Two or three old foam pillows placed in an area where two coyotes or foxes have been seen will attract the few residents in the area. Sometimes such pillows become scent posts within the territory and can then be used as potential points from which to try calling.

Dale Friesen, a well-known gunsmith and hunter-friend of mine, tells the story of a fox that fell in love with a discarded powder puff. Whatever the odor the puff contained, this particular fox found the combination compelling. Dale was able to photograph the animal while playing with the puff; and he lured the fox from a well-camouflaged spot only a few yards from where the puff was set out—to the animal's undoing. Dale went on to take three other foxes the same way, using the same powder puff placed in different parts of the range.

Predators will become wise and wary about scents and odors. Had Friesen not taken those four foxes with the first shot on each occasion, you could bet the animals would have smartened up considerably. At the mere smell of the puff on a second occasion, the animal would have headed for new country.

It is important, then, when using lures or masking scents, to be sure your animals are taken. Missing at close range or spooking the animal by inappropriate movement or the reflection of light from equipment will only educate the animal to keep clear of other similar situations.

All scents and lures can be detected by the predator's nose long before visual contact is made. Should the animal spook for one reason or another, it will likely have done so after receiving a good snoutful of odor. The association of this odor

and a close escape with man will never be forgotten.

In sum, several factors will influence your success with a scent or lure. The time of year, the physiological condition of the animal, the animal's age and its sex are all important in how an animal reacts to a scent. Important, too, is the animal's previous experience with the smell. A smart adult coyote will respond differently to a scent he associates with danger, even though that smell may be one of a female coyote in heat.

The Art of Camouflage

Most modern-day hunting activities ignore, or at best play down, the need for camouflage clothing. For decades duck and goose hunters sparingly used this type of gear. Big game hunters in most jurisdictions are prevented from using this type of clothing because of the legal requirement to wear brightly colored, sight-responsive safety clothing. In recent times, the bow hunting fraternity has discovered the importance of camouflage clothing to their sport.

For hide hunters, camouflage is mandatory. It serves to provide some concealment and lets the hunter blend into the surrounding environment. Camouflage functions to prevent, or at least reduce, the opportunity for the animal to identify the hunter visually. Clearly, when dealing with lynx-eyed predators, this is crucial to success.

Remember, too, that most resident predators are very familiar with the cover characteristics within their home range. Anything that looks out of place will be given a wide berth, or at least noticed and investigated from a distance. Also, the animal will attempt to circle the suspicious object and catch any scent. The trick is to look a part of the environment and not to look out of place.

Enough studies have been conducted to date to prove that predators see only in shades of black and white. Man, of course, can see the colors. However, although the animals view the world in shades of gray, they are capable of doing this very well. Wearing the same colors as the surrounding countryside ensures that the same shades of gray will be detected by passing predators.

Man has good depth perception, the result of the location of our eyes in our head. They are far

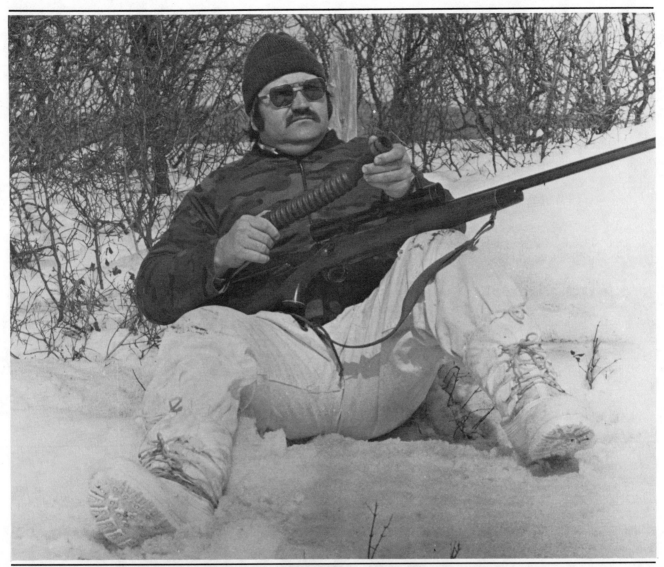

Ron Pyle shows himself in action using a Scotch bellows-type call. Note the camo method used here. The white pants and boots blend well into the snow below while the woodland camo pattern of his jacket fits into the background made up of willows, tag alder, poplar bush and snowberry.

enough apart on the same plane that binocular vision results. Most predators have not developed depth perception to the same degree as man. As a result, they have more difficulty sorting out conflicting or crosswise lines in their environments. Using clothing of the same color as the surrounding vegetation confuses the animal's depth perception by presenting lines that do not look out of place.

The clothing you wear as a hunter, therefore, must match the surroundings. Manufacturers are now universally recognizing this fact and the variety of products is probably better than ever before. Choose your clothing to match the vegetation around which you will be hunting and take into account the season as well as the terrain.

Any hunter looking at camouflage clothing for the first time will have no trouble finding some-

All-white camouflage for winter use is efficient when snow cover is 100 percent. Coveralls offer added protection to the back region during frigid calling sessions.

thing he needs. For most predator hunting done in the autumn, a dead grass or tan pattern is best. In treed areas with lots of color, a forest pattern will work well enough among the bare trees.

Hunting clothing should be chosen with care and attention to detail. It must serve the purpose for which it is intended. Pockets that are easy to get into are important. Full-cut and roomy clothing is best, since much time will be spent walking or sitting. Tight-fitting clothing restricts blood flow and promotes uncomfortableness. Depending on the season, the clothing or combination of clothing should be appropriate for the temperature.

Hunting clothing must also be soft-surfaced. Hard or coarse materials scrape on bushes and create noise when movement is made. Nylon is out for this reason. Cotton or cotton duck still remain the best fabrics for hunting jackets. The same applies to rain gear and some ponchos. The plastic or waterproof material used in these makes too much noise. Rubberized material, such as is found on older rain gear, is likewise worthless for camouflage. It has no place in predator hunting and will prove costly in terms of furs taken. Since camouflage clothing should not reflect light, material with any kind of sheen should also be avoided.

Winter Camouflage. In the winter, a pure white outfit is best. I have an outfit made by the Duxbak Corporation that is nearly pure cotton and it serves very well for this type of hunting. It consists of a jacket with two large pockets and a pair of oversized pants that are held up with a draw string. I bought the largest sizes they made, as I wear this over my winter clothing. The pockets in the coat are particularly useful for holding winter gloves or a pocket call.

For winter hunting, two-piece outfits offer versatility. This allows you to put on an extra sweater or jacket when you're calling. You can then peel off the jacket when skinning or walking back out with a hide or carcass. The two-piece set is also easier to get on and off than a pair of coveralls.

An inexpensive source of winter white suits is painters' or plasterers' clothes. Most work clothing stores will have such garb and the price is usually moderate. Most of these pants and shirts are made from heavy cotton or twill and will make a durable work-wear product in itself. They are full cut, and buying one of a large size will ensure a fit over win-

The author displays his favorite method of camouflage—white above and camo below. This fits well with the intermittent snow pattern common in some years in the areas hunted.

ter clothing and room for shrinkage due to washings.

It is best to have two sets of winter white clothing. This way if one pair is in the wash, the other is still available for use in the field. A clean set of white camouflage is vital if good blending with the surrounding snow is desired. Invariably, white clothing becomes soiled and it shows very quickly. The knees, the elbows, and the seat will be the first to stain, but, depending on the winter and the conditions under which the clothing is used, the whole suit will not stay white for very long. It is wise to remove the outer clothing when skinning or working with hides. Blood stains and grease very quickly detract from the prime white color that is needed, and they are difficult to remove.

Some hunters have used off-white or almost gray

oversuits as winter camouflage. It was their opinion that these particular colors blended in better with the white poplar trees that grew in their areas. The trees have a white- to gray-colored bark, prominent in the winter when all the leaves are stripped off the trees and the surrounding shrubs are bare. The hunter sitting against one of these trees and calling out across a prairie opening is well-camouflaged in this type of garb.

Winter camouflage parkas or jackets should be equipped with a hood. White winter camouflage clothing, used by the NATO and Warsaw Pact armies, is outfitted with large hoods. This serves as weather protection and camouflage by covering the head and dropping slightly over the face to shield it from all sides. The design helps conceal the face, or at least breaks up the overall features that would identify the object as human. This is valuable for any hide hunter. Indeed, if the winter clothing is not equipped with a hood, a white material can be used to make a reasonable facsimile.

Some hunters use a white sack to cover their face; others use a pillow case. While these items work and provide adequate camouflage, a hood that is part of the garment will never be left at home or forgotten in the truck. Since the hood is always attached, it is always with the coat and this is a major advantage.

Woodland Camo Gear. Cast-off military camouflage clothing can be used in areas that lack

Trick or treat anyone? Blending in with the snow is critical for winter predator calling, and a face mask made from a white sack, pillow case or preferably an attached hood offers superb concealment.

snow cover. In my hunting area, snow is usually prevalent during the prime season, but there have been years when the ground was not snow-covered at the beginning of the fur season. For this reason, I have a complete set of bushland and desert camouflage that see routine use.

One of the best sources for this type of clothing is still the various military surplus stores and suppliers. In more recent times, the demand for this kind of clothing has risen sharply and the bargains that previously characterized our surplus stores are fast disappearing.

In addition, wearing camouflage clothing is becoming fashionable. Who knows, maybe it will become fashionable again to be a hide hunter. Anyway, this spread of fashion has made the clothing more accessible to the average hunter, and it is no longer necessary to become familiar with the old outfitting catalogs, such as Eddie Bauer of the former dynasty of Herter products to find camouflage clothing.

Military clothing that makes it to the marketplace these days seems to be definitely surplus. Throughout the 1950s when the governments of the world were dumping the remains of World War II on the market, nearly new camouflage clothing regularly showed up in the dealers' stores. Now the clothing is well worn and often patched when it becomes surplus. It is wise to check any such articles closely for damage and the extent of repairs that may be needed. If the cost and damage equation doesn't seem to balance out, then shop around for newly manufactured camouflage. Many times it will be the better buy.

For woodland hunting, I currently use an army surplus camouflage jacket that came out of a store in South Dakota about four or five years ago. It is of Italian make and the pattern is particularly good. The jacket is three-quarter length and I have had my wife add pockets at the waist. Elastic in the cuffs gives the jacket a snug fit at the wrists and this prevents other clothing from working its way down the arm. The jacket is full cut and large enough that it can be worn over any type of clothing. This general type of jacket should be a major part of any hunter's kit.

Camouflage pants are not as important as the jacket. However, it certainly will benefit the hunter to dress in camouflage from head to foot. Many

Don't let lack of camouflage clothing stop you from having your fill of predator hunting. Dark-colored clothes, especially deep blues and greens, will provide at least some color protection and blend into the surrounding environment.

times the lower part of the hunter's body is covered by vegetation or, when calling, the legs and lower torso are not seen by the predator.

If camouflage pants are not worn, dark pants should be part of the garb. This applies in all seasons except winter when it is imperative to dress entirely in white. Dark pants will absorb light and contribute to the low visibility the hunter is trying to achieve. I wear a full-cut pair of military-style pants that an old friend of mine traded from a member of the local Swat Team. These pants have the large-capacity pockets on the thighs and regular button pockets at the other points. In addition, they feature a draw-string closure at the ankles. This prevents my inner pants from sliding out and provides a tight fit where my boot and pant meet.

While this type of pant is nice and raises questions from those who see me in them, they are not essential for successful hide hunting. Nearly any comfortable, dark-colored pants will work.

Many hunters consider a pair of coveralls as the best and least expensive hunting clothing available. Be sure to buy cotton for the reasons outlined previously. I have to be the first to admit that I hunted using white coveralls for years before I found the two-piece suit I now use. In the fall and summer, dark green construction coveralls were just as effective.

For the hunter who has no camouflage clothing, all is not lost. Tie-dyed equivalents work just as well and non-camo clothing with patterns or checks will work some of the time. Plaid shirts in either green or brown are good. Blue jeans or other dark pants can be used also.

Dyeing Your Own Camo. Many hunters think that it is necessary to select camouflage patterns that are commercially fashionable. This is not so. Tie-dyeing white cotton coveralls can give a custom-made product that is not available in stores. You need only select the dyes and tie-dye the article in true hippie fashion.

Here's how it's done. Choose your dyes—three or four colors that are integral to the habitat you will be hunting in will do.

Begin your tie-dyeing project with a white garment. Prepare the dye by following the instructions that come with the package. Start with your lightest color first. Begin with a fairly deep yellow that resembles the shade you'd see in the fall. Place the entire garment in the dye until you have achieved the desired color. Let it dry.

Next, tie areas throughout the garment. Some hunters do this by using stones about the size of marbles, which are tied into the garment by string, elastic or strips of rawhide. The stones serve to measure off even amounts of cloth to be knotted and tied. The fabric in between the knots will be dyed, but the knots will not be. Try to keep the knots evenly spaced so a pattern will evolve over all parts of the garment, rather than show large areas of a single color.

Now, with the knots in place, dye the garment with the second lightest color for your area, perhaps a light green. The tied areas will have the wavy yellow color and the remainder of the area will be green. Again, allow the garment to dry.

Do not untie the knots that were used to hold the yellow color in place. Instead, now add more rocks in order to tie the green dye in place. You would use twice as many rocks and consequently tie twice as many knots in the material as you did for the yellow color. In this way, you are getting more green into the material than yellow.

Your third and final dye could be a light brown. On top of the green and yellow, this usually gives a sufficiently dark garment for forest and light tree use.

When you want more green in a set of clothing, use the yellow, then a very light brown. Follow this with a dark green and the results should be very pleasing.

The knotting of the stones, dyeing and drying requires a little time, but, in my opinion, the end product is not only unique, but also works well. Others would say, in the end, it would be cheaper and easier to use newly purchased camo clothing. The advantage of making your own lies in the correct color combinations and an added bonus is that you can use old clothing that would otherwise get thrown away or used for cleaning rags at skinning time. It can also allow you more than one set of camouflage gear. I usually keep a full set at my cabin, another in my truck, and another outfit that I use routinely from home.

Care of Camouflage Clothing. The hunter after furs and concerned about scents and human odor would do well to keep his camouflage clothing separate from his usual hunting clothes or everyday wear. Some hunters store their camouflage clothing in a plastic bag and only take it out when they're in the hunting area. It's also a good idea to store a few sprigs of vegetation from the immediate area in which you hunt. This works particularly well if you hunt in an area of pines or coniferous trees. In my area, lodge pole pine are common and I routinely store a few pine needles with my coat. It keeps the camouflage clothing smelling as if it had come from the forest.

Sagebrush twigs work well from the prairie uplands that I hunt, and a few poplar leaves provide the correct odor for use in the parkland areas I frequent. I have also used scrub oak leaves and mast from one of my other favorite areas. This is one trick that definitely helps reduce the odors of ur-

Always store hunting gear with some of the vegetation from the area in which you will be hunting. This keeps the clothes smelling like the area and reduces the chance of a sharp-nosed predator picking up human scent at a crucial time.

ban living from your hunting clothes. When I hunted on the farm I simply stored my hunting clothing in one of the outbuildings, usually the barn. The result was the same.

A final note on camouflage clothing. Don't wash the jacket or pants or coveralls unless absolutely necessary. Most modern soaps and cleaners leave far too strong an odor of their own. Any predator can smell this yards away and will be tipped off long before the hunter even realizes there is a long-hair present. Store this type of clothing in its own special place away from the odors of modern-day society.

Wearing Gloves. Cover your hands with white gloves in the winter and multi-colored camo types the rest of the year. The hands will be seen as they move the rifle into position and could easily signal a close-in predator. Gloves will help blend white hands into the background. In the winter, they will also keep you warm while you wait or call. As with the other articles of camouflage, be careful what you touch or handle. Do not wear these gloves to pour a can of oil into your truck, for example. They should be stored with your other camo gear in a plastic bag and scented with vegetation from the surrounding area.

What Type of Hat? Avoid wide-brimmed hats for camouflage use. These hats are obvious for miles around and they are easily knocked ajar by surrounding vegetation. They are great when riding horseback, but when hide hunting leave your western-style hat at home and wear a watch cap and hood in the winter or a long-peaked cap with a camouflage mask or headpiece in the other seasons.

Completing the Disguise. Clothing is only part of the overall camouflage story. Such items as your eyeglasses, face, rifle and any equipment must also be camouflaged, or the total goal of concealment will not be achieved.

Eyeglasses are the single most difficult thing to camouflage. Lenses and frames both reflect incoming light. This reflection telegraphs your location for miles around. Everybody is familiar with the typical cowboy show where the ambush is foiled because the hero spots the glint of a rifle barrel at the last minute. The same thing can happen in real life. Coyotes and foxes are particularly sharp at spotting reflected light.

Little can be done to reduce the shine from the lenses of your eyeglasses. An old wives' tale is to rub freshly cut onions over the lenses. This, it is alleged, will reduce the reflectivity. It might, but it also mucks up your eyeglasses and makes your eyes water, and in this type of hunting visibility is vital.

If you are like me and have to wear your glasses in order to hunt successfully, the best trick is to use a long-peaked cap and always try to be conscious of the direction the sunlight is coming from. Try to keep your eyeglasses in the shadows, and the chance for a quick glint of light going out across the prairie will be greatly diminished.

Reflections from the face can also be a problem, especially when predators are coming in close in response to a call. During calling, there is always

Well-known outdoorsman, Bob Elman of Stewartsville, NJ, uses a camo stick to reduce the face features and further the blending into the background.

some movement of the face as your cheeks funnel air from your lungs down into the call. Sometimes even the neck moves when calling becomes intense. Light can easily be reflected off the face at this time.

One of my favorite remedies is to wear a face mask. During the winter I use a white face mask and in the other seasons a camouflage head net. My white face mask is nothing fancy. It is an old pillow case and I tuck the long end down into my white jacket. The ample size allows me to place the cover over any other head gear I might be wearing at the time. In the winter, this can range from a peaked cap to my parka hood and toque. The holes that

have been cut for my eyes are a bit larger than one might normally expect. Some hunters cut only slits. However, with eyeglasses, fogging can occur. The large holes let your moisture-laden breath escape. Be sure to cut a mouth hole large enough to allow you to use your mouth-blown call if you are not using an electronic caller.

Some hunters paint their faces with leftover military surplus camo stick or newly manufactured stuff made for the bow hunting fraternity. Others streak their faces with burned cork. Frankly, I never do this, and it surprises me the number of predator hunters that will go to such pains. They argue that it is much more comfortable than wearing a mask and sometimes this may be true. However, I have found that traveling around the countryside with my face painted like a commando officer does nothing for my public relations image. In some areas, the survivalist movement is decidedly unpopular and to be associated with this group is not my idea of how to win farmer friends and gain access to posted places.

In the end, the decision to paint your face is up to you. I see no reason for it, and can see several negatives. The same or better can be accomplished by using a mask, and no clean up is required. It also takes less time to slip on a mask than to paint your face properly. Most hunters do not consider face-painting as a fine point in public relations. However, try to gain access to a stranger's posted farm sometime when you are all painted up. If the farm dog doesn't take a run at you, you're lucky. As far as any additional head gear goes, my camouflage headpiece is the remains of a military helmet cover. It has several pieces of vegetation tied into the net and this hides my face and glasses well enough that no reflection escapes.

As mentioned, gun barrels can be a real problem. In the summer and fall seasons, use camouflage tape to cover the barrel and stock. Bow hunters use this tape all the time and it does have a positive effect. In the winter, use a piece of old bed sheet torn into strips and wrapped around your rifle barrel. Cover the scope as well. Split one end of the bed sheet into two strips and use these to tie the sheeting in place.

One last point about light and reflection: Guard against silhouetting yourself when you are setting yourself up to call or hunt. Obviously, situations exist where the hunter has to cross a valley or a high hill and can be seen for miles. Other less obvious occasions occur when the light is behind the hunter and there is insufficient cover. The key is to sit in the shade of whatever is available. While there may not always be trees and shrubs to crouch under, it is critical to use the available cover to break up your figure or outline. Camouflage clothing will be of little help if your figure is plainly visible for yards in any direction.

In any discussion of camouflage and its uses, the topic of portable blinds will surface. There are now many advantages to using portable blinds to call from or to station yourself in with an electronic caller placed a few yards up the trail. Well-designed blinds can be extremely comfortable for extended use. Modern-day, well-made blinds can be set up in seconds and are lightweight and easily portable. Blinds with a top that either pops back or has a slit to shoot from are better than the open-topped varieties. One of the major advantages of a solid, well-placed blind is that the hunter has room for some movement inside it without alerting the animal.

On the negative side, blinds that are constructed from nylon blow about and rattle in the wind almost like a poorly erected tent. This noise will alert animals for yards around. Aside from this, the blind will have to be carried into the hunting area along with your other equipment. It also means that the hunter is exposed longer while trying to set up the camouflage. Blinds, like a tent, require a fairly flat piece of ground to set up in, and the veg-

Portable blinds are useful to the predator hunter, especially when hunting near carcasses or garbage dumps.

The Careful, Concealed Hunter   139

etation has to be cleared away from the walls and floor. Also, like a tent, some models require that ropes be strung out from the poles to hold the covering in place.

In short, I do not often use a blind because of these problems. However, I have used a blind when hunting garbage sites or when hunting over an old carcass that I know is being visited by coyotes. I have used the commercial models and I have used old military netting. I will leave either of these in place for as long as the area yields productive hunting. Homemade blinds ranging from white sheeting in the winter to natural vegetation in the fall can be used under these circumstances.

In using any permanent blind, the key is to have your approach established so that it is out of sight from the area to be watched. This type of setup works best on valley walls where the blind overlooks the valley below and the trees and vegetation provide natural cover to the entrance way of the blind.

Remember, too, that blinds only let you look in one or two directions. Animals have been known to sneak up on a camouflaged caller and almost step on the hunter before sorting out the danger. In addition, the odd porcupine has been known to take up residence in a little-used blind.

Chapter 11

Any Bullet,
Any Caliber?

The whole area of choosing which gun, which action, which caliber and which bullet is fraught with controversy. The broad range of circumstances and many different ranges under which game is taken make the choice all the more difficult. There are confirmed gun enthusiasts who can quote ballistical statistics until the sun comes up and own more guns than they can reasonably shoot. In contrast to this group are those who think that nearly any gun is good enough and a rifle is little more than a tool needed to complete the task at hand. Many campfires will burn to ashes before the controversy will be settled.

For the predator hunter, selecting the correct combination of caliber and rifle will take on different dimensions. For some, the choice of caliber and rifle will be what is currently on hand and used for other types of hunting. Others will have been first attracted to predator hunting through firearms and the opportunities this kind of hunting provides for extended shooting. In addition, there are those who view predator hunting as a business and want the most efficient combination of cartridge and rifle available.

Meeting the Needs of Predator Hunting. Cartridges for predator hunting must meet some very demanding criteria not always necessary in other types of shooting or hunting. First, the cartridge must be adequate to dispatch the predator humanely. Wounded animals caused by impotent cartridges cannot be tolerated. Second, since this hunting exists to harvest hides, the load used should not be overly destructive to the fur and skin of the animal. The cartridge must also be accurate. Finally, any load or cartridge and bullet combination must leave the greatest part of its energy in the animal. Bullets that pass through an animal are losing part of this energy.

It seems that most hunters go through several stages in the selection of a predator rifle cartridge. The first stage is the "any cartridge, any bullet" school of thought. Most often this is followed by an intense romance with high-velocity, flat-shooting, extended-performance cartridges. Somewhere after this, the hunter begins to think about loaded-down versions of these high performers. This thinking can extend to the point that the hunter begins to believe that low-velocity, heavy-bulleted cartridges just may be best. Along these lines comes the notion of using lead bullets in modern-day cartridges loaded-down to mild velocity levels. Then there is a short period where the shotgun becomes the favored predator gun. The last stage is the hard-point or full metal-jacketed bullet craze. Once the hunter has experienced these steps in the search for a better predator cartridge, he seems to reach a calm and selects what seems to work best for him.

Some Cartridges To Consider

The "any gun, any bullet" school of thought is hard to thwart. It is in here that rimfire cartridges are usually tried and the hunter vows to take animals only within range and under ideal conditions. In truth, most rimfires are capable of knocking over predators, and the lightweight bullets driven at low velocity destroy little hide. The cartridges are also remarkably silent. However, for the most part, the .22 rimfires are too weak to be considered for all predator hunting situations. This is especially true of the .22 short, long and long rifle versions on the market. In recent times, a noble effort has been made to bolster the power of the rimfires. The Stingers (as made by CCI), the Viper (Remington), the Yellow Jacket (Remington), the Spitfire (Federal), and the Xpediter (Winchester) are attempts in this area.

The same generally applies to the 5mm Remington and the .22 Winchester Magnum. The Magnum develops just over 2,000 feet per second (fps) and could be considered a predator cartridge under the right circumstances and when the hollow-pointed version is used. It can produce good hits at 70- to 80-yard distances, but suffers from a rapid loss of velocity and questionable accuracy beyond this limit. The 5mm Remington, which is no longer on the market, performed slightly better than the .22 Magnum, giving 2100 fps and still retaining 217 foot pounds of striking energy at 100 yards. This cartridge never did develop the kind of following among American shooters that was necessary to ensure its survival. It seems to have found a niche somewhere between the old-time performers like the .25-20 and the .22 Magnum. In short, these two should be dismissed for serious predator hunting.

In the country, a hide hunter will still come across a surprising number of old rimfire performers in the hands of farmers, wood cutters, share croppers and general backwoods' loafers. The .32 rimfire Stevens that currently decorates my basement wall was gleaned from one of these sources. Cartridges purchased in the late 1950s and early

The .25-20 and the still useful .32-20. Both refuse to die, although no firearm has been manufactured for these cartridges in years.

The .22 Savage Hi-Power and the .25-35 Winchester were both once thought of as useful predator rounds.

1960s are still in the hands of these people and function well when it comes to dispatching a marauding porcupine or skunk that burrows under one of the outbuildings. They are also useful for "shooting away" foxes or coyotes that become attracted to the chicken coop. It is in these places that the idea any gun can do the job still persists; it will draw guffaws when the hide hunter shows up with his brand-new, high-powered rifle designed only for shooting fox.

The lower velocity, older centerfires have proven to be good cartridges for predator shooting. Throughout farm country today the .25-20 and .32-20 still hold a favorable reputation as reliable performers that dispatch quickly, with little damage to meat or furs. They are still thought of as "meat guns" that are used to put sick animals—from horses to pigs—out of their misery, or for butchering healthy fattened farm animals. In addition, these two cartridges still hold their own for keeping vermin away from the chicken coop or from denning too close to the yard. This performance accounts for the fact that .25-20 and .32-20 cartridges are still being manufactured, even though no rifle has been made for either cartridge in the past 40 years.

These cartridges would suit a lot of hide hunting situations, especially where the animals were taken within 100 yards and presented good targets. However, they are ineffective beyond this range, and the .32-20 in a 100-grain, soft-point bullet retains only some 250 foot pounds of striking energy at 100 yards. I have used an iron-sighted Model 53 Winchester in .32-20 for years. Loaded with 10 grains of 2400 and a 100-grain, hollow-point bullet, it is good in many calling sessions. Beyond short range, it is woeful and best left in the truck. The same applies to the .25-20, which gained a reputation as a small varmint rifle cartridge back in the early 1920s.

Other cartridges in the lower velocity, semi-obsolete category have proven to be good predator cartridges. The .22 Savage Hi-power, although no longer made, was thought of as a capable predator cartridge, especially when teamed up with the Model Savage 99. As well, the .25-35 Winchester held a reputation as an early form of all-round cartridge useful for everything from fox to deer. The most impressive shooting I have ever seen was with a Model 94 Winchester in .25-35. A sheep herder friend by the name of Jack Bonnell stepped from his trailer one evening and shot a coyote at 475 measured yards with the combination by resting the rifle on a corral post.

Early on I discovered that slow-moving lead bullets did extremely well as close-range predator cartridges. The first bobcats I ever shot were taken with long, obsolete .38-56 Winchesters in an ancient and heavy Model 1886 Winchester. Interestingly, the 255-grain, soft lead bullets seemed to tumble around inside the predator, anchoring the animal for good. There was little pelt destruction, and very few, if any, made large exit holes.

Again, the problem in shooting these kinds of cartridges lies in the distance at which the animal can be taken. Sometimes fox and more often coyotes would come within only 150 yards of a calling site. At this range the predator was quite safe. Other times animals would be seen when leaving the calling site. These could be put up at any distance, but with a modern, high-powered rifle, they would be fair game up to 225 yards or more, while the older rifle severely limited the shooting.

For most hunters, it is natural to select a modern, high-velocity, flat-shooting cartridge. Most of these have good wind-bucking ability, especially with heavier bullets. High energy is retained so that good killing hits can be delivered at extended ranges. High velocity means that little lead is required on moving predators; sighting error is reduced as is the need for holdover at longer ranges. The trade-off for these features is the amount of pelt damage that can occur, however.

Any predator taken with a modern, high-powered hunting rifle will suffer severe pelt damage. The .30-30, incorrectly thought of as weak by many of today's hunters, will devastate a coyote. A 170-grain loading in this caliber will almost cut a fox in two. The same holds true for any of the .30 calibers with hunting-weight bullets. The results are a difficult cleaning job at the time of skinning and an equally hard sewing job prior to drying the pelt.

Effective Predator Cartridges

It is for this reason that, under most circumstances, a .22 caliber centerfire cartridge will give the best results. At all but close ranges the bullet will be retained within the animal. This means less hide damage, and that all the energy the bullet was carrying stayed within the animal. In addition, the hole made by the bullet's entrance is small.

Bullets will enter from a great variety of angles, since the animal rarely presents itself broadside to the hunter. In short, most bullets will enter a predator at some angle other than 90 degrees to the hunter. This translates into a hole that is actually slightly larger than the caliber of the rifle used. This is, of course, a strong argument for using the smallest caliber possible and is one that gives credence to recommended calibers such as the .17 Remington. Anyway, the size of the entrance hole is of importance to the hide hunter since bullet holes lower the value of the fur. Given the list of variables, the .22 caliber is about the best choice.

Fortunately, there is a great selection of .22 caliber centerfire cartridges from which to choose, plus a wide range of bullet weights and types. The centerfires run the gamut of those on the weak side to those that are nearly too highly powered for the tasks required. The .22 Hornet is one of those on

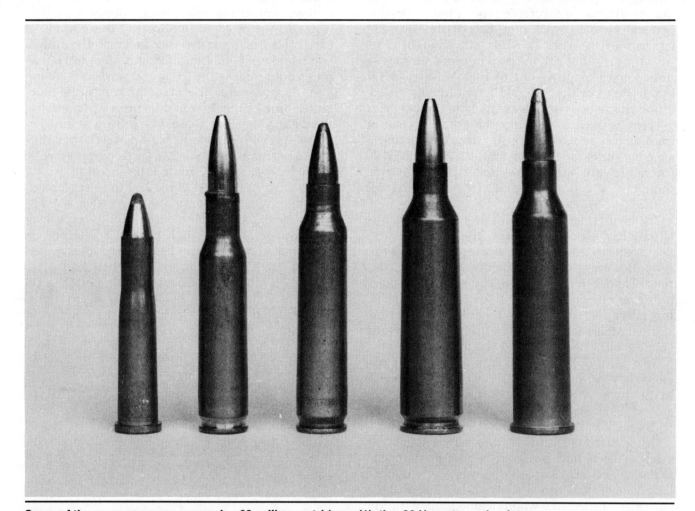

Some of the more common or popular .22 caliber cartridges: (1) the .22 Hornet, an obsolete cartridge, but one that was a valuable hide hunter's combination; (2) the .222 Remington and (3) the .223 Remington—these both have good followings in American hunting circles; (4) the .22-250 Remington, perhaps the most popular .22 of all time; and, finally, (5) the moribund .225 Winchester, used extensively by the author.

the weak side. It is now considered by many to be on the semi-obsolete list, and no rifle, save for the Ruger No. 1, has been made in the cartridge for years.

Next in line is the .222 Remington. It is slightly under-powered for long shots or shots taken at an angle to the animal. It is adequate for fox and will dispatch a bobcat at close range. The same roughly applies to the .222 Remington Magnum, which is little more than a slightly blown-out version of its cousin, the .222 Remington. The .223 Remington, the current civilian version of the 5.56mm military cartridge, is also suitable for most close-in work. Close-in, here, means up to 125 yards.

The current darling of the pro-.22 caliber cartridge is the .22-250. Although loaded in only one, factory, 55-grain offering, the choice of bullets for the reloader is immense. The .22-250, a 250/3000 necked down to .22 caliber, travels at 3800 fps and still has two-thirds of this velocity left at 300 yards, where it has 622 foot pounds of energy. This cartridge should be sighted in at one-inch high at 100 yards and will then be dead on at 200 yards. It will require some holdover at 300 yards, but should the hunter even get the opportunity, holding the cross hairs along the back of a standing predator will neatly place the bullet into the vital heart-lung area.

The .225 Winchester, which I use, is very similar in performance to the .22-250. It, unfortunately, suffered from poor acceptance by the shooting public, mostly because it was first introduced in the redesigned Model 70 that was dumped on the shooting world back in 1964. Nobody interested in firearms needs to be retold how this rifle and anything associated with it failed in the marketplace. Gun scribes universally decried the shape of the stock, the checkering, the finish, and the free-floating feature that was described as a "canoe route." Needless to say, the only route that rifle and the accompanying cartridge ever followed was the one leading straight to the scrap heap. That is where the .225 Winchester sits today.

So it was when I found the gun, clearly the ideal choice for a rough-and-tumble predator hunting rifle. At the time, its low purchase price and an abundance of bargain-basement ammunition made the .225 Model 70 the rifle to use. Even today, the Model 70 in .225 is one of my least expensive

The .243 and 6mm Remington are very popular dual-purpose cartridges. Valuable as hide-hunting loads, they are good for taking any of the wildcats.

pieces of hunting equipment. For me, the rifle and cartridge that were universally despised has performed extremely well. It may soon need a new barrel, but uncounted factory and handloaded pills have been fired in this tossed aside rifle.

Next in line to the .22 calibers are the .243 or the 6mm's. Known as the .243 Winchester and the 6mm Remington, these are considered useful cartridges for all types of hunting up to whitetailed deer. As predator cartridges they are tough to beat, especially at long ranges or under windy conditions. A shooter equipped with either cartridge in the open Northwest would be well outfitted. Factory-loaded cartridges in the 80- and 85-grain weights are especially designed for varmint hunters.

Many serious bobcat hunters prefer a .243 or 6mm, because enough energy is there to dispatch the animal at good ranges, and if shots are well placed, there is little chance of wounding. This reduces the need for a tracking job. Moreover, since bobcats are particularly tenacious, a good-sized cat needs a surprising amount of killing. This is provided by the .243.

Many hunters who use solid or full metal-jacketed bullets prefer the .243 calibers. This is because of the high-flying velocities that can be produced and the excellent accuracy nearly any bullet produces in this caliber. For example, a 90-grain FMJ Speer bullet can be propelled at 3300 fps measured at the muzzle to give a point-blank range of nearly 240 yards. This means that a standing coyote can easily be taken without any estimation in range. Hard-point bullets usually require that most predators be downed with neck and head shots, and the kind of velocity and inherent accuracy common to the .243 clan of cartridges make this possible.

The .25 caliber is found in a broad array of cartridges and is indicative of the love affair for high-velocity, light-bulleted cartridges currently alive in North America. Indeed, the .257 Roberts is a cartridge that has made a comeback in the last few years. More recently, the aged .250 Savage made a return to life and is now offered in more rifle models than it was 30 years ago.

As varmint cartridges, the .25 calibers can't be beat. However, as predator-taking cartridges,

Any of the .25 caliber cartridges are popular hunting loads. The .250 Savage is very useful, the .257 Roberts in the middle is currently on the comeback trail, while the .25-06 (right) is a bit much for most hide hunting.

where keeping the hide intact is of uppermost importance, this line of cartridges can pose some problems. The .25-06 is the first to come to mind. In the light-bulleted loadings available from most of the factory ammunition makers, damage is virtually assured once a predator is hit. Hits in the back and lower body are particularly destructive to the hide and fur. In addition, the bullets do considerable damage to bones and other tissues, breaking these into fine pieces which, in turn, become projectiles in their own right, further damaging the hide. Large, jagged exit holes are the result. These are difficult to repair and hard to clean. Sometimes bone fragments will make separate exit holes some distance from the actual bullet hole. In nearly all cases, the exit holes are enlarged by pieces of bone.

The .257 Roberts is well known as a cartridge capable of long-range connections on distant predators and still capable of serving double-duty on deer and antelope. With an 87-grain bullet, the .257 Roberts will produce slightly over 3200 fps in most rifles. This cartridge is about the maximum ever needed for any kind of hide hunting. Handloading is required to make it a usable predator cartridge, since the available factory loads come into 100-grain bullets. As such, these do much damage to long-haired hides and perform much like the .25-06 on soft-skinned predators.

About the best .25 caliber available in factory cartridges is the .250-3000, now commonly called the .250 Savage. It, too, is on a mild comeback, having almost been beaten into oblivion by the onslaught made by the .243 calibers back in the 1950s and '60s. It has been available for much of this time in the Model 99 Savage, which has a good reputation as a trapline or backwoods gun. A surprising number are still in use and anybody working back country will come across them.

The .250 Savage travels at 3000 fps in the factory 87-grain loading. This is the traditional load first marketed in the cartridge, and some modern-day offerings claim to exceed this. The factory 100-grain loadings travel around 200 fps slower than the .257 Roberts and a large 500 fps slower than the .25-06 at 200 yards. Most bullet velocities should be compared at the 200-yard distance rather than at the muzzle, because many more predators are shot nearer this distance than at the

SELECTED PREDATOR CARTRIDGES

Cartridge	Bullet Weight	Muzzle Velocity (fps)	Muzzle Energy (ft. lbs.)	Value for Hide Hunting
.17 Remington	25	4040	906	Adequate calling cartridge
.22 Hornet	45	2690	723	Once-popular critter cartridge
.222 Remington	55	3020	1114	Excellent medium-range performer
.222 Remington Magnum	55	3240	1282	Useful, but losing popularity
.223 Remington	55	3240	1282	Military cartridge, good
.225 Winchester	55	3570	1556	Used extensively by author
.22-250 Remington	55	3730	1699	Most popular varmint cartridge
.220 Swift	55	3630	1609	Waning popularity, but useful
.243 Winchester	80	3350	1993	Should be down-loaded for fur
6mm Remington	80	3470	2139	Dual-purpose load
.25-20	86	1460	407	Short-range performer
.250 Savage	87	3030	1773	Good hide-hunting cartridge
.257 Roberts	100	2900	1867	Very versatile cartridge
.25-06 Remington	87	3440	2286	Factory load is a tad powerful
.30-30 Accelerator	55	3400	1262	Extends the use of the Model 94
.32-20 Winchester	100	1210	325	Good candidate for handloading

muzzle. Anyway, the striking energy of the .250 Savage is sufficient at all ranges, including 300 yards, to down any of the long-haired species covered in this book.

The .257 Weatherby Magnum is mentioned to round out the discussion of the quarter-inch caliber. However, it should never be selected as a hide hunter's cartridge—it is much too powerful. Any hit on the soft-skinned predators would mean terrible hide damage and no doubt coyote burger would rain down for days afterward. It is not recommended for even the most casual hide hunter.

Although most hunters do not consider calibers above the .25 suitable for predator work, a surprising number will use .270's, .284 calibers and the various .30's for all their hide hunting. Many serious callers, who specialize in calling predators only for sport rather than for the fur value, like to use these calibers. They contend that when so outfitted there is no possibility of odd surprises—like a cougar coming in answer to the call or a pair of wolves bringing up the rear. They feel that these heavier hunting loads give them all the power and perform-

ance needed to dispatch the predator. A case for such use can be made.

Tailoring Hide Hunting Loads

The use of big game hunting cartridges brings the subject of handloading up for consideration. Handloading nearly any cartridge lets the hunter tailor his combination to meet the needs of the specific kind of hunting he is engaged in. No hunting endeavor benefits from this more than hide hunting.

Lightweight bullets have been available for the big game cartridges for years. Early on the .30-06 was loaded with 110-grain bullets to super-high velocities. For some reason, this combination gained a reputation of breaking apart on the shoulders of game animals and shattering on tree branches. However, with bullet technology at its highest point to date, bullets, when loaded to appropriate velocities and used on the correct game, will generally perform as the catalog says.

The absolute maximum in predator cartridges, the .284 Winchester, home-loaded with lightweight bullets, and the .308 are both effective for coyotes and wildcats.

Most loading manuals now offer reduced, or starting, loads; these are to be used as a beginning load and increased until the maximum listed in the manual is reached, or the cartridge and rifle start to show signs of reacting to the increased loadings.

Many of these beginning loads are very good general predator hunting loads. They are usually 10 percent below the maximum load listed and this slows the bullet down sufficiently, so that in many cases there is less hide damage than with hotter loadings.

Additionally, recent reloading manuals have begun responding to the specialized need of the predator hunter by providing reduced loadings where full metal-jacketed bullets are used. For example, the third edition of the Hornady Handbook of Cartridge Reloading presents reduced loadings in .224 Weatherby, .22-250, .220 Swift, .243 Winchester, 6mm Remington, and .240 Weatherby. These are some 10 percent lower than the suggested starting load for the given caliber, and they are as much as one third below the maximum recommended for the cartridge.

Powder Requirements. This type of specialized loading means that different gun powders become necessary. Reloading-down is not simply a situation where less powder is placed in the case. Special, faster burning powders are required to mesh with the increased empty space available within the cartridge case. Space and the time in which it takes the powder to burn are crucial factors in determining the optimum pressure under which the cartridge will function. Moreover, the pressure built up must be consistent from load to load, both for the safety involved and bullet accuracy.

The hunter after furs would do well to select powders that provide for these considerations and still give the edge needed to take predators. Most shotgun powders can be substituted in these kinds of loads, and the old standby 2400 is very useful. Shotgun powders handy for down-loading include Red Dot, Blue Dot and 700X. The IMR 4198 is about the only extruded, single-base powder that can be used safely in down-loading. The powder labeled SR4759 is also currently favored for use in old cartridges such as the .38-55, where heavy at-home cast lead bullets or jacketed bullets are given moderate velocities. Another favorite in down-loading is IMR 4227, used in large cases where medium velocities are desired. An example might be loading the .30-06 with lightweight 110-grain bullets to velocities of around 2100 fps or just a little faster than a .22 Magnum, but having considerably more killing power. In short, some selection and consideration of the powder is needed for down-loading to be successful.

A recommended scaled-down load for the .243 that will work well for most predator hunting out to about 175 yards is 23 grains of SR 4759 and the Hornady 80-grain FMJ bullet. This produces about 2500 fps at the muzzle and will be about three inches high at 100 yards with a 200-yard zero. Most predator hunters, especially rank beginners, would have trouble sorting out the three-inch distance when shots are taken at less than 175 to 200 yards. Those hunters should consider a dead-on 100-yard zero, which would be only six inches low at 200 yards. Shots made at this distance could still result in reliable hits by placing the cross hair of the scope along the back of a standing predator and letting the bullet drop into the heart-lung area.

A recommended lower velocity load for the .243 places the 75-grain, hollow-point Hornady bullet behind 36 grains of IMR 4320. This will give a muzzle velocity of about 3000 fps or a little less occasionally. The 75-grain, hollow-point bullet shoots through the average predator only when ranges are less than 50 yards and tends to do so more often on fox than on any other animal. At 100 or 200 or more yards, there seems to be sufficient energy for the bullet to open up and leave its entire energy inside the animal. Entrance holes are small and as yet no bullets have broken to pieces on the shoulder of the animal. Any shot that strikes at an angle, especially from the front or rear, never leaves the body of the animal.

Another useful predator load is a 60-grain Sierra hollow-point bullet with 37 grains of IMR 4064 to produce 3380 fps at the muzzle. This bullet can be loaded to nearly top levels such as 44 grains of IMR 4320 and still perform with little hide damage when predators are taken at extreme ranges.

A load that gives serious competition to the .243 calibers in terms of reduced hide damage and predator effectiveness is the .250 Savage. Outfitted with a 60-grain Speer spire-point bullet and 25 grains of IMR 4198, the nifty little .250 produces 2700 fps at the muzzle. A predator hunter should sight this in to be dead-on at 100 yards. The result will be a bullet that is nearly five inches low at 200 yards.

Many of the .22 caliber cartridges can also be loaded-down with some success. This is particularly true when full metal-jacketed bullets are used. Although the effectiveness of the full metal-jack-

Ed Sceery at his loading bench preparing some .22-250 loads for coyotes. A full-time hunter is wise to tailor his own cartridges, because hide hunting puts special limitations on the kinds of cartridges used and the results produced.

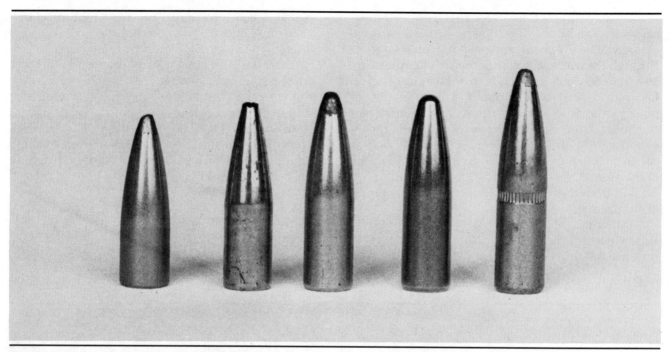

Popular varmint bullets include the .243/6mm 70-grain Hornady spire point, 75-grain Hornady hollow point, 87-grain Hornady spire point, 90-grain Speer full metal jacket, and the 100-grain Hornady spire point.

eted bullet is sometimes a hot topic of debate among predator hunters, it can result in less tissue damage than the standard soft-pointed or hollow-pointed bullet will produce. However, to achieve this in the .22 calibers, muzzle velocities must be in the range of 2300 to 2700 fps.

In terms of down-loading, the smaller case volumes characteristic of the .22 caliber cartridges allow for the use of powders that cannot be used in larger cases. In particular, IMR 4064 and IMR 4320 can be used with no sacrifice of safety.

Four loads that would produce 2700 fps using a 55-grain solid Speer bullet include 21 grains of IMR 4064 in the .222 Remington, 23 grains of the same powder in the .225, 24 grains in the .22-250 and the .220 Swift with 26 grains of IMR 4064.

Speer was the first bullet manufacturer to offer a 90-grain, full metal-jacketed bullet for the .243 Winchester or the 6mm Remington. This was hailed as the perfect bullet to allow reduced hide damage and yet be combined with the inherently accurate .243 caliber. It was soon found that bone fragments, high-velocity tissue damage, and tip-

ping of the bullet under some circumstances all combined to produce as much or more damage as any soft-nosed bullet would offer. Added to this was the increased chance of ricochet and the concern of having an adequate backstop against which to shoot. The answer to the problem was to opt for reduced loading of the cartridge. A favorite recipe was 34 grains of the eminently practical IMR 4064 to yield 2700 fps out of the .243 Winchester case. A sister load of 35 grains was used in the 6mm Remington. This improved the full metal-jacket performance in the .243 calibers, but reduced the useful range at which shots could be reliably made.

The Performance of Hard-point Bullets. The effectiveness of hard-point or full metal-jacketed bullets is, as yet, unresolved. Some hunters would not be without them, while others are less enamored. It has been pretty well established that a full-power load using these bullets can do as much or more damage to a soft-skinned predator and its fur as a soft-pointed bullet. This is especially true when broadside body hits are made. Hard-points are very good at dispatching predators when head and neck

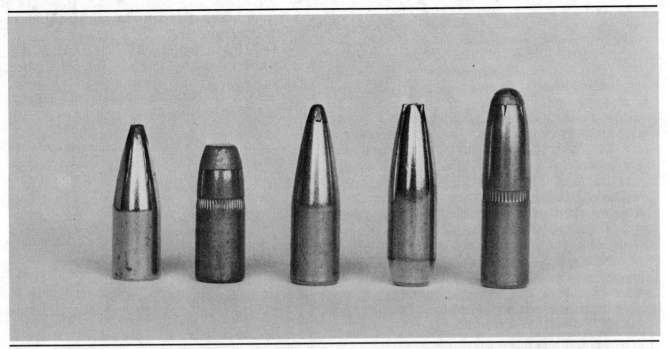

Some .25 caliber bullets that have made good names among hunters are the 75-grain Hornady hollow point, 86-grain old CIL soft point for the .25-20, 87-grain Hornady spire point, 90-grain Sierra hollow-point boattail, and the 117-grain Winchester for the defunct .25-35.

shots are routinely made. This, of course, is only possible when medium- to short-range shots are taken and most often at standing targets.

Another problem lies in the potential for wounding the animal. Poorly placed hits, especially in the lower body too far back or in the legs may result in the predator escaping to suffer a lingering death and the loss of a valuable hide. It seems that solid body hits are devastating, while anything other than this produces a wound that does not necessarily anchor the animal and will often allow the animal to escape. As told before, tracking a predator is very difficult unless conditions are optimal, and many times a minor hit with a solid bullet will leave no telltale sign.

The strange performance of hard-point bullets is not new to anyone who has burned up surplus military ammo. As a kid I cut my shooting teeth on a P-17 Lee Enfield rifle shooting cast-off war surplus .303 British ammunition. One of these solids, as the English call them, would punch a neat hole through a two-inch poplar and then keyhole to nearly mow down a four-inch or so poplar only feet away. Experience with the ancient .303 at least taught me not to try full metal-jacketed bullets in anything above the .243 caliber.

Many of the same problems exist with home-cast lead bullets. Perhaps the saving grace is that most homemade bullets cannot be driven as fast as the commercial jacketed versions. Hard-cast bullets can drive clean through an animal, even at long range.

Casting Lead Bullets. One of the big problems most hunters have with homemade bullets is poor accuracy. However, the key is to do more load development and experiment with different powders. Fundamental in using any cast-lead load is to slug (with a ramrod gently push a slightly oversize lead core down the length of the bore) the barrel of the rifle the bullet is going to be used in. Then measure the lead core to find the diameter necessary to match the bullet to the barrel. Be sure to size the bullets to match this diameter or certainly no more than .001 inch larger than bore size. Smaller bullets should never be used and the greatly oversized discarded as well.

Two duty-proven hide hunter's bullets in .22 caliber. A 45-grain Speer Spitzer soft point and a 55-grain Hornady spire point.

Greasing is also important. Many commercial bullet lubricants are now on the market and these are much better than some of the older versions. I well remember paying a call on a trapper in the northern Alberta bush in the dead of winter. Opening the door of the cabin, my nose was assailed with the strangest smells coming from the hot stove. It turned out he was melting together vaseline, bear fat and bacon drippings into a concoction to grease bullets for his .25-20.

Another problem is the alloy used for making the bullets. For years, reloaders have read that Lyman No. 2 alloy was the best for all-round bullet making. However, for predator hunting a much softer bullet is required. A bullet of nearly pure lead, much the same as is required by muzzleloading shooters is best. This is necessary so that the bullet will tip on contact with the predator's body. A soft lead bullet will deform greatly on impact. This tipping or deforming acts similar to expanding or mushrooming in jacketed bullets.

A bullet of pure or nearly pure lead cannot be driven to the same velocity levels as one composed of much harder alloys. This is fine for most close-in predator hunting, but precludes these kinds of loads for long-range use.

Most lead that a hunter will find or scavenge from friends and local acquaintances will be of wheel weights, salvaged plumber's lead and other junked items, such as car batteries. Much of this contains tin, which is used to harden the lead. Any long-hair hunter using such sources of lead would do well to remember to heat the metal until it melts and then let it settle for a few minutes under high temperature. This will extract the tin as well as any dirt and other foreign material that salvaged lead always seems to contain. This can be scraped off the top of the melted lead and discarded. Fluxing, the act of placing a substance, usually wax or paraffin (bees wax was an old favorite) into the heated mixture to promote the fusion of any tin with the lead, is recommended in most cast bullets. Therefore, as much tin as possible should be scraped off before fluxing is done. Although this is a deviation from the standard recommended procedure, it will give the hide hunter the kind of bullets needed to perform the highly specialized job of effectively dispatching the animal and producing little damage to the skin and hair.

A big, although often overlooked, advantage of home-cast, soft lead bullets over their jacketed counterparts is that they allow larger caliber rifles to be used for predator hunting. I use my Model 70 in .30-06 with lead bullets, for example. Long ago a load of 10 grains of Unique in front of the 170 or so grain Lyman mold number 311291 made a very useful close-in load for long-hairs. Another good load was to size the cast .32-20 bullet down to .308 and use it on top of 15 grains of 2400 in the .30-06 case. It worked extremely well.

Cast bullets can be used in the smaller calibers, such as the .243 and the .25. A .25-06 can be downloaded in much the same way as the .30-06. The .243 Winchester and the 6mm Remington, using the now discontinued Lyman 245496 round-nose bullet and 10 grains of 700X, make for a good load where fur bearers are coming in at short and intermediate ranges. The .250 Savage performs well using the 106-grain Lyman 257231 mold that was originally designed for the .25-35. Another discontinued mold that works well in this caliber is the 257388, originally designed for the .250 Savage. It leaves a nominal 80-grain bullet that can be loaded to equal the .243 with 10 to 11 grains of 700X or Red Dot.

Gunsmith Dale Freisen, whom I mentioned in the last chapter, used Red Dot exclusively in his many rifles. He was able to make small-game and predator loads for nearly every caliber and cartridge using this powder.

The hunter after furs may well have to spend some time scouring gun shows and flea markets looking for some of the discontinued molds since the current crop gets smaller every year.

How Lead Bullets Compare. Hollow-pointed, cast-lead bullets do not have the same dramatic expansion characteristics as commercial bullets. However, a soft, hollow-pointed bullet will tip inside the animal very readily and do much internal damage. The .32-20 bullet cast from the 31133 Lyman bullet mold had a very deep hollow point. Bullets recovered from the insides of downed predators showed that sometimes the lead bullet would break apart at the hollow. Sometimes the impact would compress or deform the nose of the bullet to

Handloaders are advised to use softer than normal bullets. Outdoorsman Ed Pyle, former soldier, farmer, carpenter and jack-of-all-trades, experimented for years with lead bullets in an ancient .40-82 Model 86 Winchester. He reported good success with soft cast bullets on coyotes and foxes.

such a degree that the hollow was completely closed. At times, the bullet was almost bent into a slight C-shape. Simply, a soft, cast, hollow-pointed bullet is better than a plain-nosed version, and a flat-nosed type is better than a round nose. Although these bullets definitely do not expand in the manner today's hunters have become accustomed to seeing from commercial bullets, they do perform the expansion function by tipping, bending and keyholing inside the animal.

While there are good points to the use of homemade, soft, cast bullets, some less positive features appear. The major drawback is the need to be very familiar with where the rifle is shooting. Using the same scope setting for full-house reloads and then again for slower lead bullet reloads is asking for a clean miss, even at close range. Usually the vertical point of impact is markedly lower with the underpowered load and different bullet weight. The .30-06 load quoted earlier shot a full 12 inches low at 100 yards compared to the regular hunting load used in the rifle. Otherwise, it was horizontally correct.

There's nothing quite like having a coyote respond to a calling session only to have the animal stand off just over 100 yards away while the hunter has a short-range lead load up the spout of his rifle. Sometimes it is possible to change, quietly working the bolt of the rifle, expending the weaker cartridge and replacing it with a full-power load. At times, cartridges of the different loadings will get mixed up unless plainly and carefully marked— and always accounted for. Anyone who has hunted predators will be able to tell stories of letting fly a pipsqueak load when expecting a full-bore cartridge to go off. However, lead bullet loads are easy to tell from jacketed versions, and keeping them stored in different containers will go a long way to preventing embarrassing mix-ups.

Lead loads, as you can see, require a lot of development, work and experimentation. Some hunters do not have the time for this or are unwilling to put effort into this kind of development. Once two or three acceptable loads are put together, a hunter will not usually change unless there are some real difficulties.

Besides the need for development and a fair amount of shooting, most hunters will find that shooting many lead loads will mean more frequent barrel cleaning. Leading can become a problem with soft bullet loads in as few as 20 rounds. Unburned powder and other residues will also build up far more readily than with copper or gilded metal-jacketed bullets. Rifles used during the winter and moved in and out of warm places, such as the cabin or the truck cab, attract considerable moisture. This is held by the powder residues and lead fragments and can damage the bore through rusting and corrosion.

Lead bullets in the .22 calibers are not generally recommended for predator hunting. The light, fragile bullets used in these calibers do not frequently shoot through the average-sized predator. The entire bullet remains inside and it does not matter if the bullet breaks up extensively or holds together. Lead bullets offer no advantage over the factory versions in these cartridges. As well, the small bore size of this family of cartridges is difficult to clean and scrub, although it can be done.

A Word About Accelerators

In recent times, there has been a growing interest in using sabot-outfitted cartridges with bullets of smaller caliber. One of the first on the market and to receive some critical acclaim was the Remington produced .30-30 Accelerator. These were sold with the intent of filling a need for a fast-moving varmint cartridge that could be used in the aging Model 94 Winchester. The idea was to turn the old saddle gun into a varmint-dispatching, long-range number that would let the hunter have a true dual-purpose rifle all wrapped up in one package by merely changing cartridges.

This strategy has been partly successful. There is a place in the open West where, to this day, nearly every pickup truck is outfitted with a Model 94 Winchester in .30-30. It is a badge for many, almost like a pair of cowboy boots. There is need for a high-speed loading in the .30-30, although a 90- or 100-grain bullet would probably do just fine. The Accelerators should not be loaded through the magazine of the typical Model 94, as this places the sharp bullet in contact with the primer of the cartridge in front of it. Indeed, countless predators marauding around sheep camps and calving fields have been felled with this relatively new combo.

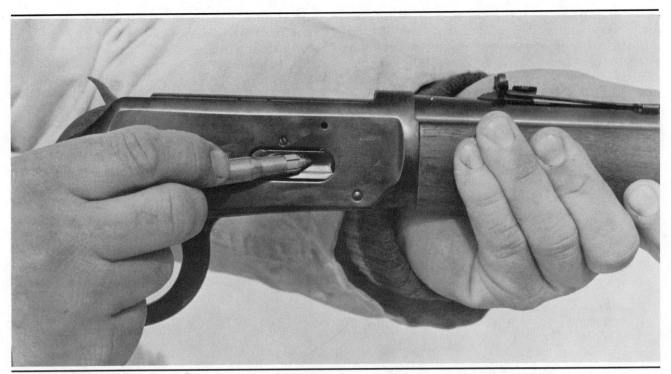

The .30-30 Accelerator has potential for hide hunting. However, care must be used as the sabot and bullet can produce two wounds on predators taken at ranges under 50 yards.

Having said this, the cartridge has to be used cautiously on predators taken for fur purposes. The bullet from the .30-30 Accelerator travels at 3400 fps from the muzzle. Although this would be reduced in a short-barreled Model 94 Winchester, the potential for hide damage is high. The sabot does not always separate from the bullet, and at close range the sabot and the bullet could hit the animal. This, of course, results in two wounds, or at least two damage points on an already delicate hide. The potential for damage to hides by high-speed bullets has already been reviewed and those observations would apply to the .22 caliber, sabot-held bullet as well. Unfortunately, the sabots and their associated bullets are not yet available to the reloading public. If they were, there would be room for load development and the potential for use in hide hunting could more appropriately be determined.

The family of .30 caliber accelerators has grown. There are now accelerators of the .30-06 (actually the first cartridge so outfitted), the .308 Winchester as well as the .30-30.

Accuracy can be a problem in some rifles of all of these calibers, but Remington claims that performance in this department solely depends on the rifle used. The .30-30, the only one I have used, performed reasonably well and accounted for a recent coyote using the Model 94 Trapper model. However, it did shoot through the coyote, leaving a large exit hole. Yet, as an auxiliary cartridge where the fur is of little or secondary importance, the accelerator will work fine.

In the final analysis some combination of cartridge and bullet—be it factory ammunition, commercial bullets in handloads or homemade cast bullets—is what most hunters will choose. A few may use accelerators. The .22 calibers are favored, in particular the .22-250. While the hunter will see many types of firearms and cartridge combinations in use, remember that the hide hunter's needs are different from any other hunter's. He must preserve the hide with the least amount of damage possible and yet deliver a killing blow that is both humane and efficient.

Getting and keeping a good load or cartridge and bullet combination is an important facet of hide hunting. The greatly varying distances at which predators will be seen, and the array of habitat conditions and weather situations will all give the hunter's loads sufficient test. Load development takes time and effort, but the reward of the perfect combination saves great amounts of time when the skinning and hide preparation side of the hunt begins. Remember, the cartridge you use *can* influence the price received for any raw hide harvested.

Chapter 12

Improving Your Shooting Proficiency

Compared to selecting a cartridge, choosing the right rifle for hide hunting is easy. Nearly any type will do. The action is unimportant; it could be a bolt, a lever, a pump or a semiautomatic. Bolt-actions are preferred, simply because the most effective cartridges tend to be available in these. Recently Browning Arms introduced their lever-action rifle in .22-250, which might offer some challenge to this direction. It still stands that any rifle can be a predator or hide hunter's rifle.

Bolt-actions are capable of handling a broad range of reloads and are more tolerant of high-pressure loads than most lever rifles. My Model 100 carbine in the uncommon .284 Winchester requires that special small-base dies be used to bring the cartridge down to the minimum chamber size used in this rifle. The same applies to the Browning lever. Bolt-action rifles, such as the traditional Model 70 Winchester and the Remington 700, let the hunter get by with standard-sized dies.

A hunter outfitting for his first hunt would be in good company choosing a bolt-action rifle. The wide array of cartridge choices lets you use the rifle for the dual purposes of long-hair hunting and big game hunting. In addition, a bolt-action rifle is probably the easiest to learn to shoot well.

For most hide hunters, one of the tough decisions that has to be made is whether to choose a lightweight rifle for the majority of the shooting, or to pick one of the many models that comes outfitted with target-weight barrels. The debate will hinge around the high accuracy level of the heavy-barreled rifle versus the weight that will be carried through heavy bush, across snow-choked coulees and up and down sundry hills.

In some of my recent hunting I used a lightweight Sako Deluxe bolt-action in .222 caliber. Built on the Sako A1 action, it weighs in at a scant 5¾ pounds or 2.6 kg.—one of the lightest of the lightweight rifles available. Right off the top the hide hunter would find this weight saving helpful. It means less to carry and pack. In addition, the shortened rifle is quick to throw to the shoulder and hold on target.

However, accuracy is an important factor in this type of hunting, especially since most predators present small or obscure targets. Tight-shooting firearms are a must under these conditions, and if necessary light weight can be sacrificed in favor of tack-driving accuracy. It is for this reason that many shooters will tolerate the extra pounds of bull barrels on their rifles.

In the past, lightweight rifles have suffered from the reputation of being slightly inaccurate. Three-inch groups are common in carbines, mountain rifles and Mannlicher-styled rifles. Coupled with this

The bolt-action rifle is probably the best overall type of firearm for hide hunting. Here are some excellent examples: (left to right) the Model 70 Winchester; the more recent Model 70 Featherweight; an early, post-1964 Model 70 in .225 Winchester; and a heavy-barreled Model 700 Remington in .25-06.

At 5³/₄ pounds (2.6 kg.), the Sako Deluxe rifle is a lightweight bolt-action that produces tight groups—a must for hide hunting.

is the difficulty of holding a light-weight steadily on the target. For most sporting arms there is a heft that seems to help the shooter hold steadily or at least feel as if there is less wobble.

Right out of the box and without any fine tuning, however, the Sako Deluxe shot 1¹/₄-inch groups. The load was one that I had been successful with in other .222 rifles: 24.4 grains of IMR 4320 behind a 55-grain Hornady spire-point bullet. With further load development consistent three-quarter inch groups would no doubt be possible. Any hunter who wishes a highly specialized rifle for calling only

should consider the .17 caliber; where longer range shots are anticipated, either the .222 Remington or the .223 will be adequate. Light weight and accuracy are combined in few rifle packages today, but the Sako bolt-action has both.

A case could be made for a semiautomatic rifle where quick follow-up shots are needed. However, in practical hunting of long-haired species, there is usually little time or opportunity to make a quick second shot. And when sufficient time is available, a bolt-action can be worked quickly enough to meet the need.

Another popular bolt-action rifle used by hide hunters is the Model 77 Ruger.

fatty layer of the animal. They have no killing effect, but still result in a sewing job or cleaning effort. Some pellets, bound up with hair, cut much larger holes in the hide.

Having said all this against the use of the shotgun, there are special circumstances that might favor using one. Close-range shots under extremely bushy conditions will sometimes require the use of a shotgun. In these instances, head and neck shots should be attempted. Full-choke barrels should be replaced with modified or cylinder. Shot should be no smaller than BB size with the hope that one or two pellets will deliver a killing blow rather than a tight column of shot covering the entire side of the animal.

It is probably more difficult to obtain a good clean hit with a shotgun than with a rifle. "Clean" here is used to mean one that produces little damage to

What about using a shotgun for taking predators? In my opinion, it is not a good idea under most circumstances. Fur buyers greatly downgrade hides sprinkled with pellet holes, and the hunter who thinks the buyer does not notice these holes is kidding himself.

A tightly patterned, full-choked shotgun can have devastating results on any kind of fur-bearing hide. Shot sizes as small as No. 7½ will ruin a hide. Shots taken at an angle are particularly bad since the animal takes pellets from a large portion of the pattern. Broadside shots at short range blow an incredible hole in the animal.

Shots taken at longer range, after the pattern opens up, will also damage a good hide beyond repair. The pellets that do not penetrate the hide roll up in the fur. Others, slowed by the hair, yet powerful enough to puncture the hide, settle in the

A case could be made for the use of a semiautomatic rifle when quick follow-up shots are needed. Here the author uses the famous Model 100 Winchester semiauto rifle in a carbine version .284 Winchester caliber.

The Accelerator greatly extends the use of the trusted Model 94. The author particularly likes the Little Trapper version of this all-time favorite.

the hide and hair. Moreover, the potential for wounding is great. Pellets that strike too far back or too low will only inflict wounds from which the animal may, or may not, recover.

Mastering Your Shooting Technique

Collecting long-hairs demands good shooting. The target is small, the ranges are variable, and bullet placement is crucial. The animal can be moving, broadside, quartering or seen from the rear. It is rare that a predator will present an opportunity for a good shot.

For this reason, it is vital to be thoroughly fa-

miliar with your rifle. Many times opportunities to shoot will come when the hunter is cold, bundled up in bulky clothes or stiff form long periods of sitting. It is under this diversity of conditions that knowing how the rifle feels, where it shoots, and how it fits is important for consistent hitting of predators at any range. Practice throwing the rifle to the shoulder under all types of conditions.

It is important to learn the distances and ranges in your hunting area. Frequently pace off the distance to some prominent landmark from the trail on which you are driving. In my areas, I make a point of ticking off the distances to wells, stock watering tanks, rock piles, lone trees, bushes, fences, irrigation works and gates. Once you know the distance to most objects, a fur-bearer that appears near any one of these things is at a known range; this usually results in more hits than when range or holdover has to be estimated.

Knowing the distances to the landmarks and how your rifle is shooting means that most of the guesswork is eliminated before the trigger is pulled. Ranges are stored in my mind in two categories: distances where holdover is required and distances where a dead-on hold is sufficient. Up to 200 yards, a dead-center hold with either the .243 or the .225 is all that is required. Beyond that range, the cross hair of the scope is held along the back line of the animal.

Broadside shots are the best. And it is perhaps

Take into account heavy winter clothing, because bulky items could make the length of pull uncomfortably long for a short-armed hunter. Moving and placing the rifle to the shoulder may be much more difficult and should be practiced beforehand.

worth waiting for these types of shots under most circumstances. Patience is sometimes required. At other times, when the hunter knows the predator is alerted to his presence, there is no time to chance the broadside opportunity and you just have to decide to go with what is there. Sometimes a couple of toots on the predator call will slow the animal up for just a second, giving the hunter his chance for a lung shot.

Bullet placement is critical. Poorly hit predators can run for miles. Tracking, even under good conditions of snow and weather, can be difficult. The broadside shot offers the best chance of placing the bullet in the vital heart and lung area, the boiler room as it is called by many outdoor writers.

In competitive shooting, as in most other sports, the importance of psychology comes into play. It is realized that a psychologically fit competitor has an edge over others less mentally prepared. The same applies in hide hunting. The hunter must be mentally, or psychologically, prepared to shoot. He must believe that every time the trigger is pulled, a hide will grace the yard pole. His skills must be honed and he must feel he will make the shot. When the rifle is put to his shoulder, he must maintain good concentration. Moreover, the hide hunter should take his efforts seriously since the advance preparation necessary for this kind of hunting and the many skills that must be mastered are placed on the line when the trigger is squeezed. There must be a strong desire to hit the animal cleanly and effectively.

There is a kind of rifle psychology that is necessary for success. Many long-time hunters develop this without ever realizing that they have acquired the correct mix of skills and mental attitude. A soldier, for example, and a backwoods' marksman become good shots, but each arrive at that skill in vastly different ways. The soldier gains his ability through intense training, whereas the backwoodsman achieves his through necessity and opportunity. The hide hunter has to fall somewhere between these two obvious iconoclasts of modern-day riflery. He must learn the technique of marksmanship and the methods of the rural sharpshooter, yet be able to apply the discipline of a soldier.

It is difficult to convey this concept well. Perhaps most simply stated, a rifle is not a toy and it must

There is great potential for wounding animals with poorly placed shots. Make every shot count by keeping your rifle on your knee, always ready for a short-range response from a predator.

be used like a fine tool or a precision instrument. The hunter must come to terms with his rifle, he must understand its every quirk and why it performs the way it does. He must understand himself. In the end, the rifle and the hunter become one as a fur-gathering tool.

Scopes and Other Shooting Aids

No other single article of hunting equipment has done more to improve hunting than the rifle scope. Well-made, good-quality, high-resolution rifle scopes are now an integral part of the American hunting scene. There was a time when scopes were delicate instruments made more for surveying

than a day in the back country. Fortunately, that day is long past.

The rifle scope has really helped make modern-day hide hunting possible. Where iron-sighted rifles made taking a coyote or a fox at 100 yards a rare event, the glass and steel scope made it uneventful and increased the chances of connecting out to well over 300 yards. Indeed, the scope gave the hunter the opportunity to shoot as far as his rifle could accurately place shots.

Scopes are classified by power, or magnification. Most predator hunters prefer scopes at the higher end of the power scale, but for hide hunting a four- to six-power scope is best. Scopes in this medium-power range offer less waver as the hunter draws a bead. They also have wide fields of view. Highly specialized scopes, such as 10- to 14-power versions, really have no place in hide hunting. They are difficult to hold, and on dull wintery days, it is difficult to find the target. High-power scopes also make it difficult to discern the animal from the background. In addition, when moving shots are made, the narrow field of view requires a steady arm to keep the animal under sight.

Many hunters outfit their rifles with variable-power scopes. They argue that the higher powers *can* be used to discern a predator from its background. However, the need to adjust the variable-power ring means more movement during calling—movement that will send a sharp-eyed predator scurrying. Most serious hunters prefer single-power scopes and leave it at that for all hunting.

Rifle scopes are now nitrogen filled to prevent fogging. Many early models would lose their nitrogen filling in the cold northern winters and become fogged when cold, moisture-saturated air replaced the space vacated by the nitrogen. However, the sealing done on most modern-day scopes has eliminated this problem.

Waterproofing is critical. A scope that allows moisture to creep in from the outside will also fog. Rain will wet a scope down. Condensation will occur when moving the scope from a cold to a warm area. The surface of the lens at either end of the scope will also collect moisture. Scope covers will prevent some of this, but can be an impediment if a predator breaks from nearby cover.

Three shots at 100 yards will usually tell the hunter how the rifle-scope combination is doing.

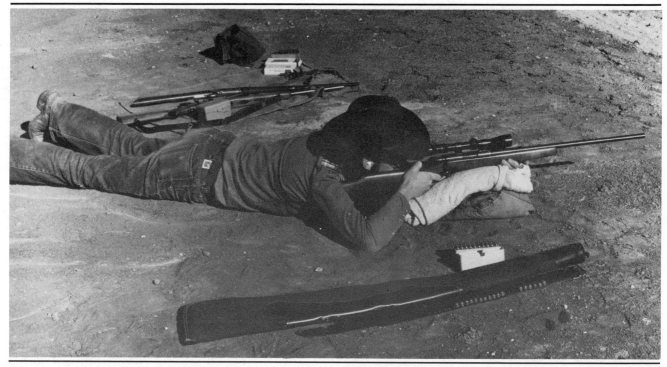

Every hunter should frequently check the zero of his rifle. In the course of a hide hunting season, more ammunition should be expended in checking the zero than is shot at predators.

Never, of course, do this shooting in the immediate area of the hunt. The noise is just too much for alert predator ears.

If the scope appears significantly off, and all other factors of holding, type of ammunition, and weather conditions have been accounted for, check to be sure the scope is properly fastened to the rifle. Carrying a screwdriver of the correct size, either in the rucksack or left in the vehicle, is a good practice. There is also a scope tightening tool once made by Weaver products that is very handy for this work. A hunter may have to do some scouting for this tool, since the Weaver company has gone the way of the passenger pigeon. A scope should be no more than hand-tight to the rifle. Make sure the bases are tight, and tighten any loose ones with a small screwdriver.

A scope should be tightened to the rifle and sealed in place with a lock-tightening compound. Many backwoods hunters of my acquaintance still use clear nail polish for this job. It works well and is remarkably waterproof. One friend uses it to waterproof the bullet into the case and the primer into the flash hole of reloaded ammunition.

The need for iron sights, when a scope is fixed in place, is often questioned. Opinions vary on this as they do on all shooting topics. In the end, it will be a personal decision, with some hunters believing a rifle looks better without the sights, and others feeling that a rifle looks incomplete without the front sight. A hide man would do well to leave the iron sights in place. In fact, any hunter after furs should be able to use his iron sights equally as well as the modern steel and glass combination.

A hide hunter should be able to hit a coyote-sized animal consistently out to 80 or 90 yards using factory iron sights. This is vital should the scope fog up, break, or for some reason deliver clear misses. While it may be more difficult, it is still possible to shoot a predator with iron sights.

Scopes can be mounted with specially designed swing-off mounts that will let the hunter get the scope out of the way and allow use of the original sights. These were originally invented to allow a hunter to bypass a fogged-up scope. Many hunters use these types of mounts, but it is still strongly held that these combination mounts will not return a scope to true zero every time. In reality, the jury is still out deciding whether or not these mounts meet the rigorous needs of hide hunting.

"See-through" mounts are also available to the hunter. These place the scope high enough above the bore to allow use of the iron sights below. Manufacturers include Redfield, Kwik-site and Clearview, among others. Again, this is an area of intense personal choice, but it is becoming clear that many more hunters are beginning to use this type of mount. Ten years ago there were few manufacturers. Now there are many, and this must mean an acceptance of the product. These mounts are the kind to have if iron sights may be needed.

When it comes to reticles within the scope, about the best that can be used is the dual-thickness cross hair. This is the kind that is relatively thick from the outside and steps down to a thin portion in the center of the scope. This design lets the hunter get his sight picture quickly and remains visible even when looking against a dark background. The dual-thickness cross hair is currently the most popular reticle on the market, and its use in hide hunting is part of the reason.

If you are going to use your scope to maximum advantage, you must become familiar with the scope and be able to find your target quickly. Practice is needed to become proficient at locating targets and getting the eye to line up at the correct distance from the eyepiece. Winter clothing may sometimes interfere and it will be necessary to crane your neck slightly forward to get a proper image. Be sure the scope is mounted to give the correct eye relief with the rifle squarely in place. Sometimes the thickness of a winter parka will cause a hunter to cant his rifle-scope combination, and this makes accurate, reliable shooting almost impossible at long ranges. Develop the ability to find the target quickly by throwing the rifle up to

A well-adjusted scope is a must in predator hunting. Three shots at 100 yards will usually tell the hunter how the rifle-scope combination is doing; also check to be sure the scope is properly secured to the rifle.

your shoulder and sighting on some object a hundred or so yards away. Things look strangely different through a scope compared to the unaided eye.

Learn to discern detail through a scope. Bright light against white snow will make a hunter's eye feel as if it is being pulled out of his head. Ground fog will appear thicker through a scope. Looking into the sun or toward a sunset will cause an animal to appear silhouetted and sometimes difficult to sort out from trees and shrubs. Practice under these varying conditions is essential, since a hunter usually gets only one chance for a shot.

To keep your scope in its best working condition, use a scope cover, especially during wet or snowy weather. A warm day with soft, nearly wet snow flakes is probably worse than a driving blizzard in terms of blurring the ocular or objective ends of the

scope. A scope end will fill with snow and water and make it impossible to get a good clear image when needed. An effective cover actually consists of two covers, one for the front end of the scope and another for the rear, often times with elastic stretched between the two. A quick pull and release on the back cover will put enough stretch into the elastic that the front cover will fly off at the same time. This gets the covers off in a hurry and still allows time for a quick shot in many instances.

Another good idea is to carry a soft cloth or towel with which to wipe condensation or moisture from the scope lenses. A small cloth can usually be carried in the ammo pouch. In inclement weather a scope lens can fog while the hunter is calling. Checking the lenses and wiping them when needed will make sure a clear sight picture is always possible. There is also the chance of knocking snow

A shooter should use any opportunity to steady the firearm before shooting. One of the most common shooting rests is across the hood of a truck or car.

While many of us, the author included, prefer to carry a rifle in the barrel-down position, it can easily result in a barrel plugged by snow.

from surrounding trees and shrubs onto the lenses. This can frequently happen when sitting down or setting up to do some calling.

Any hunter after furs should frequently check the zero of his rifle. In the course of a season of hunting, far more ammunition should be expended checking where the rifle shoots than actually taking animals. When a rifle is shooting well, a single shot fired to check the aim is good enough. But if a rifle has received some rough travel over rugged terrain, a more detailed check is in order.

Shooting Rests. Some hunters, especially varmint hunters, suggest the use of a bipod or shooting sticks. There is little doubt that these shooting aids do greatly steady the rifle and enhance shooting. However, in most hide hunting work they would be difficult to use, especially when calling from a blind. There would be some opportunity to use the bipod out on the open prairie where extreme long-range shots were being attempted at a standing animal. The bipod would also work well for younger shooters who have trouble steadying the firearm. Any shooter who has had problems hitting consistently at long ranges might consider giving one a try.

A shooter should take every opportunity to steady the firearm when making even close-in shots. One of the most common shooting rests is across the hood of a truck or car. In places where this is legal, it makes an excellent rifle rest for taking long shots at animals spotted off the road or trail. As well, most callers rest against a tree or shrub during calling, and often this cover can be used to steady the rifle. When shooting from the sitting position, the elbows can be braced against the knees. Use a rest at any opportunity.

The Sling As a Shooting Aid. Although many hunters do not consider it as such, a sling is a valuable addition to any hunting rifle. A military sling can help hold the rifle in place during shooting or be used in carrying the rifle to the calling site. A sling should be fitted to the rifle with detachable swivels. In this way, it can be removed when working heavily vegetated or shrubby areas, where it may snag on vegetation.

Rifle Care and Precautions

Most fur-bearer hunting will be done under cold or snowy conditions. In most parts of Canada and the northern U.S., bitter cold, snow, and winds capable of producing high wind-chill factors are common. Under such conditions, a wise hunter should take several precautions that relate specifically to his rifle and shooting technique. For many far northerners, these tips will seem laughable, but those not familiar with the ravages of winter should take heed.

Snow in the rifle barrel is one of those unique winter problems. Most hunters know that any rifle barrel plugged with snow can be dangerous to the shooter. Blown barrels, or at least bulged muzzles, are a common result. However, many outdoorsmen do not realize a rifle does not have to be plugged tight to be a problem. Any amount of snow that restricts bullet travel down the barrel can result in a bulge. The same applies to accumulations of moisture inside the barrel.

Carrying a rifle in the barrel-down position in snow conditions can easily result in a plugged barrel. Dropping the rifle can do the same thing. It may seem trivial to warn a hunter not to drop his rifle, and almost no one would ever do so deliberately, but with winter clothing in place, deep snow, and winter-weight gloves or mitts, a rifle can slip. Sometimes crossing a fence or tripping on fallen branches covered with deep, soft snow will send a prize rifle flying. For this reason, always carry a cleaning rod, broken down, in your pack. With 10 minutes work, a plugged barrel can be cleared and you can be on your way.

In really tough snow conditions, or when carrying the rifle while snowshoeing or on a snowmobile, use a muzzle cover. A piece of tape could be used, but a simple cloth cover that shrouds the

Any hide hunter working under snowy conditions should carry a broken-down rifle cleaning rod in case a plugged barrel should result from a fall by the hunter or from the rifle being dropped into snow.

barrel for about six inches down from the end is preferable. It should be tied in place with string. This allows it to be quickly shaken or pulled off should a coyote or fox burst from the brush.

Remember, too, that condensation can be deadly during the wintertime. Any firearm taken from the cold outdoors and into the warmth will collect condensation. Taking the gun in and out of a vehicle under such conditions can quickly freeze the action closed, especially on semiautomatic guns. Water can collect under the free-floating barrel and cause rust when the piece is stored. The firing pin, usually heavily greased when leaving the factory, can become stiff and fail to deliver a sufficient blow to strike the primer.

Any firearm used during winter hide hunting should be prepared for the cold weather. The main spring should be stripped out of the bolt and the grease removed with solvent or other such cleaning fluid. Also, the magazine and/or clip should be cleaned of grease and any foreign material. Grease under the barrel or along the sides and bottom of the action should also be cleaned away, as this only acts like a trap for moisture during the winter. These parts should be reassembled dry and left that way. There are some modern-day lubricants that claim and actually may be unaffected by cold, but I wouldn't take the chance. A rifle can always be re-oiled or greased if necessary in the spring.

Though most hunters do not consider it, cartridge primers are less effective during the cold winter. The chemical becomes less sensitive to the sharp blow needed to detonate the primer. In extreme cases of cold, pistol primers may have to be used, since they do not need to be struck as sharply. This is not a practice that should be approached lightly; some rifles with very strong main springs, especially some older military rifles, will easily pierce a thin, webbed pistol primer. At temperatures around 40 below zero, and where the rifle and ammunition are at the same temperature, this trick will work well. Use large pistol primers, the same ones that a handgun shooter would use in his .44 Magnum.

A good tip on rifle storage is to use an open-topped rifle case or saddle scabbard. This makes the firearm reasonably accessible, yet gives some protection to the barrel and stock. When the rifle is not needed, the cover should be fitted in place, but

Practice calling whenever in predator country and always travel with a rifle. Most important, come to terms with your rifle. Know how it shoots, how it performs, how it feels.

when it is in the hunting area, the top cover can be stored out of the way.

Another good idea is to store the rifle out in the cold. For many, especially those who must travel to the hunting sites, this is not possible. But for the lucky hunters who live on farms or right in the area they hunt, storing the rifle outside means that condensation will never be a problem. An unheated outbuilding, such as a garage or pumphouse, would work in the same fashion. The rifle would always remain at the same temperature as the surrounding air and there would be no alternate heating and cooling. This would eliminate condensation.

Remember to take into account the problems of any added winter clothing. It only takes a few clothes to make the length of pull uncomfortably

Taking long-hairs demands good shooting technique: precise bullet placement, range estimation and familiarity with the rifle. Early-season hides such as this one (turned hair-side-out for this photo) are the mainstay of fur hunting.

long for short-armed hunters. Heavy winter hats can also interfere with sighting. A winter cap, especially one with the ear flaps pulled down, is harder to bump out of the way with the scope than a summer cap. Sometimes it is difficult to place the rifle to the shoulder when fully dressed and the gun can catch on bulky chest fronts or the bottom of a parka sleeve.

In conclusion, the boundaries of modern-day predator shooting and hide hunting have been extended by a number of factors. Any average-skilled hunter outfitted with good ammunition, a reasonable rifle and an adequately powered scope should consistently be able to hit a small soda bottle at 200 yards from the sitting position. With a rest, he should be able to repeat the event at 300 yards. While standing, a hide hunter should be capable of hitting a cardboard dinner plate set at 100 yards three shots out of three without dropping the rifle from his shoulder. This kind of shooting, demanded of hide hunting, is possible.

Preparing the Hides for Market

Chapter 13

Before You Begin Skinning

Once the shot has been made and the elated hunter retrieves his kill, a new set of skills is demanded. It is in the use of these skills that the true title of "hide hunter" becomes clear. The animal must now be skinned and the hide prepared for market.

Most predators taken with well-placed heart-lung shots will not require finishing-off shots, as is sometimes common with big game animals. A well-hit predator will usually fold within 100 yards, and one taken with a hit to the central nervous system will drop instantly. Animals that are poorly hit should be dispatched quickly, as they can claw a hunter in a last-ditch escape attempt. This should be done with due care to the hide and hair of the animal, however.

A hunter should be able to locate his kill. Many times the rapport and recoil of the rifle obscure what happened at the moment the animal was hit. However, a wise hunter will have mentally marked where the animal went down in relation to some obvious feature of the landscape. Called animals will usually be close enough that relocation will not be a problem. Animals taken at 100 yards or so will be easy to find. Marking the spot where the animal was last seen is required when shots are taken at longer ranges.

It is vitally important to be mindful that you are hunting hides. This means the condition and qual-ity of the hide must be preserved, and it is particularly true when the hides will be marketed or sold to buyers. Poor handling at this point can result in reduced profits later on.

In preparing the hides for market, the hide man must take his hides through a number of processes to ensure high quality and marketability: skinning, fleshing, washing, stretching, and drying or curing. But before we begin explaining these stages, the hunter should get the proper tools together and be aware of some of the dangers involved in handling the hides.

Knives and Sharpening Tools

Knives play an important role in many outdoor activities. Hide hunting is certainly no different, and in some respects demands a knife of much higher quality than is necessary in those other pursuits.

Knives are available in many grades and shapes. Indeed, if you want to get the campfire debating society going some evening, just extol the virtues of your favorite blade and someone will surely take the opposing view. Use, design, and personal taste all combine to give the modern-day knife its form and character.

Like many other hunters, I have indiscriminately

175

used my knives for such jobs as rooting baked potatoes from the hot ashes of the campfire, shaping tent pegs from uncooperative plains poplar, and striking the blade with axe or stone to help cut through green boughs for a fall bivouac. I have then expected the same knife to see me through skinning coyotes and fox that very evening. For me, the knife must be a rugged and highly serviceable tool.

However, when possible, the hide hunter's knife should be a well-looked-after implement, useful in the task of skinning, and perhaps fleshing. In particular, it should be kept well sharpened. Being a knife user, rather than a knife maker, I asked Glen Gentels, a well-known Regina area knife maker, just what was needed in a knife designed specifically to meet the hide man's needs. Together we enlisted the aid of professional skinner and hide dresser, Steve Repka, also from the Regina area. From this joint effort, we set out some specifications for a hide hunter's knife. Glen would then

Knives are available in a variety of grades and shapes. Regardless of the style you use, knives are important to the hide man, since all steps in hide preparation demand a good-quality, sharp knife.

The traditional skinning knife with a preferred design to the blade and handle. It serves as a more general tool that will take care of camp chores as well as skinning and fleshing.

provide a working version.

We agreed that most hide men could do all their work with one knife that had a six-inch blade, although a four- or five-inch length was also satisfactory. There was no need for a finger guard, and the handle could be any material from ash to hickory. However, the handle should be about four and one-half inches long. Any longer would make the knife unwieldly, and any shorter would make it difficult to grip. The handle should be square and in strict line with the blade. This, it was felt, would provide firm control of the knife and let the user know at all times where the cutting edge was working. There would also be less tendency for the knife to turn as fat, hair and other material worked onto the hands.

The question of the amount of curve needed in a practical knife blade was given considerable thought. A wide curve would be acceptable on a knife used purely for skinning because this shape is known to be very efficient. With such a knife, it is possible to skin a hide clean; in other words, very little follow-up fleshing would be required. However, a straight blade with only a little down turn was chosen because a slightly more general-purpose knife was being selected. This knife would do other jobs as well as skinning.

It is important that the blade hold an adequate edge. Any knife used solely for skinning and absolutely nothing else can be resharpened anytime during skinning. However, in the field, a knife that retains its edge longer is far more desirable.

Today, stainless steel is preferred for blades. Many readers will know that steel hardness is compared on the Rockwell scale of hardness. Hard tempered steels, such as 56 to 59 C on this scale, will hold an edge for a long time, but it may be difficult to replace this edge. On the other hand, Rockwell values down around 50 C will readily resharpen but will need frequent touch-up jobs to stay keen and useful. A knife used for hide hunting, where skinning would be a major task and other more general chores done infrequently, could have a milder blade and still perform satisfactorily.

Knife blades can be either hollow ground or flat ground. In outdoor circles, much noise is made favoring the hollow-ground types. It is true that these blades can be sharpened to a higher degree and perhaps will cut finer. However, hollow-ground knives are difficult to sharpen and appear to be more delicate. Generally, flat-ground blades are stronger than their hollow counterparts and have the added advantage of being easy to sharpen with anything from a file to the finest of steels. These are clear advantages to the hide hunter who is short on time.

Many hunters are now carrying folding knives, using them for all purposes, including skinning. However, it was our collective experience that in continuous use these knives simply became too dirty. Various unwanted materials filled the inside of the handle and internal rusting, resulting from repeated washings, became a problem in all but the most expensive models. For these reasons, a solid-blade knife in the traditional one-piece or full-tang style was considered best.

About the only concession made in design could be a thumb rest on the back of the blade. In some models, machine cuts along the back of the blade would be useful for gripping during fleshing, but are certainly not a necessity. Such cuts on most knives are made to lighten the blade, rather than serve any functional purpose.

In short, a plain knife of simple design was considered most practical for continued hide hunting. Many new to this hunting will not at first realize that skinning and fleshing will wear away a knife blade over the course of a year's work. How fast a blade wears out will be determined by the amount of use and the frequency of sharpening. A hunter who processes a couple of hundred hides will see considerable wear to his knife. It is not unreasonable to go through one or two knives per year.

The sheath is equally important for safe transportation and storage of the knife. One that rides high on the belt has real advantages when driving or sitting and calling. A heavy leather sheath is best and stitching is preferred to rivets.

In summary, then, the perfect hide hunter's knife probably does not exist. However, a short-bladed knife that has an excellent point and a good handle that is squarely mounted would be about the best. The blade could err to the soft side of modern-day steels to allow for quick resharpening. With the sharp point a slight down turn to the blade would make a knife that was an excellent skinner, yet leave enough design room to be used in a myriad of other tasks from fleshing, when necessary, to doing camp chores.

Aside from the hunter's knife, a surgeon's scalpel is handy for skinning around the eyes and ears of

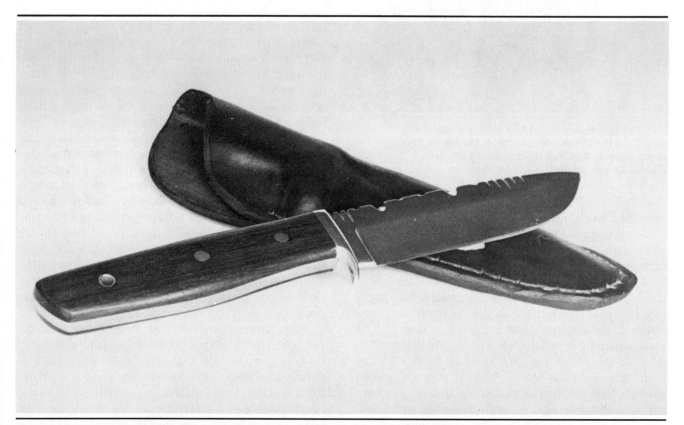

The machine cuts along the back of the blade make this knife a very useful hide hunter's design. While decoration on most other knives, these cuts help the hand grip the back of the blade when the knife is used for fleshing.

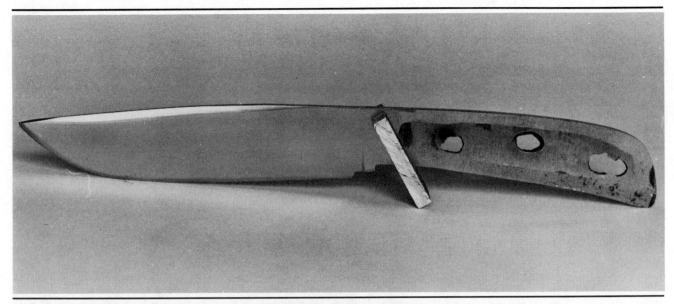

After consulting with a knife maker and a professional skinner, the blade shown here—the drop point—was chosen as the most useful design for the practicing hide man.

a long-hair. Wild animals have very strong bones, and the effect of skinning next to these is akin to dragging a knife over rough stone. Scalpel blades are very expendable and cheap to acquire. A trip to your local veterinarian will equip most hunters with a year's supply at little cost. The handle that accompanies this can also be purchased there. Aside from this, the package is compact to carry and quite effective for field use.

Sharpening and Care of Tools

A sharp edge is necessary for hide work. A dull one requires greater force to use during cutting, and this can lead to accidents of misjudgment, or simply destroy or greatly devalue a hide.

Until fairly recently, the tools used for sharpening remained virtually unchanged for centuries. A file, a butcher's steel, and a whetstone were all that were used. Now space-age ceramics, the same kind used on the tiles of space shuttles, are common sharpening tools, even in butcher shops and meat packing houses.

Nearly every little town and all the cities have people who specialize in knife sharpening. This is most often extended to saw blades, machine tools, and household knives. While it is easy and inexpensive to use these services, the hide hunter would be wise to learn how to sharpen his own implements and use only commercial services for an incredibly dull knife or one that has become damaged. Aside from the expense, there is the need to have your knives sharpened "now" and not to have to wait for a sharpening service to schedule your needs. In addition, it is not inconvenient to carry sharpening tools with you in the field.

A file is the simplest tool for resharpening any knife. It is best to use an extremely fine type. Nearly every hardware store has good files at cheap prices that will work well for most sharpening. However, using the file is a bit tricky. If a knife is so dull that filing is required, some practice with the tool is needed before attacking the knife blade.

For most, sharpening with a whetstone is best. There are die-hard traditionalists who insist the only way to sharpen a knife correctly is with a natural Arkansas or Washita stone. Carborundum, a man-made stone, will, however, work just as well.

Four standard grades of whetstone are currently available. Hide hunters can largely ignore most of these and pick the Washita or soft Arkansas stone.

A good-quality leather sheath that rides high on the belt is best for carrying a knife safely.

Sharpening is done by running the blade along the stone. Lift up the back of the knife to make an angle of about 20 degrees to the surface of the stone.

This has a grit level of 800. Many stones come with a coarse grit level on one side and a lighter, or finer, grade on the opposite. This combination will cover most situations.

Some hide men, depending on the quality of the blade used, will stop and sharpen the knife two or three times in the course of an extended skinning session. Some consider sharpening a fine art or something akin to magic. It is neither, really, and with practice anyone can master the angles needed to keep the blade well honed.

To sharpen an all-purpose skinning knife, begin by placing a few drops of oil (any oil will do) on the surface of the stone. Place the blade along the stone and lift up the back of the blade to an angle of about 20 degrees. In most cases, this means the back of the knife will be about one-eighth of an inch up from the stone surface.

Just to keep the record straight on the sharpening of all cutting tools associated with hide hunting, the angles at which they must be held to the stone vary. An axe should be held around the 30 degree mark. A fleshing tool should be sharpened at about 40 degrees to the stone. A scalpel blade is sharpened at 17 degrees.

Using some pressure, push the knife down the stone from the heel to the tip of the blade. Be sure to use some force, as light strokes will not be as effective. Work as if you are cutting a shaving off the surface of the stone. Be sure to maintain the critical angle of 20 degrees while sharpening.

The number of strokes required will depend on

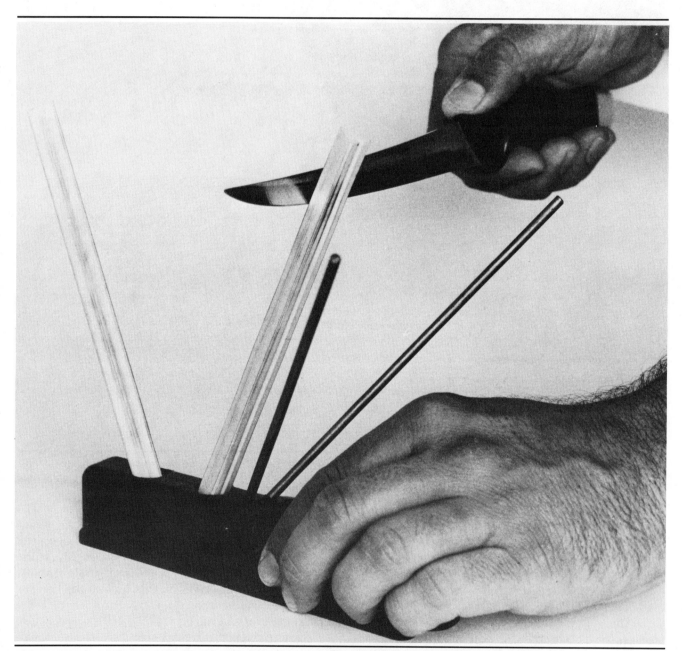

Ceramic sticks, now sold in many forms, are made of alumina and a bonding agent, the hardness of which equals the traditional Washita stones. They are very portable and offer the hide hunter a quick and easy alternative to other sharpening devices.

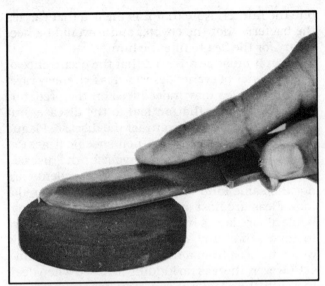

A pocket carborundum stone is excellent for touching up a blade in the field.

the dullness of the knife. Usually about a dozen strokes per side will hone up a knife enough to get the average-sized coyote hide off the carcass. Keep track of the strokes, turn the knife over and repeat the process with the same number of strokes.

Many times in the field it is necessary to touch up a knife blade in order to get through a skinning job. In this case a pocket carborundum is recommended, but any of the new ceramic rods will also work well. A few quick strokes while maintaining the crucial angle will have the knife in condition to complete your skinning job.

A word about the unique ceramic sticks that are now taking many forms and being sold to the outdoor public. These started out as kitchen sharpening tools, and it was soon found that they did as good a job on harder steel hunting knives as on the kitchen utensils. These are made from alumina, a man-made sapphire plus a bonding agent. The rods are lighter in weight than traditional oil stones and much cheaper to produce. Their hardness equals the older-type stones. Other advantages include ease of use and cleaning, which requires only water.

Bascially, the rods, sold under dozens of names, are held in a base at about 60 degrees. The knife blade is held to the rod at a 90-degree angle or, in other words, perpendicular to the base, and drawn down the rod from heel to point with a fair bit of pressure applied by hand. This is done for an equal number of strokes on both sides of the blade until the desired edge is achieved.

For the hide man, a set of these rods will work very well on knives that are already in good shape. Overly dull knives or those that have become damaged will still need the file and the hone treatment. Think of these new rods as an extension of the butcher's steel and use them in the same way. Thus, for most skinning jobs, they will perform best for touch-ups and offer the added advantage of being lightweight for field use.

One final point. Keep all working knives clean and free of fat and animal material. While animal oils and fats will not actually ruin a knife blade, they will clog the pores in all types of sharpening tools. Hair, as well, will gum up sharpening tools, especially files. Blood, because of its unique chemistry, will stain any knife blade unless quickly wiped away. Tools that are not kept clean will be difficult to hold and will discolor quickly. Keep knives, fleshing tools, and axes clean by wiping them with a cloth. Washing in cold water will remove blood, and a warm, soapy water bath will quickly and easily remove fats and oils. Immediately wipe the tools dry and store them where no harm will come to them or others, especially children. Keep them separate from other kinds of working tools, and they will always be ready and in usable shape when needed. The final step in preparing any hide is to wash and care for the tools that made your skinning job such a breeze.

Be Alert for Diseases

Long-haired predators are amazingly free of disease, no doubt the consequence of a long evolutionary process with the disease organisms. While a practicing hunter will rarely see a sick animal, it still can happen. The hunter should be alert to the diseases and follow precautions in handling animals that may be afflicted.

All predators can carry the fungal disease *coccidioidomycosis*. Sometimes called *San Joaquin Valley Fever*, it is anything but a fever. The disease is a fungal infection of the respiratory tract that produces fever-like symptoms. Man can catch this unpleasant disease by inhaling the spores left behind by the fungus. A hunter who finds an animal with any fungal growth around the mouth should leave the animal behind. If possible, the carcass should be burned.

Distemper is a familiar disease in domestic dogs but can occur in foxes and coyotes. It is a major canine affliction, but does not seem to be transferred to man. Among animals, it is a virus that is spread by direct contact. Fortunately, it is uncommon in free-living canids and no problem exists in handling the hides from infected animals. About the only thing a hunter will notice from an infected animal is a lack of luster to the hide, or it may appear shabby for the time of year.

Another well-known, chronic disease that, interestingly, dates to as far back as 500 B.C. is *rabies.* Most hunters already realize the dangers of this virus, which attacks the central nervous system of mammals. A bite from a rabid animal can transfer the disease to man, while sometimes only a scratch is required. Any animal, especially a fox, that behaves in a strange or overly aggressive manner is probably suffering from the disease in an advanced stage. Foxes that show no fear of the caller should be treated with suspicion and should be dispatched at once. In most areas, rabid animals must be turned in to local authorities either to confirm or to reject the presence of the disease. If a test is found positive, a program or alert is usually begun in the area to clear up the rabid animals.

A disease of immense importance to the practicing hide hunter is *wild rodent* or *sylvatic plague.* In man the disease is called *bubonic plague.* What really happens is that man is bitten by a particular flea and thus accidentally interferes with the rodent-to-flea-to-rodent life cycle of this horrific disease. The odds of a hunter becoming infected are very low and it would take an incredible series of events before man could pick up this disease from a predator. However, the coincidence would have to run something like this example. A coyote would have to have eaten a prairie dog or other rodent that harbored a flea carrying the dangerous bacteria. The flea would have to attach itself to the coyote. This could only happen while the coyote was actively taking the rodent. A hunter would then have to harvest that particular coyote and, in the process of handling the hide, the flea would have to

bite the hunter. Note that it is the flea that carries the bacteria, not the coyote, and it would be necessary for the flea to bite the hunter.

Again it must be stressed that the occurrence of the sequence of events described is extremely rare. An infected flea may indeed feed on the predator, thereby exposing that animal to the disease, but the predator does not contract the disease. Plague is more related to rats and their specific fleas. Rodents, it seems, act as a reservoir for the disease. As well, the kinds of fleas that live on rodents are not the same kind of fleas that live on the predators. Fleas are host specific, as the biologists say. While all predators harbor fleas, it is only in a rare instance that any of these itching arthropods would be fleas from a rat or other infected rodent.

However, there is no kidding involved when dealing with the plague. Everybody knows about the three major outbreaks of the disease. The first lasted for 50 years, occurring around the sixth century A.D. The second, the Black Death, swept over Europe during the 14th century, killing off an estimated 25 million people. The most recent epidemic began in the late 1800s, and ran its course just before World War II, devastating India and the Orient as it passed. Although there has never been an outbreak in North America, the odd case continues to surface each year, keeping public health officials on the alert.

It is against this background that the hide hunter should become familiar with the symptoms, if for no other reason than peace of mind and to dispel fear in others. The disease strikes suddenly, starting out much like a cold or the flu. The major lymph nodes called buboes (hence the name bubonic plague) swell, producing much pain. Chills and fever followed by thirst, headache, and a general dull feeling are the key reactions. Delirium may also ensue. Black spots, giving the name Black Death, formed from the swollen lymph nodes, appear in about three or so days.

Another disease, called *pneumonic plague,* can be associated with bubonic plague. This form is very life threatening, as it affects the lungs and air passages.

Fortunately, certain drugs can now combat the disease if it is caught within the first day of the appearance of the symptoms. There are also preventive medicines. Any hunter who feels he may have

Jerome Knap approaches a fox just taken. The wise hunter examines an animal for ticks or fleas before handling it.

contracted the disease through handling pelts or flea bites should consult his doctor at once. Explain the symptoms and mention that you have been working with hides that may have been flea infected. Streptomycin in usually given for the disease; it may be wise to mention this.

Tularemia is another plague-like disease that should be watched for. Commonly known as "rabbit fever," it is a bacterial infection that affects rabbits and rodents. It can be transmitted to man by handling pelts containing infected fleas, mites, and ticks, and also by handling diseased animals. The predators we are dealing with in this book

rarely contract the disease, although they can readily carry the different arthropod vectors that hold the bacteria in their mouth parts. For many years, tularemia was considered an occupational disease of trappers, hunters, game wardens, and fur buyers.

The disease begins with chills and fever followed by vomiting, nausea, and weakness. Usually a small sore develops where the bite was inflicted, which will ulcerate and provide some discomfort. In many cases, the lymph nodes will swell, especially in the neck region and the lower groin. A red rash may also appear. Untreated, the fever can run

DISEASE ALERT: SIGNS AND SYMPTOMS

Although long-haired predators are incredibly free of disease, the following checklist is important to keep in mind for anyone who handles hides. In general, it is difficult to detect disease-carrying insects because hair provides an excellent hiding place. The more obvious signs of infestation will be patchiness of the fur, lack of sheen or an emaciated-looking body. A wise hunter would always check for signs of disease or infection before handling animals and would wear gloves when handling them. Also, keeping a supply of good-quality flea powder at arms' length, and using it liberally, is beneficial.

Disease	Symptoms in Man	Signs in Animals
San Joaquin Fever (Coccidioidomycosis)	Fungal infection of the respiratory tract that produces fever-like symptoms.	Fungal growth around animal's mouth. Carcass should be discarded.
Distemper	This virus does not affect man.	Lusterless or shabby-appearing hide for time of year. Transmitted by direct contact among animals, few free-living canids contract this disease, which results in inflammation of nasal membranes, obvious fever, diarrhea, convulsions.
Rabies	Virus that affects central nervous system. Choking, convulsions, inability to swallow and eventual death could result if not treated.	Bizarre animal behavior, overly aggressive or overly docile, excessive salivation; of the predators, it is found more commonly among foxes, although all mammals are subject to infection.
Tularemia (Rabbit Fever)	Bacterial infection transmitted to man by handling pelts that contain fleas, mites, ticks or by handling infected animals. Symptoms: chills, fever, vomiting, nausea, weakness, swollen lymph nodes, red rash. Disease is not fatal, although affects may linger. Antibiotics are the treatment.	Long-haired predators rarely contract this, but they can be carriers of the arthropods that do the infecting. Rabbits are most commonly affected, with high fever, sluggish behavior (liver would appear spotted).
Wild Rodent Plague (Sylvatic or Bubonic Plague)	Bacterial infection carried by fleas produces swelling lymph nodes (buboes), followed by chills, fever, thirst, headache, possible delirium and death. If caught early enough, antibiotics are effective treatment.	Host-specific fleas that live on rodents transmit this rare disease. They must bite the animal directly to produce infection. High fever, pneumonia and inflamed lymph tissue are key reactions. Experiments prove that animals can be treated effectively if during the early stages. Stay away from wild rabbits and rodents that appear ill.
Pneumonic Plague	Similar to Bubonic Plague (above), but affects lungs and air passages.	

for months, leaving the victim listless and drained of energy.

Treatment of the disease in humans means the use of common antibiotics such as tetracycline, streptomycin, and chloramphenicol. While tularemia is not fatal, its lingering effects can be distressing to the hunter who would rather be outdoors in prime season.

The presence of these diseases, although uncommon, do indicate that the active hide hunter should take certain precautions when handling freshly taken animals and pelts. Hunters should wear gloves and sufficient clothing so that mites, ticks, and fleas will not have easy access to the body. Clothing used for hide preparation should be kept apart from other apparel and laundered with strong soap when necessary. A clean working environment will also help.

Since most prime hides are taken during the coldest part of the year, the low temperatures greatly reduce the arthropod vector activity of most of these diseases. Thus, it is unlikely that disease will be transferred during this part of the year. Some hunters will deliberately leave a predator with hide in place, waiting for the animal to cool down before skinning. In areas where disease has frequently occurred, this is a good idea. In the north, this usually happens automatically because of the ambient cold temperatures.

Use Gloves and Flea Powder

The use of gloves is highly recommended when skinning any predator. In the winter, soft cloth or cotton gloves are good for this purpose. Surgical gloves are also excellent and better to wear when working indoors or during warm weather. Rubber gloves of the type used for kitchen work are suitable, although they are hot to work in and may cause rashes in individuals who have sensitive skin. Industrial rubber gloves, in some lightweight models, are excellent for skinning and fleshing out a predator. All gloves give protection from minor cuts or abrasions and prevent bugs from biting the hands.

In warmer areas of the predators' range, the use of a good-quality flea powder is also a good idea. As soon as the animal is taken, dust the carcass with flea powder, giving it a few minutes to take effect on the resident insects. Then place the carcass in a plastic bag or burlap sack routinely used for this purpose. A burlap feed sack that has been heavily laced with flea powder is a great temporary place to store a freshly taken carcass. The sack also soaks up any blood or body material, thereby keeping the hide cleaner than if using a plastic bag. For those who really want to be cautious, the feed sack could be placed inside a large plastic bag. This would ensure that no arthropods would escape the flea powder treatment.

In most flea powders, the active chemical ingredient is usually one of the organophosphorous compounds. When choosing louse or flea powder, purchase the kind recommended for animals, rather than humans. In small quantities these are not dangerous to man. However, a hunter who is dusting predator carcasses should try not to breathe in any of the powder during the process. Spray compounds such as Raid or other house and garden bug killers will also work. A friend of mine always keeps some on hand in the skinning room. Should some bug be discovered during skinning, it is quickly killed with the spray. Sprays are more convenient to use than louse powders, but the powder lets the hunter see where it has been dusted. Gloves should be worn during this part of the job.

Remember that when handling any furred predator, there will be few signs indicating the presence of fleas and other bugs. The hair provides an excellent hiding place for these creatures and the skin gives the animal much protection. Only in severe infestations will there be obvious raw spots on the carcass or signs of secondary infections. Patchiness or lack of sheen of the hair are indications that something is wrong. An extremely emaciated animal would suggest a heavy lice or flea load. Observe the animal carefully for these signs and use the louse powder accordingly.

Chapter 14

Skinning and Fleshing Techniques

Since decomposition of the hide starts almost at once, it is wise to begin skinning at once. Digestive juices, body acids, and the various enzymes start to break down the gut and muscle tissue of the animal. In addition, animals taken with bullets will have entrance and perhaps exit holes that are sources of body fluids and blood spilled onto the exterior of the hide. This can add to the decomposition process.

Many hunters remove the hide even before the carcass has cooled. This has several advantages. One is that all the mess of skinning is left behind in the field. There is less weight to carry, no further trips to dispose of the carcass, and the hide can be more easily stored and transported to where it will be stretched and dried. Also, the animal is easier to strip while warm than if it is cooled, or even frozen, then thawed out. Some hunters choose a different route and will sell the animal, complete with carcass, the same day. This leaves no trace, especially of the smell of an un-field-dressed carcass.

In the north, where hide hunting is done during the winter, the carcass can freeze solid in a matter of a few hours. This, in turn, means that a warm place will be needed to allow the carcass to thaw, usually in a heated garage or barn. Sometimes, however, the only warm spot is inside a porch or in the house and the odor can be unpleasant, to say the least. Thawing will require several hours, usually overnight, before the hide can be removed easily.

Some hunters will store a carcass, complete with hide, leaving it until they have some time to work on the animal, perhaps in the evening or on a stormy day. One such day or a couple of evenings can account for several skinning jobs. It is up to the hunter and the time constraints under which he works. In the north, storing can be done simply by leaving the animals in an unheated outbuilding; in a warmer climate a deep freezer used solely for hide work serves nicely. Frozen animals thawed prior to skinning are more difficult to work on, but sometimes this has to be traded off against the time available that could be used for additional hunting.

The Cased Method of Skinning

This brings the hunter to the actual point of skinning the hide from the carcass. All long-hairs are skinned in what has come to be known as the "Cased Method." Essentially, the hide is removed by peeling down toward the head, with the fur side in and the fleshy side out. It is later reversed during the drying process to be presented fur side out. This lets the buyer view all the fur, his chief concern, since such things as rubbing and other damage cannot be seen from the leather side. Traditionally, the hides have been prepared cased so as to provide the processors with a full back and full belly area to the hide. From this shape, long strips can be cut from the entire hide, or the back can be used to make pieces for a coat.

1. With the carcass either lying on the ground or hung up, the first cut is made at the large joint of the hind leg. Cut completely around the leg as shown; complete the same kind of cut on each rear leg.

2. Now, while holding the hind leg with one hand, or if the animal is hung, then by holding down on the animal, make a cut that runs along the inside of the leg down to just behind the vent hole. On all the long-haired predators, there is a distinct demarcation between the underfur and the fur on the top or uppermost part of the animal. The line made by the union of these hair types should be used as the guideline along which the cut should be made. In doing this, the cut can run just behind the anus, next to the base of the tail and continue up along the opposite leg. Skilled

Animals that have been frozen must be allowed to thaw. Under most circumstances, it is best to skin an animal shortly after it has been taken.

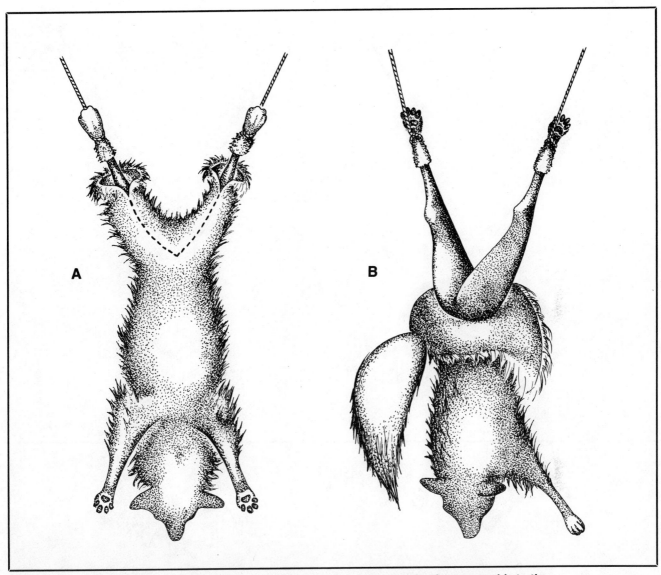

To skin any predator, (A) cut completely around each hind leg, between what is comparable to the ankle and knee; cut along the inside of each leg down to just below the vent. (B) Pull down on the hide, using the knife sparingly. At the vent, cut around the anus, then cut the tail bone beyond the vent. Leave the bone in place until the skinning is completed.

skinners can make this cut in one swoop. The cut should also be made from under the skin, pointing the blade upward, rather than cutting through the hair side, which dulls the knife easily.

3. From here on, it is most efficient to have the carcass hung at a comfortable working height. Unlike big game, it is not necessary to hang with sturdy poles through the gambrel joints or to use a reinforced pulley. The long-hairs to be skinned here are relatively light in weight, so hanging with rope, baler twine, sash cord or even soft wire will be just fine. Tie both legs between the first two joints (what is comparable to the ankle and knee) and suspend the animal from a garage rafter, tree, corral fence or whatever. The important point is that your eye level should be at about the middle of the

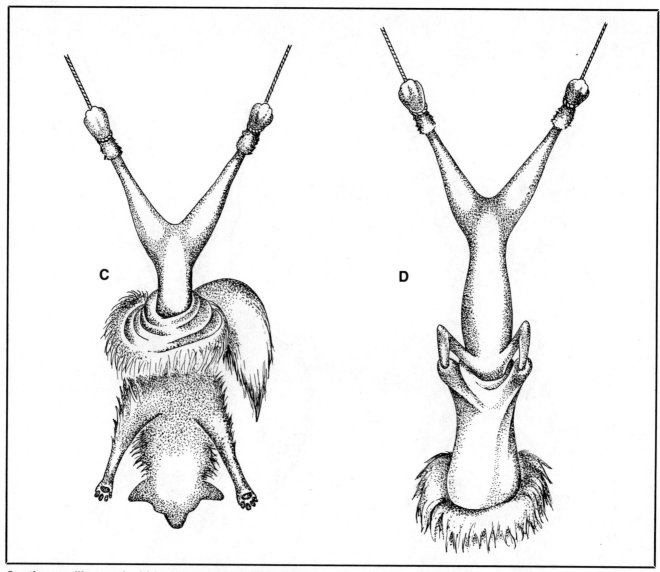

Continue pulling on the hide down over the torso (C) and to the shoulder area; (D) cut the fore legs free as you did with the hind legs and work the hide down over the shoulders, bringing each leg up through the hide. This is usually a tight section, so patience and care are required.

carcass. This gives enough room below so that the hide does not touch the ground or floor during the skinning operation. It will also let the hunter use his own body weight to pull down on the hide. A lot of muscle is required at certain points in the skinning, and it is important to use leverage whenever possible.

Begin skinning the legs. Work the knife deftly and carefully along the skin, and pull as much as possible on the hide with your hands, using the knife only when the hide has to be freed from the carcass. When the hide is removed down to the vent, cut around the anus. This will leave the tail still in place.

4. The tail must now be worked on. Very good skinners working with fresh materials in prime condition can pull the bone right out of the tail. This is done by using two small blocks of wood that

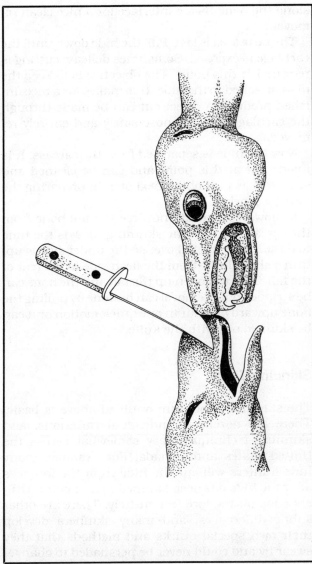

Very gingerly pull on the hide, cutting through the cartilage at the base of each ear, through the translucent membrane around each eye and the cartilage of the nose. You should now have a completely cased hide.

have been carved to allow a place for the tail bone to pass. The wood blocks are held together surrounding the tail, and with some effort, are pulled downward, using the body weight to help in the pulling. For most hunters, this is a difficult trick to master and it is better to cut the tail bone out of the fur with a knife.

The tail bone must be removed by whichever means you prefer—but it must be removed. Many beginners feel that this step can be passed over. They simply cut off the tail bone just beyond the vent during skinning. Unfortunately, this will cause considerable spoiling along the tail. Hair will slip and any buyer will severely downgrade the most perfect hide. Most will pay less for any hide whose tail bone is still in place.

In practice, it is best to cut out the tail along the underside. A cut should be made along the entire length of the tail. Unless the hunter has become particularly skilled at removing the tail bone, leave the bone in place until all the other skinning is completed. Simply sever the tail bone from the carcass and leave it in the tail. Be sure not to cut the hide during this step.

5. Once the tail bone is free of the body, the hide can usually be pulled down to at least the shoulder area of the animal. The hide will be coming off the animal much like an inside-out sock at this point. All the fur will be to the inside, with the flesh on the outside.

6. At this point, cut the fore legs free of the hide in the same manner used for the hind legs. Make this cut about six or so inches up from the foot. Cut completely around the leg, but be careful not to cut unnecessarily into the muscle tissue of the leg. A cut made too deeply will allow some of the meat tissue to cling to the hide, making it more difficult to clean later.

7. In any case, the front shoulder area will be the most difficult portion of the animal to skin. The best advice is to proceed slowly, use your knife sparingly, but, when necessary, make small cuts that will free the hide from the carcass but not nick the hide. With an animal hung up at about eye level, it is possible to pull the hide with considerable force. On some animals, if they're hung properly, a hunter can almost lift himself off the floor when pulling the hide.

Now work the hide down over the front shoulders and pull the front legs through the hide. Sometimes this will be hard work. The hunter will have to use his fingers to grip the hide and slowly work it forward. Once the skinning is to the point that a finger can be slipped under the front leg, a quick, powerful pull will usually bring the front leg up through the hide. Never cut the inside of the front legs to free the hide. This is considered amateurish by the fur buyer and it can be used as an excuse to downgrade a hide.

8. The head is the final part. Pull the hide further until the bases of the ears are exposed. Cut through the cartilage at the base of the ear where it originates from the skull. Press the knife tight to the skull to prevent cutting through this delicate portion of the hide.

An additional pull should place the hide down to the eyes. This is a very important area for a nice-looking hide. Surrounding the eyes is a translucent membrane which must be cut through. The key is to remove this lymph tissue intact, and to do so you must cut tight to the skull for best results.

All that's left now are the lips and nose areas. The lips should be cut free and clear of the skull. Carefully pull the hide away from the mouth area and cut close to the skull. Never cut the fur portion. Always keep the cutting as close to the jaw as possible. Once the lips have been freed at one end, it is possible to pull on this part and work the knife along the bone-tissue interface for a nice clean removal.

The nose area is last. Pull the hide down until the cartilage is exposed. Sometimes delicate cutting is required at this point. The objective is to keep the nose attached to the hide; this makes for a nice finished product. A direct cut can be made through the cartilage and the nose safely and entirely removed.

Now the hide is separated from the carcass. It is inside out at this point and can be cleaned and stretched as part of the next step in preparing the hide for market.

If, however, you did not free the tail bone from the carcass early in the skinning, now is the time to do so. Turn the tail over so the under side is up. Run a sharp knife from the flesh side to the rear of the tail. This will open up the tail and the bone can be stripped out. Removal can be done by pulling the bone upward and out in one quick motion or it can be skinned out with the knife.

Skinning Tips

The skinning procedure outlined above is basic. There are dozens of individual variations, and skinning techniques vary somewhat across the United States and Canada. For example, many hide hunters will cut the hide from the fore legs after the hide has been skinned to that point. Others chop off the fore feet entirely. There are other subtle differences, and many skinners develop their own special quirks and methods that they swear by and could never be persuaded to change. Some hunters use machines to assist in skinning. The point is that the hide must be taken from the carcass and any trick that helps to accomplish this has to be appreciated. What may be convenient or faster for one hunter may not be so for another.

In short, while some of the fine points may differ, the important thing is to get the hide off the animal in as good a condition and as quickly as possible. Skinning is necessary to hide hunting and a hunter should feel free to experiment and try different methods.

It is imperative to use the knife sparingly during all steps in the skinning process. If the hide can be pulled toward the head without the need of making

Once the skinning is finished, take a sharp knife and cut on the flesh side along the tail bone to remove it from the hide. This can be done at any point; the important thing is that it must be done.

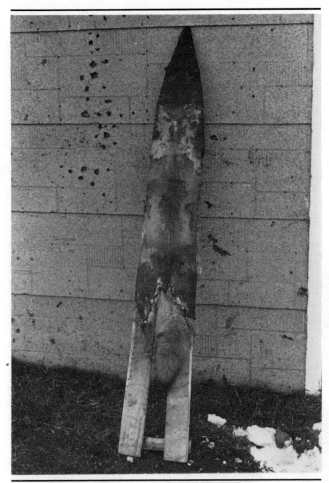

A cased hide prior to fleshing. Note the areas of fat distribution on the skin. The tail end usually has much of the animal's stored fat; this hide is quite heavy to the front as well.

cuts in the tissue holding the hide to the body, the knife blade will stay sharp longer. Pulling the hide requires some strength. On large animals, the effort can sometimes be considerable and the beginner can end up feeling frustrated with the progress. However, using this technique produces a cut-free hide that will flesh out easily and sell for a better price. Knife cuts are downgraded greatly by the buyer or trader.

When working the legs of any hide, use your fingers to work in around the leg. Strong and long fingers help in this step. However, even a beginner can do this job and, amazingly, strength will build in the fingers as the fur season progresses. Using the fingers also means there is less opportunity to nick the hide. At first work slowly, putting your body weight or leaning into the skinning. Once the finger has been worked around the fore leg, placing the second hand along the wrist of the working hand will help strengthen the working arm and put additional pressure on the hide.

Working around the nose and skull areas will quickly dull even the best skinning knife. Use the knife with this in mind and always use no more knife pressure than is needed to do the job. Never grate your knife along the cartilage portions unnecessarily. Some skinners will clean the knife blade by rubbing it across the skull. This is a superfluous gesture and, while it does clean the blade of tissue and fat, it will also speed the dulling process.

Again, individual style has to be stressed in the skinning process. While the overall technique is straightforward, there is a lot of room for developing techniques that the individual finds work best for him. Some skinners can make one cut across the hind legs and with one mighty pull have the skinning job nearly done; others, lacking the same type of strength, need to free the hide with more knife work. The heights at which different hunters will hang a hide also varies. So, while a few hard and fast rules apply, there is plenty of opportunity to develop working styles that are unique and efficient for the individual hunter. Always keep an eye open to where you may adapt your own methods; it will help immeasurably.

Finally, how long should it take to skin out the typical long-hair? Given an average-sized animal, a really good skinner working with fresh, clean carcasses and set up to handle the job could probably skin out a coyote in 10 minutes. A competent amateur with practice should be able to do the same job in 20 minutes. Anybody requiring a half hour to skin an animal should not complain; speed is achieved only through repetition. Hunters who shoot only a few animals per year will never develop the speed of the hide man who routinely skins out 300 animals in a season. For those who are just starting out, don't worry about the time as a factor in skinning. Take all the time you need because it is the quality of the job that determines how much money a hide will be worth.

Fleshing Techniques

A major task in properly preparing a hide for market is fleshing. This is the removal of all fat and tissue that clings to the skin side of the hide. The amount of fat found just under the skin of any long-haired fur bearer changes with the seasons and varies with latitude. Animals taken in the extreme southern parts of the range will often lack great quantities of fat, while those from areas farther north will carry considerably more. As mentioned, all fur bearers store fat as part of their survival mechanism to live through food-short winters and as an insulating factor against the cold. In some years, depending on food supplies, animals will be able to store greater amounts of back fat, while in others, less will be stored. All fur bearers attempt to build fat stores, and nature has modified their metabolism to provide for this at the appropriate time of year. There is also considerable variability in amounts stored by the same species of animal within the same area. Old animals tend to accumulate less, while prime breeding adults build up more. Fat, while frowned upon in modern-

The fleshing beam is an important piece of hide preparation equipment, and has been in use for centuries.

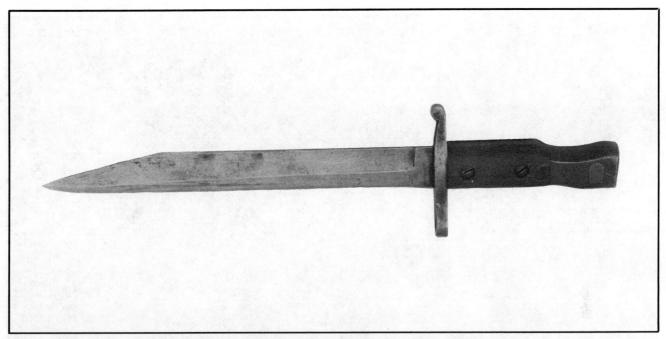

The bayonet—a favorite fleshing tool in the western part of the predator range. This one is an unsharpened World War I Ross rifle bayonet. Although valued as an antique by military collectors, it is a very practical fleshing tool.

day human life, is essential in the animal world.

Right off the top, all fat and flesh must be removed from any long-haired hide. Failure to do this interferes with drying and causes what the hide buyers call "grease burn." Grease burn is simply a rotting process that results in a breakdown of the root hairs. Hair will slip where fat and tissue are not adequately removed.

Hides cannot be stored for long periods of time unless they have been properly fleshed and cleaned. The fat continues to decompose and the breakdown in tissue eventually reaches the fur. The problem escalates when a few improperly prepared hides continue to perpetuate bacterial growth that affects correctly done hides stored in the same package or next to one another.

A hide must be fleshed when it is still "fresh." At this time little enzymatic breakdown of the tissue has occurred and the hide is still tough and resilient. Hides that are not fleshed directly rot very quickly and hair slipping is assured. Also, the greater the time that elapses, the more liquid the fat and adjoining tissue becomes and the more difficult it is to remove both tissues properly. Best results are had when fleshing is done within minutes of skinning. Old hide men call this "green fleshing," meaning when the hide is "green" or fresh.

Most long-haired species flesh out easily. With practice and the right tools a coyote can be done in 20 minutes. Fox, which accumulate more fat than coyote, may take longer. Bobcats usually have little fat, while a lynx may have its entire back saddled with pearly white fats. The hind end of all species is the area that carries most fat.

As in the many other aspects of hide hunting, having the right equipment and knowing how to use it is crucial to success. Fleshing demands two important tools: the first is a fleshing beam; the second, a fleshing tool.

Fleshing Beams. Fleshing beams have been used by hide handlers since the beginning of time. They serve to provide a place over which the hide is draped, enabling the hunter to remove the layer of fatty tissue easily. The beam is really a specialized workbench consisting of a six or so foot long two-by-four or two-by-six which extends upward from

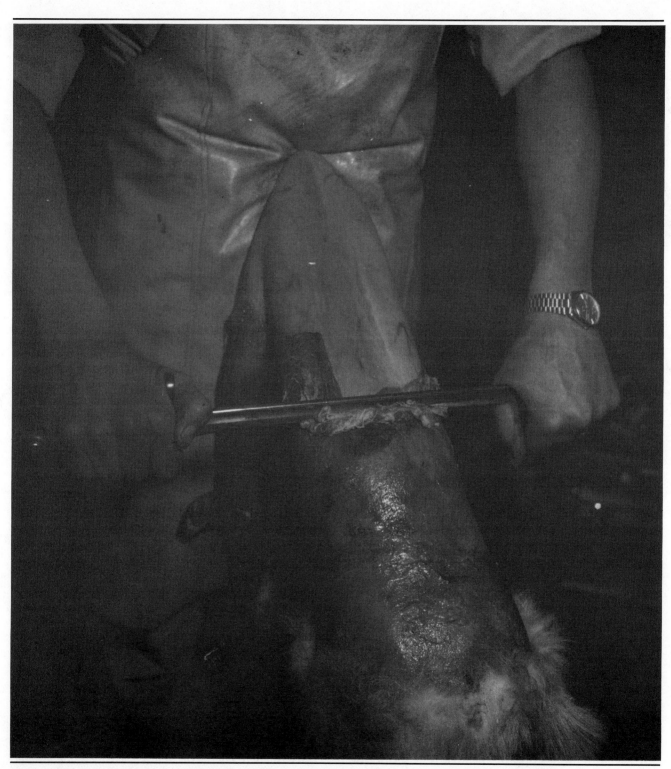

Here the fleshing process is demonstrated using the beam. The hide is fleshed from the head end to the tail. Note the fleshed area compared to the green or unfleshed portion.

the floor at about a 45 degree angle. It is supported at approximately two-thirds of its distance from the floor by a set of legs that are about three feet long. The head end of the beam is rounded to accept the head area of the hide. The working portion should be about waist high.

Since all long-hairs are skinned by the cased method, the cased hide is placed through the beam with the head end held at the top of the beam. Thus, the fur side of the pelt touches the beam, leaving the fat-laden skin side facing upward, with only one layer of skin touching the beam. The opposite layer hangs safely below.

Fleshing is begun by stretching the hide tautly over the beam. Some hide men use clips to hold the hide in place, but no matter what is used, the top surface of the hide should fit snugly to the beam. On the fleshing beam shown here the skinner uses his body to hold the hide in place.

The hide is always fleshed from the head end to the tail. This is because there is typically more fat at the back end of the animal; the fat toward the front is usually thinner and peels off more easily. During fleshing, much blood is also removed from the skin side. This helps in the cleaning process and presents a better looking hide.

Fleshing Tools. There is tremendous variation in the choice of fleshing tools. The Short Rib Indians of the Northwest Territories got their name from the fact that they always used a "short rib" for fleshing. Old bayonets that have never been sharpened are preferred by most skinners, however. Some hunters use the back of a knife and others use two-handled homemade things that have their origins in car springs, buggy seat springs or saw blades. Of course, commercial fleshing tools are also available.

The objective in fleshing is to remove the fat and tissue layer—the ultimate goal being a hide that overall has a neat, slightly oily appearance. Sometimes it is necessary to cut small areas of skin and fat free from the bottom of the hide.

It is crucial not to overscrape. This will cause the hair to fall out and downgrade a hide greatly. For the beginner, it is hard to tell when the hide is being overscraped. However, considerable pressure must be applied to the skinning tool in order to cut deeply. The trick is to use only enough pressure to remove the fat from the hide, and in order

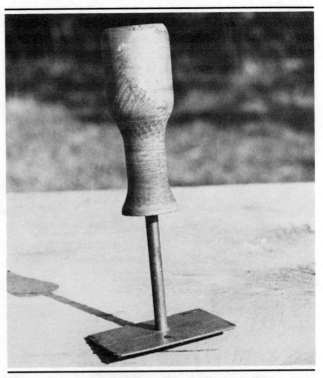

The commercial fleshing tool is of simple design, with good hand-holding qualities.

to do this, the fleshing tool must be dull. Unsharpened bayonets are best, as they have a peculiarly rounded cutting edge. Bayonets were, of course, never to be sharpened when used for combat, and the original factory edge is very useful for fleshing.

The inside of the tail and legs are the most difficult to flesh out well. A beginner should proceed slowly and try to lay the portion he is working squarely on the beam.

In the process of fleshing, fat sometimes finds its way onto the fur side of the hide. This can easily be removed with a damp, warm cloth. It is far better, however, to do a careful job and avoid the cleanup all together. Use the scraping tool diligently and wipe excess fat from the blade with newspaper or other material. Keep the fat clear of the hide. Stubborn spots do occasionally resist the pass of the fleshing tool. These have to be treated carefully and worked with the tool or a knife until removed.

Sometimes fat stains that are the result of poor handling or poor techniques will be found on

The simpler fleshing tools in action. Try to sit in a comfortable position in plenty of light.

hides. These should be removed using a cloth dampened with unleaded camp fuel. Dry cleaning fluid will work also. Either of these tricks can save a misbegotten hide from the junk pile, but be sure to use cleaning fluids with extreme care. Any pelt left smelling from gasoline or cleaning fluid will draw a suspicious call from the hide buyer. In fact, the best advice is to rewash the hide several times to remove any hint of cleaning fluid. One final tip is never to use coal oil, kerosene, diesel fuel or home heating fuel for these kinds of cleaning jobs. The odor will never come out.

Many thousands of hides are fleshed every year that have not been done on a fleshing beam. The hunter simply places the hide skin side out on a stretcher and begins fleshing. Most often a small knife is used and the hunter sits with the hide over his knee to do the work. Others flesh the hide over their arm or lay it on a bench with the head end fastened to a nail. Still others attach the hide to a building and cut away at the fat, while yet others never bother to do any of this and simply pick off the larger pieces of fat with a sharp knife. No doubt this will continue for eons to come. But the point is that the fleshing beam does a much better job, more quickly and cleanly than any other method. It helps in the job of presenting the perfect hide.

Chapter 15

Washing, Stretching And Drying Pelts

Once a pelt has been skinned and fleshed, it has progressed through two major steps in the hide preparation process. From here on, each process is designed to show off the fur's character and improve what nature has created. With continued care and attention to detail throughout the remaining steps, the outcome should be a hide that is picture perfect—the embodiment of what the hide buyer wants, his raison d'être for being in business.

Washing, stretching and drying, or curing, the pelts are the final phases of hide preparation. Through these stages, the hide handler should always be mindful of how he wants the finished product to look. General appearance is one of the chief factors the hide buyer takes into account when he evaluates the furs. Other considerations over which you have some control are damage to the skin or to the fur and the straightness of the top hair. These are critical factors in grading furs and, along with all the other elements, are discussed at length in the following chapter.

Washing the Fur

All long-hairs, by the nature of their life-styles, have dirty fur. Soil, twigs and in some areas burrs,

pine balls and other material become stuck to the fur and hide. In addition, animals taken by rifle will usually show some blood clotted onto the hide or other material that has become intermingled with the hair. The washing process cleans the hide thoroughly, making it appear brighter and more sparkling.

Use Cold Water. Washing in cold water, specifically, will remove most of the foreign matter. Cold water is well known for its effectiveness in removing fresh blood stains, and it is best for use in washing bullet-taken hides; usually all of the stain will flush out. It will also remove any dirt or mud that has adhered to the hide.

Wash By Hand. Hides are best washed by hand. Many professional hide men still use the old-fashioned scrub board. They gently rub the hide and water together along the board until the water runs clean from the hide. It works amazingly well and actually improves the hide by removing or washing out loose hairs and breaking down matted parts of the fur. Interestingly, hides that are washed will show much more of the actual color variation naturally present in the pelt.

Long-haired hides that have blood or other organic material clinging to their hair are greatly downgraded. In the washing step, be sure to break down any clots of blood with the fingers and sepa-

203

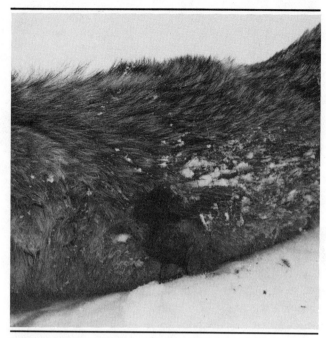

Large-caliber or high-powered, medium-caliber rifles can leave large exit holes in a hide. The hide must be washed free of any blood and other debris, then the hole must be sewn. Otherwise, this is a good, thick hide.

light-colored coyote pelts will stain permanently within hours. Furs with greater amounts of white hairs will turn yellow and this is downgraded. Speed and the knowledge of what to do to keep the hide looking natural are important here.

Resins or pine pitch in the hair of lynx and bobcat can also be a special cleaning problem. Such balls mat the top hair and the underfur. Sometimes evidence can be seen where the animal has gnawed at the bothersome knot, and the fur will be permanently damaged. The pitch-stained areas should be softened with cleaning fluid or white gas. This should be followed by working the hairs free of one another by hand. Wash thoroughly and then comb the hairs to restore the pattern and flow.

Partial Drying. Drying the hide—actually partial or pre-drying would describe it better—is an equally important step. The soaking-wet hide should be gently wrung out and rinsed at least twice prior to the final drying. The hide is usually

rate the individual hairs. Rinse such spots several times. The same applies to mud. Most long-hairs can pick up incredible amounts of mud and dirt in their fur. This occurs most often toward the end of the season when fur quality is generally on the decline. Sometimes the animals appear to be rolling in the mud to comfort themselves from bothersome arthropods or an ill-fitting hide. These furs should be washed well and the mud worked out by hand. Many times hair will come off with the mud, but this is no problem and is more the result of the time of the season than any other factor. The key is to work such spots with the fingers. Separate the hairs and elmininate any matting of the underfur. If this procedure is not done at the time of washing, the matting will remain with the fur and look awkward, interrupting the fur flow.

It is important to clean any kind of stain as quickly as possible. White furs, like the arctic fox, clear-colored furs like the southern bobcat, and

The author prepares a freshly washed hide for drying in a tumble dryer. This greatly speeds the drying process and improves hide appearance.

hung to drip-dry for a few minutes and then placed on the stretcher. However, a more efficient means of drying is to use a clothes dryer to bring the hide to a "just damp" stage. This is easily done by regulating the heat and timing cycle of any contemporary dryer.

Many old-time hide men may balk at the thought of placing a good hide in a tumble dryer, to be bounced and tossed around for 20 or so minutes. However, the truth is that all hides are passed through many spin dryer operations on their way to final processing. Generally, the hides can take this tumbling with no damage or decrease in value. However, in order to prevent the hides from becoming twisted with each other in the drying cycle, it is best to place each hide in a separate sack. Old pillow cases or cloth feed bags, tied tightly, work very well for this job. The average-sized household dryer can hold four to six coyote hides in this way with no damage to the dryer or the hides. Use the low heat setting and set the timer around the 20-minute mark for best results.

By the way, be sure to have your wife's permission to use the family clothes dryer for this kind of stunt. If enough hides are put through the dryer, a typical hide odor will soon pervade the machine. This can rub off on other clothes, and smelling like a coyote dressed in your Sunday best may not be your wife's idea of a joke. Believe me, I know. If possible, use a separate machine for this job. Also, in the city or an apartment, venting may be a problem.

Once a hide has been nearly dried, it is then ready for the next step in preparation: stretching. You will find that a hide washed and dried as described here will have less fat remaining than a hide handled differently. As well, any hair that may have later fallen free of the hide will be removed and this has the added benefit of not coming loose just as the hide buyer runs his hand over the hair and casts a disparaging look.

In instances where a hide can only be washed and not spin-dried, hanging until drip-dried will be sufficient. It is important to let the air circulate around the hide to promote drying in a general environment where the hide can dry properly. In damp climates or at rainy times of the year, this can be a problem. Also in cold climates, hides will not dry as well as desired. In really cold temperatures, the water may freeze and this slows the drying. A hide that freezes solid can break when bent and the hair is easily broken. So keep these points in mind when you're debating about the clothes dryer.

Samples of Summerberry or Northwestern-type long-hair hide stretchers. These are essential for any hide operation.

Stretching the Hides

Stretching is an absolute must before a hide can be marketed. Unstretched hides are limp and poorly sized. When dry, they shrivel and twist, resulting in a poor product.

Furs are stretched for two reasons. First, it prevents wrinkling and binding of the hide; and second, it allows the fullness and denseness of the hair to be correctly displayed. Stretching also gives a hide its shape. In short, it enhances the appearance.

Stretching is a very important part in the overall drying of a skin or pelt. Essentially, drying preserves the skin for further processing. It is a natural chemical reaction that is brought into place by the steps of fleshing, washing and stretching. Stretching is a vital step in the overall process because it provides the means by which the hide will

dry. Considerable attention to detail during this stage is a must. A beginner should think out just what the final hide should look like and try to make his product approach the accepted norm for his area.

Crucial to the proper stretching and drying of long-haired hides is a proper fitting stretcher. The wrong shape will quickly negate the best cleaning efforts; hides will wrinkle, shrink and dry unevenly on such stretchers. The result, of course, will be greatly discounted hides and lower hunt profits. Overstretching is equally as bad. This pulls the skin apart and greatly weakens the fur. Hide buyers are quick to spot this sort of thing, due to the thinness of the long hairs at the shoulders. Another indication is the paper-like feel to the skin. These conditions can be overcome by using correct stretchers.

Types of Stretchers. Basically two types of

PATTERN FOR PELT STRETCHING BOARDS

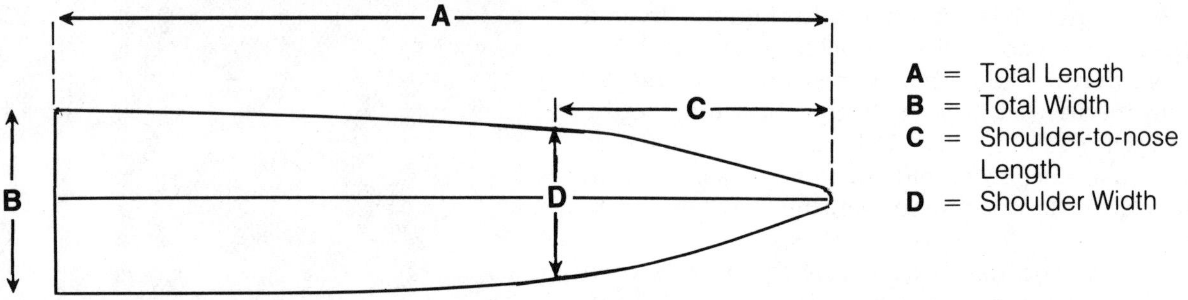

A = Total Length
B = Total Width
C = Shoulder-to-nose Length
D = Shoulder Width

	A	B	C	D
Coyote (Large)	80	16	16	10
Coyote (Medium)	80	13	15	9
Lynx (Large)	60	8	12	6
Lynx & Bobcat (Small)	48	7	10	5
Bobcat	50	8	11	5
Red Fox	45	8	11	5
Arctic Fox	45	7	11	5
Gray Fox	40	6	9	4

All measurements are in inches.

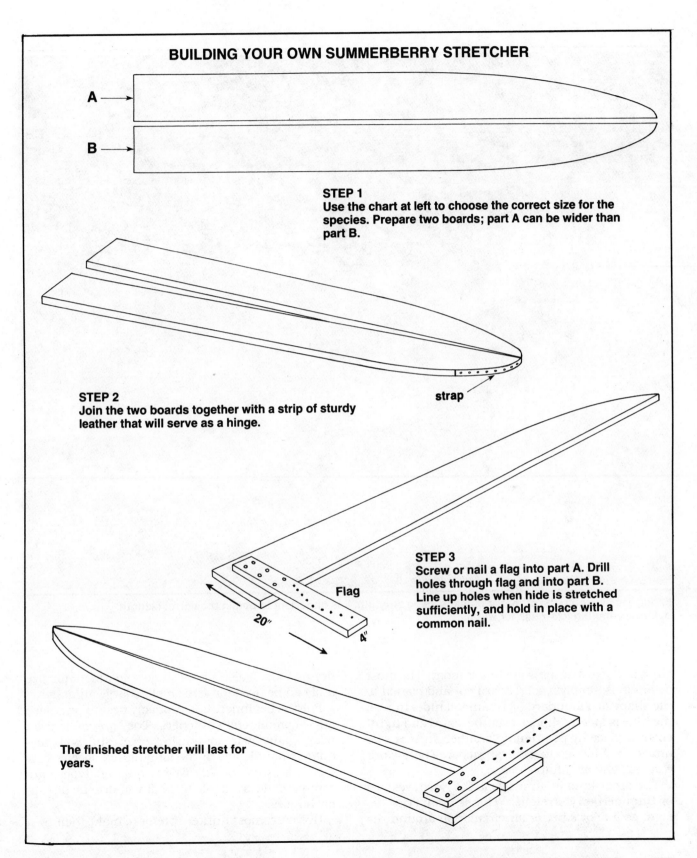

BUILDING YOUR OWN SUMMERBERRY STRETCHER

A →

B →

STEP 1
Use the chart at left to choose the correct size for the species. Prepare two boards; part A can be wider than part B.

strap

STEP 2
Join the two boards together with a strip of sturdy leather that will serve as a hinge.

STEP 3
Screw or nail a flag into part A. Drill holes through flag and into part B. Line up holes when hide is stretched sufficiently, and hold in place with a common nail.

Flag

20"

4"

The finished stretcher will last for years.

Fitting the hide onto the stretcher requires some strength. It is important to obtain the correct length before attempting to stretch for width.

stretcher board designs are in use today. The most common is simply a solid board cut and planed to the shape of a standard-sized animal hide. In use, the hide is merely slipped over the board and tightened in place by positioning another stick or two under the hide against the stretcher. These work very well and are simple to use.

The other kind of stretcher is the Northwestern or Summerberry stretcher. This is a superior design, as it allows better air circulation around the drying hide. It also allows some adjustment for size and can be used for very small to large animals.

For the beginner, it is probably best to purchase a few commercial stretchers. They are made from heavy-gauge wire or spring steel and will adequately handle any of the long-haired species covered in this book. Good quality types are commercially available from any of dozens of supply houses.

However, most hunters prefer to make their own

Professional hide men like Steve Repka use a large wedge to separate the jaws of the stretcher in stretching for width and to keep the jaws open while the hide is tacked to the board. This is done after any repairs are completed.

stretchers. This seems to be a deep tradition based on the early days of the fur trade when commercial stretchers were uncommon and difficult to have shipped to remote parts of the country.

For those who wish to make their own, measurements are given in the previous diagram and table. These sizes are for average long-hairs, but should an exceptional animal come your way, an inch or so in width may be added.

Constructing your own Summerberry stretcher requires a little effort, but is not difficult; besides, many of them will last for years. Begin by getting some hardwood (oak, spruce, poplar, etc.) "dimension" lumber of 1/2-inch or 3/4-inch thickness. Match the outline shown in the diagram, using the dimensions from the chart for the size animal you have. Pencil the outline on the wood and saw it out as you would for any other carpentry project. Cut up the center of the board to the nose end, leaving two oblong pieces, one of which could be wider than the other if you didn't cut precisely up the middle.

Join the two pieces of wood together at the nose with a strip of leather. This piece should be thicker than regular garment leather, but more like latigo strength, the type used on saddles. It should be 6 inches long and ½- to ¾-inch wide, depending on the thickness of the wood. Tack the leather strip with nails or screws to the nose ends of the wood strips in about 1-inch intervals. You now have a hinge that will keep the "jaws" together.

At the bottom of the stretcher, you will nail or screw into place a cross piece called a flag. The flag should be between 16 and 20 inches long by 4 to 6 inches wide, depending on the overall dimensions of the stretcher, by the same thickness used in the boards. Pulling the "jaws" or stretcher boards apart wedges the hide into position, and the flag holds the jaws open after the hide is in place.

In practice, the flag is nailed to the opposite jaw to hold the hide in place. Many hide men drill holes into the flag and the jaw, then use wooden plugs or nails to hold the stretcher sides apart. Drilling three or four holes will cover most hide widths.

How a stretcher is used will greatly determine the final quality of the hide. After it has been washed and is nearly dried, it is put on the stretcher with the fur side in. It is left in this position to continue drying. The key is to let the hide dry only to the point that it can still be taken off the stretcher, turned fur side out, and returned to the stretcher for final drying. Under normal conditions, it takes anywhere from a few hours to overnight for the skin-side-out drying to be completed.

The danger is in allowing the hide to remain skin side out for too long a time. This makes it difficult to turn the fur side out. However, should a hunter forget to remove the hide, the solution is to rewash the hide and repeat the process of stretching.

Place the hide on the stretcher with care. Sometimes a beginner will be in a hurry and twist the hide as it is placed. It will dry in this position and look awful when removed from the board. Hide buyers say that such hides appear to have no back. In addition, the hair flow and pattern will be broken.

Place the hide on the stretcher and pull with some vigor down the length of the board. It is important to obtain the correct length first before attempting to stretch for width.

When dealing with the long-hairs, it is worth keeping in mind the ratio of length to width in the final stretched hide. It is easy to overstretch foxes and coyotes. In a typical red fox out my way, a length of 30 to 33 inches would have a corresponding width of 7 inches at the hind end. In general, coyotes have a 4 to 1 ratio. Thus, a 44-inch coyote would come out 11 inches wide at the bottom of the hide. These figures will vary somewhat, being generally smaller for animals taken in the southern part of the range to slightly larger farther north.

Stitching Repairs. When the hide is mounted on the stretcher skin side out and has not yet been firmly fixed to the board, this is the time to do any sewing of cuts or bullet holes. The whole area of sewing is extremely important to the hide hunter and is one where practice and skill will really pay dividends.

Sewing up the holes offers real advantages to both the hunter and the hide buyer. Naturally, the hunter receives a better price for a sewn fur than one that sports a gaping hole. The buyer receives a better product because the hide has been handled in such a way that proper drying around the bullet

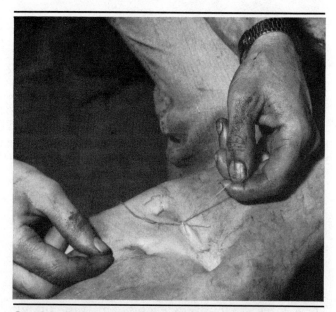

Careful stitching will ensure unbroken fur flow. Sew on the flesh side with a heavy needle and coated thread, with a simple overcast stitch that butts the edges of the hole together.

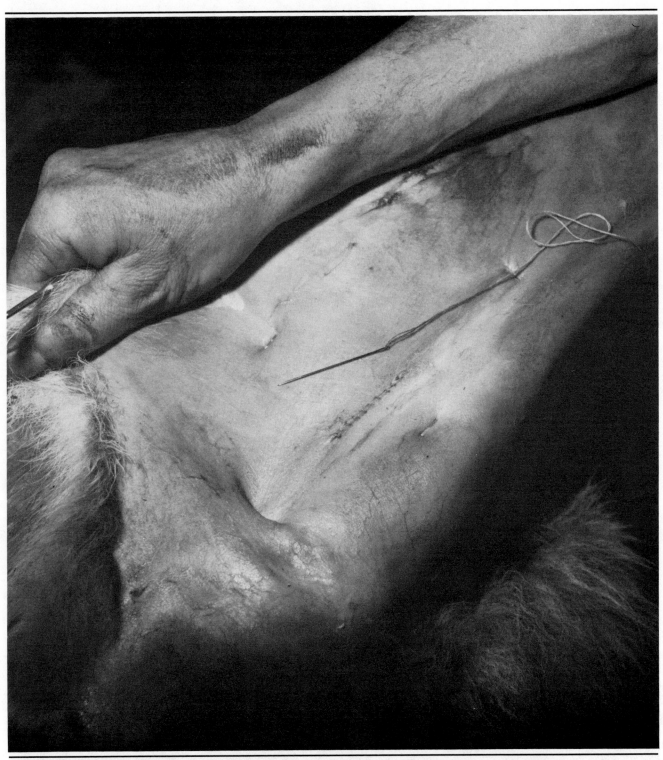

A neat and functional finished product. Many well-done repair jobs are left in place and become part of the final garment.

hole has taken place and any damaged hair has been cleaned and straightened. Unknown to many is the fact that hunter repair jobs, if done well, are not altered when the hide goes through the dressing steps. Many times the final fur product will have hides that still hold the original repair job made by the hunter. These articles suffer no reduction in quality or beauty. In addition, sewing the hide shows the buyer that there is no break in the fur flow or pattern. In his mind, this means the hide will be good enough for the end product and

no second guessing about appearance is required. Under these circumstances, the buyer will risk the higher price.

With the damp fur placed on the stretcher, turn the stretcher so the holes or cuts are easy to reach. Most bullet holes are not really round and many are somewhat jagged or rough edged. It is best to cut these out using a very sharp knife. The hole is extended slightly, with a bit of hide being removed from each side of the hole. Cut lengthwise along the edges of the hole in the shape of two triangles, with

The hide is tacked to the board. A large staple gun is an excellent aid for this phase of preparation.

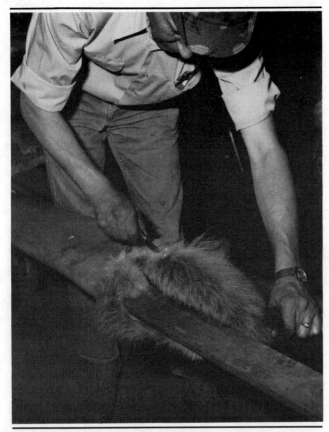

If you haven't done so prior to this point, now is the time to cut the tail bone from the tail.

in the stitch. This ensures the flow of the hair and the pattern, and leaves no bulk where the sewing took place.

Once the length has been determined and any sewing done, width can be set very easily on the Summerberry stretcher. Professional hide men use a wedge to separate the two halves of the stretcher. The wedge holds the hide in place while it is tacked down at the hind end. It also allows for the setting of the flag. Again, be careful not to overstretch for width. Gently open the stretchers until the halves become firmly in contact with the hide. Any vigorous pulling apart of the halves is actually reduced by the use of the large wedge. It brings the halves apart about evenly and divides the pressure equally on each side of the fur.

Those who do not have a wedge to separate the stretcher halves can simply use hand power. Spread the stretcher until it is firmly in contact with the hide, but be careful and do not overexert during this step. No crinkles or wrinkles in the hide should be visible, and the skin should look smooth and flat. There should be no wave-like contours to the hide if it has been put in place properly.

The fore legs of the animal are held open either with pieces of wire or wooden sticks. These can be stapled in place or, in the case of wire, left hanging to spread the leg open just like a stretcher. Some hide men place paper cones inside this part of the hide, while others use wedges made of cardboard. Still others omit this step entirely and leave the legs dangling.

The hide can be affixed to the stretcher with tacks or nails; a large staple gun may also be used. This is quickest and most efficient and also very neat, since the little holes left by the staple gun are of no consequence. It also saves the stretcher from becoming pitted by repeated nailings.

Once the hide is nearly dried, remove it from the stretcher and turn it fur side out. Brush the fur several times at this point to reset the lay of the hair and pattern. Check the areas that have been repaired to be sure that the hair is natural looking. Be sure that none of the long hair has been stitched over. Check areas where blood or mud might have been. Comb these carefully and reset any hair that looks out of place. Give the hide a good shaking to fluff up the hair. The skin sould have a slight crackle to it. Listen for it.

one triangle pointing upward from the center of the hole and the other pointing down. The outermost points of the triangles should be in line with each other and the center of the hole. Mending a .22- or .25-caliber hole requires no more than a one-inch cut. Straight, non-bullet-type cuts, of course, do not need any additional trimming. Then push any long hairs back through the cut to the fur side and pull the skin together. Staple the hide to the stretcher to hold the cut edges while you sew.

Use a sturdy sewing needle with an eye large enough to accept the thread you will be using. Some hunters use waxed thread, while still others use monofilament fishing line.

Sewing done on the inside of the hide will butt the two cut edges of the hide and hold them tightly together. The particular advantage of sewing in this manner is that very little of the hair is caught

Final Drying of Pelts

Once a hide has been partially or pre-dried, removed from the stretcher, turned inside out so that the fur is to the outside, and checked, it should be returned to the stretcher for final drying. Drying is a very important stage—the final phase of the hunter's involvement—in the long process of hide preparation.

Many professional hide men give the skin a good rubdown with burlap sacking or paper toweling be-

fore turning it. The goal is to be sure the skin surface is dry and free of fat and oil or any other material.

Remove the pelt from the stretcher and begin reversing it. Tuck the head inside the pelt, starting with the nose, and gently roll the hide inside out. Remove the slats, wire or wood wedges that were used to keep the legs open. Turn the legs so they are outside the pelt. Replace the pelt, fur side out, on the stretcher.

Many hide men do not retack the hide, but this

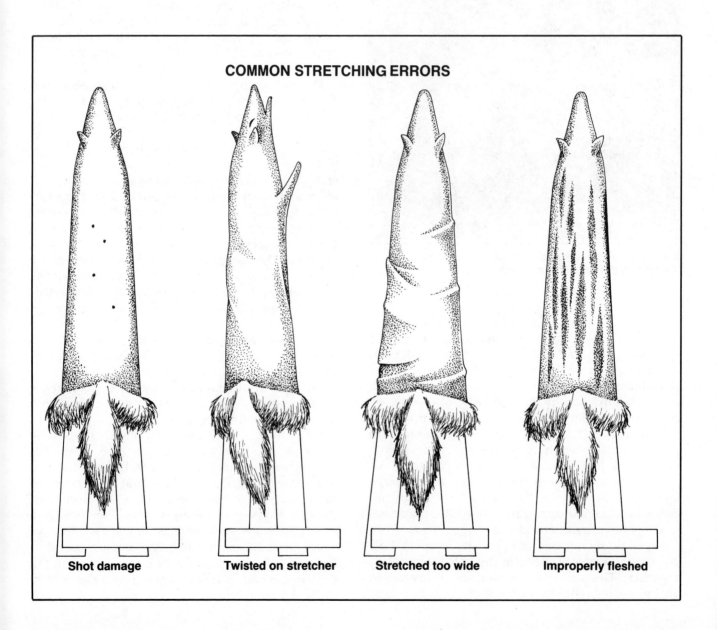

COMMON STRETCHING ERRORS

Shot damage   **Twisted on stretcher**   **Stretched too wide**   **Improperly fleshed**

is optional. Depending on the degree of dryness obtained either from a few hours or three to four days hanging, retacking may not be needed. Judgment and experience will soon tell whether the hide has dried sufficiently.

It is important to hang the stretchers up so that air can circulate around the hides. Where several are hung, air should pass uniformly around all the hides. Poor air circulation can lead to mold developing on the hides, even at a correct drying temperature.

If your hides have been cleaned properly, they will dry easily. Even at low temperatures, given enough time, a fat-free hide will dry to an overall neat appearance. Naturally, all hides do not dry at the same rate. Coyotes have thicker, oilier skin that do foxes or lynx. As a consequence, these take longer to dry. A southern bobcat dries quickly compared to a well-fattened lynx.

The kind of working environment available to the hunter is also a factor. Humid conditions, such as encountered in the southeast, demand longer

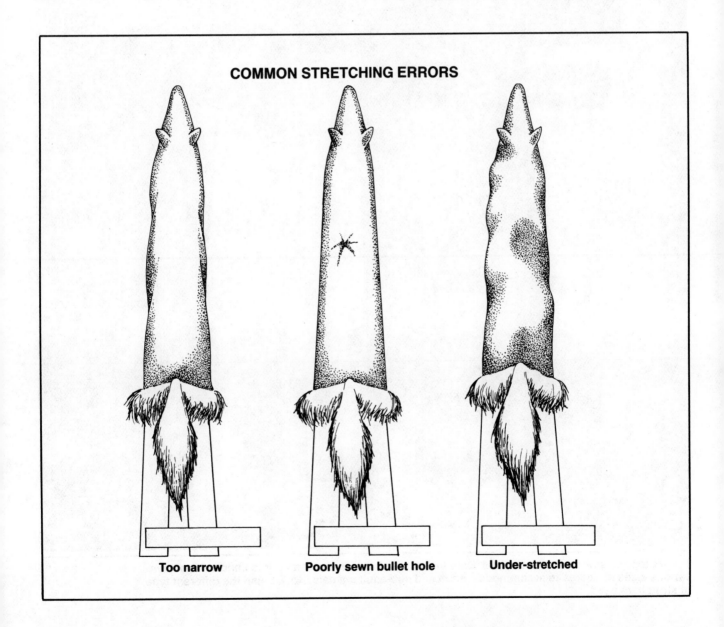

COMMON STRETCHING ERRORS

Too narrow **Poorly sewn bullet hole** **Under-stretched**

Three properly stretched coyote hides. Note the smaller board in the center. It is important to have various sizes of boards to accommodate adult and sub-adult animals. Notice also the different type of stretchers used.

drying times, even with hides of relative thickness. In the north, freezing winter conditions pose special problems for hide men at drying time.

Drying can be accomplished best in a cool, but moisture-free area where the humidity level is approximately 40 to 50 percent. Most hide men use the lee side of buildings, a garage or a barn. Optimal drying is probably achieved in the 60 degree range, but most hunters will not have facilities to control the inside temperature. Damp basements or cellars are poor places to dry hides. Direct sunlight will dry a hide quickly, but intense sun will dry the hide unevenly. Similarly, hanging hides too near a furnace can dry them too quickly.

It takes from 10 to 15 days for the average-sized, well-cleaned, long-haired hide to cure completely. Some may take longer, others less. Check the hides daily and watch for rodent or other animal damage. Dogs, and especially cats, can be a problem. Porcupines are not above nibbling on drying hides in the midst of a hard, cold winter. Weasels that hang around farm buildings may also help themselves, as may mice and squirrels.

Once a hide is well dried or cured, it can be removed from the stretcher and stored elsewhere. It is best if the hide can remain hung up by the head end with plenty of room for air to circulate around it. In addition, constant dry storage conditions are a must to keep the hide in shape. Some hunters place hides in the freezer after drying, but no advantage is gained in this, and the possibility of other damage only increases. Be sure to check hides frequently, turning them when needed and combing to bring the hair out to its fullest.

Once the hides are dry, the hunter will be able to sort them into sizes and colors. They could be sold this way, or the entire batch taken into a hide buyer. As more hides are taken over the prime season, bundles can be built up that are uniform in size or color. The choice is up to the hunter and the demands of his particular market.

A wise hunter should try to time his drying efforts with the approach of any fur sales or the needs of his buyer. It is always good to have a small inventory of furs on hand, just in case a buyer is looking to fill a package prior to a major sale. Having hides well dried before the sale date will also help in the packing, for it means that only dry furs will be sent.

Packing and Shipping

Shipping hides is often a problem at this time. The first word of warning is to ship only totally dried hides that have been carefully packed. If a hide does not feel just right, with the correct amount of suppleness, or if, for some reason, it has not dried just right, do not ship it. Instead, consider selling it locally or waiting until it has dried.

When it comes time to pack your long-hairs, remember that the long guard hairs are highly susceptible to rough handling. Although the previous processing will have removed much of the loose or near-dead guard hairs, those still in place may suffer considerable abuse during shipping. Trucks,

After a hide is completely dried, the stitched part is beat with a stick to fluff up the hair and return it to its natural flow. This is a quick way to condition a fur prior to a sale.

trains and even air-freight handlers are not particular about how they handle a package.

In packaging, never place the hair of one pelt next to the skin of another. The long guard hairs can stick to the skin and be pulled out during the unpacking. If you must ship mixed lots of furs, at least package each one individually by laying a sheet of canvas or heavy paper over the hide, and placing the next on top of this. Oil or grease can also be transferred at this time and the packing will prevent this.

Paramount in the packing or storing of long-haired furs is: *Never, never fold the pelt*. The skin will bend permanently, and dressing will never return the hide to its fullest beauty. Sometimes hides that have been rolled are received at the larger auctions. While this does not usually damage the skin, it is a bother to those who operate the auction and must sort the hides.

Pack furs in cardboard boxes, canvas bags or wooden boxes. This prevents damage during shipping and protects the hides from becoming wet if the bundle is left outside in the rain or snow on some loading dock miles from your destination. Always label the packages and, if more than one is sent, be sure to assign a number to each.

It is not so common now, but hide men used to bundle their hides in canvas bags and bind them with rope. Often the rope would rub hair off the hide or leave rope marks where the rope cut into the hide. If ropes or twine have to be used in packing furs, be sure to buffer the wrap with cardboard for protection, or tie the lines only snug enough to close the package. The best way is to ship in boxes and forget using rope or twine all together.

Finally, be sure the destination is clearly marked and a return address is visibly in place on the bundle. It should not have to be said, but be sure the correct address is on the bundle. When possible, insure your goods against loss.

Marketing Furs Successfully

Top-quality pelts require strong, resilient guard hairs that must be able to withstand trimming and bleaching during the manufacturing stage. This coyote coat speaks for itself.

Chapter 16

Criteria for Grading Furs

The single biggest concern of the hide man is the price he will receive for his furs. While he may enjoy the actual taking of the hides, and feel that preparing them requires some work, the final price is a constant source of concern. He ponders it and broods about it while working on the furs. He realizes the fur is enhanced with each operation he performs to bring out the best in the pelt. As he progresses through each step, pride develops in the finished product, and in his mind a dollar value for his effort is formed.

Many hide men do not really know what makes a pelt valuable in itself, however. Rumor and a poor understanding of the fur market lead to many misconceptions. History and tradition, both common elements in a business as old as the fur trade, also influence thinking. In addition, few written sources outline what is needed.

Yet, there is no magic to what makes one hide more valuable than another. Buyers want hides that meet distinct and observable criteria. The key for the hide man is to present a product that is the picture perfect embodiment of that criteria. Knowledge of those criteria coupled with practice and good work habits are all that is required to bring the picture to fruition. Once this is done, there will be little need to brood endlessly over the price the furs will finally bring. The hide man will know that

his furs are the best they can be, that they meet all the criteria, and therefore will bring the best possible price the market is capable of offering.

Let's look at the specific factors that influence the saleability of any particular skin. By now everyone knows that looks, condition of the pelts and any damage to them are fundamentals in establishing prices. However, these basics can be expanded into roughly ten criteria that cover every detail a hide buyer would evaluate. They are: general appearance, seasonableness, amount of fur, completeness of the fur, straightness and sheen of the hair, color and size and, finally, damage to the skin and damage to the fur. The marketability of a hide depends on how well it meets these criteria. If close to the upper end of these standards, it will be bought at a price set by the prevailing market.

Be aware that the factors interact to produce price and that the overall importance of any one factor may be affected by another. For example, in coyotes a very large hide that shows the slightest amount of rubbing around the shoulders will be downgraded. Thus, a very large pelt of inferior quality and a medium hide with excellent characteristics may bring very close to the same price. A further example is color. In coyotes color is usually ignored, but a large hide with good color would grade better than a similar hide with poorer color.

In short, the factors influence each other and it is the acting together of factors that will set prices.

General Appearance

What you see is what you get. This is a familiar axiom of modern-day life and it applies to the fur business. It is one rule nobody has trouble understanding. It is logical to expect that the best-looking hide will bring the top price.

Buyers and graders are greatly influenced by how a hide looks. Experienced buyers know full well that a muddy or greasy hide will most often dress out as well as a properly handled hide, but sometimes it doesn't work out that way. Therefore, instead of taking the risk, a messy hide is downgraded and will invariably bring a lower price. Worse yet, other hides in the same package may also be downgraded along with it.

In short, then, a nice, clean hide makes the best impression. The great looks of one hide can cause

Coyote hides in staggered stages of drying. Some are still skin side out, while others have been reversed to the fur side. Good air circulation and low humidity will promote optimal drying conditions and ultimately saleable hides.

a package to stand out from a large group of exceptionally well-handled and prepared furs. This can entice a buyer to take a closer look at that particular lot.

These first impressions often give rise to some heated bidding at large fur auctions. If the buyer is assembling a package of hides for another customer, he will, of course, want the hides that will present the most striking impression; he will be willing to offer a higher price and vie for high-quality goods. He is in the business of selling looks. Looks should be uppermost in the hide man's mind as he prepares his furs for market.

Most hide buyers—whether they are brokers, dealers or furriers—like the feel of pelts. They are attracted to dense, clean furs that are straight, supple and silky to the touch. It is this sense of touch that determines that a fur will dress out well and improve with further work. Combined with the other sensory perceptions, the desire to have one hide over another is created.

A buyer knows how many hides he has to assemble for a customer or furrier. For example, if he needs 50 hides and there are 250 at a given sale he will have little trouble meeting his order. But any buyer worth his salt wants the best-quality hides he can get for his hide-buying dollar. By his very nature, he will bid first on those parcels that have the best appearance and go down in quality as his operating money will allow. The hide man, through his preparation techniques and the quality of his fur, must create this desire.

One final point should be stressed regarding hide appearance. The entire hide business is based on impression. The beauty of one hide over another is many times strictly in the eye of the beholder. Illusion, at some point, has to have a starting point, and a correctly cleaned, well-prepared hide is the beginning of that widely held illusion of fur quality.

Seasonableness

An obvious point, seasonableness is a factor that every hide man must pay attention to. Since a hide is good for commercial purposes only during certain times of the year, it is important to know when hides reach their prime season, or simply "prime," in your area.

Depending on where you live, and to a small extent the kinds of hides produced in your area, the prime season occurs just before the coldest part of the year. Long-haired, fur-bearing animals develop the extra thick, long-haired fur and thick underfur in anticipation of this season. When the hide is most luxurious, it is also most valuable.

A hide begins to lose condition almost from the very beginning. As the animal seeks out its living, it loses hair, which is not readily replaced in the winter. The long guard hair is lost in many ways, one being that it is easily pulled out when the animal passes through bush, shrub or briars. For this reason, prairie coyotes usually maintain their prime much longer than their woodland-dwelling cousins. The seeking and taking of game will also result in some hair loss and damage.

The most common source of hair loss occurs when the animal lies down and some of the hair freezes to the snow below; when it gets up, a few hairs are left behind. Finally, as the season progresses, the warming temperatures create a lot of discomfort. The animals respond by rubbing, especially the neck and shoulder areas, and this takes a great toll on the hide's condition. Also, lice and fleas generate some rubbing. In some years, such as those with exceptionally warm winters, sarcoptic mange may ruin hides across great expanses of the range.

To help determine whether or not a hide is considered prime, veteran buyers use several tricks. For example, with fox and coyote, they will look at the root of the tail, which is the last place to show prime condition. Also, long-haired furs taken too early in the season will invariably have short fur down the center of the back. Hides taken extremely early in the season will have short hair spread throughout the entire hide. On the other hand, furs taken too late in the season will show a lack of guard hairs. In addition, the hair will look flat and the underfur will be thin.

A fur grader or buyer can determine at what time of year the animal was taken by looking at the skin side of the hide. Food habits vary extensively over a full year and the types of foods ingested will greatly change the color of the skin. The presence or absence of fat and the feel of the hide will also tell the experienced buyer when the hide was taken.

During the summer months, long-haired furs

Close-up of a well-furred coyote hide. The top hair is in excellent condition with no sign of rubbing. The animal was clearly in peak shape and was taken in the prime part of the season.

have a white color to the skin. In some areas this will be closer to a blue color. Some call this the "summer prime," but it is of no value to the fur trade. The coat will have a fuzzy appearance or look like a hairy arm. It can look like wool on some skins. Summer skin is thin and, as such, has few practical trade uses.

As fall approaches, a skin will take on a dark, sometimes blotchy, appearance. In some areas, like along the West Coast, it may become almost black. In more northern latitudes, this dark color gives way to a clear white color, with the degree of whiteness seeming to vary with the latitude. At this time, the long hair grows out, becoming longer, and the underfur increases in density. Since the changing skin condition and growing out of the long hair essentially occur at the same time, a hide is often called full furred when it is prime. Also, an unprimed skin would be called underfurred.

All other factors being equal, a prime fur will have the highest value. A pelt taken late will be worth at best one third to one half the value of a prime pelt. Pelts in this class are often termed "springy" and will show deterioration of color, much rubbing, and the scars of fighting as the mating season begins and new territories are established. A fur that is taken too early will bring about one third less, varying with how early the hide was taken.

The prime season is relatively short and, as I have tried to indicate, as each day passes, the value or condition of the hide declines. Therefore, it is important to know when the prime season begins and to have a good idea of when it ends; during this time the greatest energy should be expended to take the annual quota of furs. It may mean long hours and extensive traveling, but your perseverance during this period will mean much more in terms of return per unit of effort than at any other point in the season.

Prime season may vary somewhat from year to year. Weather conditions will greatly influence the onset of prime, and extremely warm weather during a normally cold part of the winter will usually reduce the condition of the hides markedly. No reversal in the weather will ever compensate for this. In fact, you'll often see greater deterioration under these circumstances because the animals are under considerable stress.

Hunters are well advised to begin their efforts before the prime season, so that their greatest push can coincide with the earliest beginnings of prime. When the hides are looking great, the hunting effort should be increased, then tapered off when condition declines.

It is important to note, too, that the prime season does not begin on one specific day and end on another. Animals come into prime over a period of time. This usually covers two to three weeks in foxes and coyotes. Likewise, prime condition does not just leave on the last day of the predator season. Its departure is gradual, although more abrupt than its arrival.

Areas that are in close proximity may have prime seasons that differ. This is usually due to some factor in the micro-climate, either through elevation, air temperatures, or even the effect of shadowing from high mountains or deep valleys. The condition of primeness is simply an animal's physiological response to a complex of weather and genetic factors. Within this complexity there is much room for variation.

Thus, it is clear that to err on the early side of the prime season is far better than to continue to hunt far too late. In this way, the best hides will assuredly be collected and the subsequent decline in quality will be obvious when the skinning is done. This will then be the time to slow down your efforts.

Amount of Fur

Four other interacting factors help to establish price. Amount of fur, completeness of fur, straightness of the top hair and condition, or sheen, of the fur all focus on the quality of the hair and are closely related to prime or seasonableness. These factors are largely the result of natural phenomena, but can be affected by mishandling during the preparatory stages.

The pelage or coat of hair that covers any animal varies in length and density. Northern canids have the thickest coats, while the southern members of this family characteristically have thinner coats. The entire pelage is replaced gradually by a periodic molt, usually in the early fall, so that a new coat will grow into place for the winter. Hair will grow to a definite length and then stop. As explained earlier,

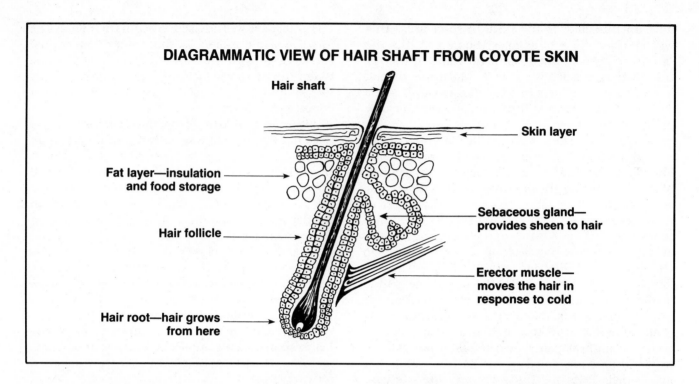

DIAGRAMMATIC VIEW OF HAIR SHAFT FROM COYOTE SKIN

Hair shaft

Skin layer

Fat layer—insulation
and food storage

Sebaceous gland—
provides sheen to hair

Hair follicle

Erector muscle—
moves the hair in
response to cold

Hair root—hair grows
from here

it is not usually replaced once lost. Molts are necessary to allow the animal to adjust to any change in body size that may have taken place over the summer. In the early winter, by the time the first cold fronts come pouring down from the Arctic, most long-haired canids are snuggly outfitted with their winter hair.

Clearly, the fur buyer wants the hide with the thickest fur. This is basic to the industry, since dense, luxuriant furs will dress out best. Typically, a hide will lose up to 40 percent of its hair in processing to the final product. Thus, hides in their prime are sought.

Each hair is set in a follicle, a cellular sac formed from a combination of the outer layer of skin and the inner layer. This forms a hair papilla and, when supplied with blood, produces a hair. The hair is forced out of the skin by growth from below. Once a hair is outside of the skin, technically it is dead. Oily secretions from sebaceous glands underneath the outer layer of skin keep the dead hair from becoming overly brittle and help the hair appear alive and healthy. One hair follicle can produce other hair by budding, but most follicles produce only one before dying back and being shed with other skin cells that are washed or fall away.

The long-haired predators discussed in this book possess two types of hair of interest to the hide man or buyer: the underfur and the guard hair. Also known as ground fur or under wool, underfur, as a hide man or buyer would know it, is comprised of closely spaced, fine, relatively short hairs. These serve to insulate the animal from the cold. They can be hollow or divided into hollow segments or compartments. These air spaces, of course, add greatly to the overall insulating ability of the fur.

The underfur can vary greatly among different animals of the same species. One area may produce pelts whose underfur is decidedly thinner than that produced in an area only a few miles away. A hide with thin underfur can show the sewing seams on a completed coat, an undesirable feature in the garment industry. Good underfur is well recognized, and areas that produce this kind of fur, such as northern Montana, North Dakota and parts of Canada, are closely watched by the fur trade.

The guard hairs are also referred to as over hair, top hair or cover hair; they are typically longer and heavier than the underfur, but considerably less in number. Guard hairs are sacrificed by the animal to protect the underfur. Sun and moisture are hard on these hairs and the general life habits of the animal cause many to be lost.

A fur grader carefully scrutinizes the condition of the top hair because it must be strong enough to withstand the processes of tanning, dyeing and cutting without great hair loss. Many long-haired pelts are used to manufacture collars. When used this way, there is no set ratio of long hair to underfur required. However, when used for coats, these hides should have as many guard or top hairs as possible. Most of these are trimmed, but a furrier would rather start off with as much fur as he can. The guard hairs must be strong and in good condition in order to withstand trimming and bleaching. Usually, if the top hair is nice, the underfur will also be good.

What more could a fur buyer ask for than thick, supple, silk-like fur that is straight, shiny and well-prepared?

Completeness of Fur

Since the hide buyer wants furs that look thick and luxurious, if the fur is incomplete in any way, it will be downgraded and will bring a lower price.

Completeness of fur is a factor that many beginners tend to overlook. Many feel that because one portion of the fur is nice, the entire pelt will yield a good price. They ignore the fact that the fur must be complete all over to bring top dollar. A good back or hind portion is not good enough for the buyer. He demands, and usually receives, furs that are complete from top to bottom, head to tail.

If a fur is incomplete or damaged in some way, it is sometimes possible for the fur dresser to cut away the damaged portion. However, this entails the use of skilled hand labor and introduces another step—and expense—into the manufacturing process.

Removing a part of a pelt and stitching it back together may make a hide look out of balance and this will limit the manufacturing potential of the skin. Clearly, these concerns are considered by the buyer with every fur or lot he handles. A misjudgment at this stage of the buying can result in diminished profits for the company further down the line. A buyer would rather pay less for a hide because of the risk of greater cost later on in production.

Long-haired pelts generally show the effects of rubbing far more than other kinds of raw furs. Rubbing is most often seen between the shoulders. The animal pushes through bushes with its shoulders first and the damage is done in this area. The remainder of the pelt may be in excellent condition but with rubbed shoulders, it will be downgraded.

Straightness of the Top Hair

In the long-haired furs such as fox, coyote and wolf, we know that the thick, luxuriant top hair is the most desirable feature of the hide. This hair should be almost silk-like to the touch and not brittle or curled. This is a relatively straightforward criterion looked for by the buyer or grader.

The condition of the top hairs is a direct expression of primeness. Early winter is the best time for this trait to be most visible. As the season progresses, the hair dries out and loses much of its sheen or natural beauty.

It is important to recall that long hairs are not replaced very rapidly. Essentially, an animal has a quota of long hair at the beginning of the prime season and this must do until next season. Hair dries from the top to the bottom and becomes brittle as the season wears on. The long hair is then subject to easy breakage as the animal passes through shrub or bush. Thus, numerous individual hairs are lost by friction as the animal secures its food and moves through its environment.

These hairs, as well as the hide, can also be affected by how the hide is handled and prepared. Hides that are placed too close to a heat source are easily damaged. Remember, each hair is only a single long protein cell or, as the biologists call it, a simple cornified epidermal product. As such, it is extremely sensitive to heat, which can cause an immediate change in appearance. For the buyer, this means it may look curled up or kinky; hides that have this will be downgraded.

Overhandling of fox pelts can cause this kinky appearance to show up, too. The work area should have a smooth table top and the amount of brushing or stroking of a drying hide should be kept to a minimum. Also, if pelts are dried in a modern laundry dryer, the temperature should be on a cool setting so the hair is not cooked until it looks like twisted wire.

Condition, or Sheen, of the Fur

Condition, as defined here, is the sheen on both the under and outer hair. The time of year at which the hide was taken will greatly determine its condition; condition is, in fact, another fine point of primeness.

Hair condition is greatly influenced by the physiological state of the animal. An animal that has been eating well during the summer season will produce a nicer hide than one that has been under some type of stress. Old or wounded animals will usually show poor coat condition. Although the hide may be almost as thick as that of a healthy animal, it will lack that nice overall sheen so characteristic of a healthy animal. Older long-hairs, although still strong and capable hunters and

Two gorgeous hides showing the kind of sheen and luster hide buyers usually look for.

such a nice sheen is the production of this sebum. Coyotes, foxes, wolves, bobcats and, to a lesser extent, badgers all have diets that include high amounts of fat. Summer-fattened rabbits and any scavenged food animals will provide good supplies of cholesterol. This is the principle animal protein found in the mainly yellow, pearly leaflets of fat in these prey species. While cholesterol has earned a bad reputation in humans, in the wild it contributes to the production of many different esters that are the main ingredient of sebum. They, in turn, create the nice sheen or luster to the hair.

Sheen must be present on all hairs of the hide—the underfur and the guard hairs. There is a natural feel to well-oiled hides that is most difficult to describe, but once felt will always be remembered. Although there is no artificial way of reproducing this, many hide men feel that brushing with a fine comb will help redistribute some of the oil that is still on the hide.

With all the dressing and preparation that goes on after the initial skinning, why should the sheen be so important? The answer is that the hide with the sheen will have hairs of good quality. These hairs will be better able to withstand the processing, and the loss of hairs from the overall hide will not be as great. It is easy to see why a hide grader will select hides with hair in good condition.

Color

The hide buyer always selects for color. However, there are few rules to follow since the demand for colors varies with the whim of fashion. In the last few years, for example, the demand has drifted toward the lighter colors.

Hair color is determined by various pigments that are contained as granules in the hair cortex. The cortex is the area just below the outer cuticle scale of the hair. These scales can be smooth, shingle like, spined or spiral in shape and can be used to tell one species from another. A substance called melanin contributes most to the various colors of hair. Where white hair is present, little or no melanin is found. Gray is caused by the follicle producing only a limited amount of melanin.

Color is genetically linked. And some geographical areas produce unique color combinations.

scavengers, will often develop bad teeth, and this logically interferes with food intake. Hide condition will reveal this almost instantly.

Hairs are kept in condition by sebum, which is an oil-like substance produced by the sebaceous glands. There are at least two glands for every hair on the body, and in long-haired animals the glands are very active during the fall and winter. The sebum also helps to keep the skin soft and pliant, and prevents excess water evaporation and absorption by the skin. Because fat is a poor insulator, the oil reduces heat loss through the skin. Sebum is worked onto the skin by the movement of the hairs as the animal hunts or the wind tousles the hair. It is also moved by the production of "goose bumps" during the cold, and this accounts for the increased presence of the oil during the fall and winter.

One of the reasons northern long-hairs have

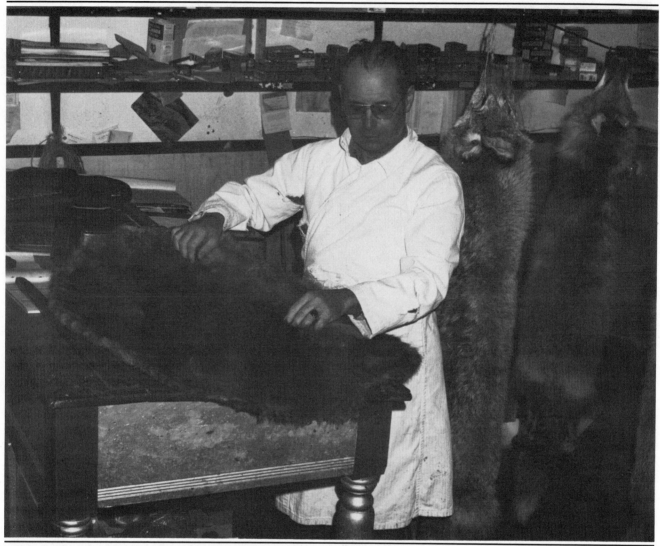

The hide buyer must be familiar with all classes and types of hides. He must know what is required in each hide and quickly be able to evaluate the quality of any given sample.

Foxes, of course, are a particular example; cross fox, silver fox and black fox are all members of the red fox species, and all display different coloring. There are four other distinct fox species with at least two color phases within, as well as local variations of these phases. This great diversity is genetic and all color types may even appear within the same litter.

Animals are usually light colored below and darker above. Thus, when you see an animal at some distance, say, 75 yards, the upper and lower

surface seem to blend into the background. A coyote that stands perfectly still will seem to disappear. One that has been standing still and then is spooked will look as if it materialized out of the prairie background. This simple observation was first outlined by the artist-turned-naturalist Abbot Thayer in the late 1800s. It is often referred to as Thayer's Principle of Coloration. What is really happening is that light reflected up from the ground is reflected back to the ground by the white underbelly. Light coming in from above is absorbed by the darker colors and therefore not reflected back to give away the animal's location.

White is the dominant color of most animals found within the Arctic Cricle, and in the arctic fox and other species such as the polar bear, this is maintained all year (although the arctic fox tends to turn grayish in summer). The sun is very damaging to this type of hair and some bleaching occurs. Some white fox hides show distinct yellowing. However, arctic fox is still a preferred pelt.

Unusual colors may occur at any time and these can command a premium price. Indeed, one of the characteristics of a top-notch fur grader is his ability to recognize a worthwhile color variation and put together a package of furs featuring this color. In the speciality business, this can be particularly rewarding financially.

Hide hunters should then group their hides by color as much as possible. With other factors being equal, a batch or run of good color from a certain area will bring additional dollars. For the individual hunter, this usually means that his few hides are picked up by a buyer or broker putting together a larger package for later resale. The broker or buyer can afford to pay a bit more for the hides in this package because he knows that his purchaser will fall in love with the great color run. Sometimes, too, a buyer will be a few hides short for his parcel and will bid substantially higher for the needed color. Under these circumstances, the hide hunter benefits.

As many will know, color became so important in fox skins that an entire industry grew up around breeding unique or distinct color phases of the fox. Ranch rearing of fox probably reached its pinnacle in the 1940s, but has since declined. Muskegon County in Michigan became famous for this many years ago. While it no longer produces the industry it once did, color in foxes still remains important.

The beauty of the lynx fur lies in its silvery hues and any hides that are dull, dark, brownish or reddish must be downgraded. A good, clear-colored or light-colored coat is preferable. It seems that lynx fur is used in the ski jacket business and light colors are preferred by the Europeans who follow this sport. Most of the American production goes there.

In summing up, color is the hardest criteria to satisfy. The animal either has the color the market is asking for, or it does not. It is very difficult for a hunter to plan to put together a parcel of any certain color because there is such great variation from animal to animal.

Size

Although the degree of importance is determined by the intended use of the hide, size is still an influential factor in the fur trade. Smaller furs usually find a ready market, but the big hides in most species are often given a close look by any seasoned fur buyer. For most purposes, a larger hide simply makes more of a product and frequently costs less than two smaller hides. In addition, it will be easier to work with, since color and hair flow will be the same.

In most long-hairs, size must be in combination with some other grading factor such as color before the prices are greatly influenced. Northern coyote and red fox usually have some exceptionally large samples at any fur auction, but if they have a mousy color, the size becomes of little import. A well-handled hide of large size would make a good trophy item or a novelty good and, in that case, color would be unimportant.

The width of the hide is significant. Pelts that are overstretched in an effort to make them appear larger may draw some attention from the hide buyer, but a quick check of the hairs will indicate a thin, overspread condition that will only earn downgrading. Typically, width may be overstretched on the bottom of coyote and fox pelts due to the shape or design of the stretcher.

Pelts that are overstretched look out of proportion. The width may seem too great for the length, or the opposite condition may exist. When the hunter is lucky enough to take a really large longhair that shows good color and excellent fur condition, proper handling procedures are far more important than trying to make the hide look larger. With average-sized hides, fur condition is more important than size. It is essential for long-haired fur to look proportionally correct to the eye of the buyer.

Size varies with the age of the animal and the quality of the diet. However, coyotes, foxes, wolves, badgers and other long-haired fur bearers tend to be of larger size in the more northern latitudes. This reduces their body surface in relation to weight and saves on heat energy. Traditional biologists call this Bergmann's Rule. Correlated with this is another rule known as Allen's Rule. It says that an animal's extremeties will be smaller in colder climates. Indeed, these old rules are borne out by the field observations of countless hunters who have seen northern coyotes with smaller ears and bigger bodies than their southern relatives. In mountainous country, the same rules will apply.

These variations in body size will evoke differing interpretations of size in the local marketplace. What is considered big in southern areas may be considered only medium size in more northerly areas. If the hunter has a choice, he should pick the area with the larger animals.

The females of any long-haired species will, on an age-for-age basis, generally be smaller than males. In most long-hairs, the value of a female pelt is still less than a male of the same species. In some aquatic furs, the price difference is as much as 50 percent. In long-hairs, the female may bring up to 70 percent of the price for males. The conclusion would seem that hunters would be better off to take only large well-developed males. However, this is not always practical. Hide hunters can, however, take heart, as there is a natural tendency for males to occur in greater numbers than females within any wild population.

Sometimes, buyers will be looking for furs of average size for collars or sleeves. In this case, most female long-hairs will fill the bill and there will be little price differential.

Damage to the Skin

The last two fur-grading factors that influence price—and do so significantly—are damage to the skin and damage to the fur. While some flaws in skin or fur may occur as the animal interacts with its wild environment, much of the visible damage is attributable to man. Unlike the previous factors discussed, here the hunter has a greater degree of control. If he exercises care and attention to detail during the skinning, fleshing and drying stages, he'll never have to worry about a buyer downgrading his furs.

Skinning Cuts. To the buyer, few things are worse than a damaged skin. Buyers will invariably frown on any hide presented to them that shows obvious signs of skin damage—cuts or nicks made during the skinning phase of hide preparation. Cuts are downgraded severely.

Almost any kind of cut will break up the fur pattern. Sewing or stitching will not help, because a break in the fur will be obvious. Fur is longer through the back and grades down in length to the sides and toward the head region, where it can be quite short. Cuts into this pattern will cause an area of more dense fur to be sewn to an area of less dense fur, and an unmistakable seam will result.

At one time, skins that were badly cut up during the preparation stage were taken and sliced into strips. These strips were resewn to recapture the correct flow and look of the fur. In more modern times, this was dropped as a viable technique in all but the most costly of raw furs. Recently, computer-run machines and less manual labor have made this old technique economically worthwhile again.

Bullet Holes. Fur damage also results from the methods of taking furs. Shooting (and other methods not discussed in this book) will leave some sort of damage to long-haired furs. Small bullet holes are usually no problem, although their location and whether or not there is any ancillary harm are important. Small-caliber holes can often be easily sewn, but the blast from a shotgun is much more difficult to repair. Close-range damage by a shotgun blast can ruin a pelt beyond repair, and it has to be stressed that shotguns should rarely be used in any form of hide hunting.

The location of hide damage is more important than the nature or extent of the damage. For example, a head shot successfully made on any longhair will have no influence on the price. On the other hand, a shot across or along the back will be sharply downgraded. Shots placed low on the hide are not viewed seriously, and a hide man can make a good job of sewing them during his initial preparation of the hide. See "Stitching Repairs," page 210.

Repairing and stitching take time on the part of the fur buyer or dresser. This is why it is vital for the hunter to know how to do his own repairs and stitching. Many buyers will not notice a well-done

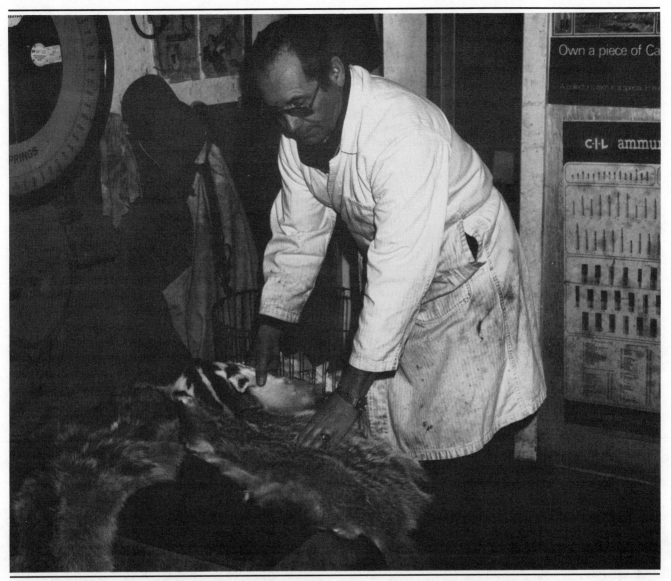

A hide buyer can tell a lot with his hands. By feeling the fur, he can establish how it lies, if there is any damage, the condition of the skin and, most important, how well it has been prepared.

mending job, and it is not until the hide is brought up for final dressing that the repair will be noticed. However, by this time the hunter has his money and the repair becomes the concern of the next handler in the processing chain. This level in the industry is, of course, well equipped to handle such repairs and does so with great economy. Also, hunter repairs do not always have to be redone. They pass through the tanning process and into the manufacturing stage with little or no effect on the final product's appearance or serviceability.

Overscraping. Another major source of damage results from overzealous scraping of the skin. When this happens, the skin becomes too thin, the roots of the hairs become exposed and the long-hairs fall out or can be easily pulled out. A grader will easily spot the roughened, raised area where the fat and skin have been cut away. A thumb passed over the spot will feel the roots. The fur is then downgraded because the affected area will have to be trimmed out.

Drying Too Quickly. Skin damage can also result from drying that has been done too quickly. Although more common in aquatic mammals, it does happen to fox and coyotes that are dried too fast and have lost their natural oils. The hide will be very stiff and, when bent over, will crack along the fold of the affected area. Natural air drying is a slow process and care should be taken so that hides don't get too close to the fireplace or the furnace.

Hides with these types of problems are worthless, especially in the long-hairs. The hides will break down when the dresser prepares them for tanning. Buyers and graders will avoid them if possible or, if the hides are purchased, it will be at a very low price, taking into account that only a small portion can be used in the final product.

Damage to the Fur

Fortunately, long-haired furs are sufficiently tough that little damage actually occurs. The most common source of natural damage to a long-hair is caused by the animal's tendency to rub. As explained earlier, rubbing is the result of the animal's habits. Little can be done about this aspect of the fur other than to be sure to present it in as good a light as possible.

Tainting. However, another type of damage—tainting—is the result of mishandling, and can be controlled. Tainting results when animals are not skinned soon enough after being taken. Carcasses that are left piled up will not allow the body heat to dissipate quickly enough and some tainting will occur. Tainting is really a polite way of saying that actual rotting has begun. Warm carcasses encourage bacteria to grow, breaking down the roots and hair follicles. In normal circumstances this does not happen, since the body produces enzymes and agents that keep the bacteria in check.

Tainting in long-hairs will also occur when the fat has not been removed. The rump, tail area and sometimes the back will have fat deposits. In fox, the tail will taint if not correctly split, cleaned and dried.

In long-haired furs, the key to preventing tainting is to skin and process the hide as soon as possible after taking the animal. Once the roots break down, there is nothing holding the hairs and they will pull out very easily. Preparing such a hide for tanning is usually a disaster, and the entire hide must be discarded. Therefore, the slightest hint of taint will cause a fur buyer to downgrade the hide severely—along with any others that happen to be in the parcel.

In the north, fur rot is rare simply because the ambient temperatures are cooler and the fur-taking seasons are usually the coldest time of the year. However, in the south, air temperatures can be extremely warm and present a real problem for the successful preparation of hides.

No matter where you happen to be, you, the hide hunter, owe it to yourself to attend to the details of proper hide preparation. Because if producing picture-perfect hides means your bread and butter, you'll have plenty to put on the table when the selling season ends.

Grading the Furs

Actual grading of the furs involves assigning a rank to a hide after all the various factors have been weighed and considered. It is a summary that tells buyers and manufacturers what the hide really looks like.

Grades serve to improve the communication between buyers and sellers. Should a broker receive a request from a manufacturer by phone, cable or telex, he has to know exactly what his customer wants to buy. Rigid grading allows this type of communication to be done succinctly and quickly. Here are the currently recognized grades.

I, or First. These are furs that are in prime condition, well furred with no damage either to the fur or to the skin. They are large and well colored. In other words, their size, appearance, and how they have been handled are nearly perfect. There are, of course, very few hides that make it to this category and this has resulted in some easing of the criteria.

II, or Second. These tend to be furs that show some, but not severe, rubbing, or the hair may appear rather flat looking. In general, a second is an average pelt with a good amount of usable hair. It is the lowest grade a manufacturer will use.

III. These are low-grade furs that show much rubbing or are very flat looking. There may still be salvageable fur, but the pelt will have to be purchased cheaply to compensate for added labor costs in cutting and further preparation of the hide. They lack sheen, will be incomplete and are often of poor color.

IV. In some places this is still a recognized grade. It refers to badly damaged hides of little value. Uncleaned hides and poorly prepared ones will fall into this category.

V. Occasionally, a fifth grade is recognized. It usually applies to immature animals with small hides and very little fur.

Along with the grade designation, a size category is most often seen with long-haired furs. The actual measurements will vary from one district to another, but the broad categories will be the same. In practice, what really happens is that a buyer will select the area from which he wants to buy. He will then channel his orders to the auctions in that area and will become familiar with the size characteristics of that particular district. The categories are—Extra Large (XL), sometimes extended to XXL, Large (L), Medium (M) and Small (S).

There are also recognized zones of fur production and the prices will vary among these areas. For example, Montana is recognized as a special area for coyotes, and hides from there will most often top the market. The Northwest, which includes much of the mountain country of Idaho, is acknowledged as a special price area and will usually place second behind Montana. The western states are also classed differently, but prices for coyotes from there can be as little as half of that of their northern cousins. Prices decline more for the two remaining areas. The Midwest, which is considered to be the large area throughout the west central part of the U.S., produces its own type of fur. The last area, which can manifest great price fluctuation, is the Northeast. The major differences that distinguish these production zones lie in the quality and quantity of fur produced as well as the length of the prime season.

The terms for grade, size and region are all strung together to describe a hide. For example, a coyote hide could be described as XL, II, N.W., meaning an extra large, grade two hide from the northwest region of the country. You most often see this in summaries of hide prices.

The jargon may be combined in other ways. For example, a buyer may quote a manufacturer that he has a good supply of "ones and twos" or "ones, part twos." Since the grade II is such a broad class, a discriminating buyer may describe his parcel as "best twos," which means that in his mind he has selected the better grade II's from several parcels. These are not good enough for grade I, but are the best of the II's on offer. Special combinations are also possible. For example, "best twos, good color," would mean a selection of the better grade II's has been made and the hides have a preferred color run.

Other terms that are self-explanatory include

"slightly shot," or "springy" and describe a condition common to a parcel. Sometimes, if enough of one type of hide can be assembled, these will be sold separately from the other grades. This is usually to the seller's advantage.

Other terms, such as "inferior seconds," "poor seconds" or "low seconds" may occasionally be heard. These reflect the overall condition of the hides and clearly denote that poorer quality pelts are on offer. However, in some years poor quality seconds are the only hides that are produced in an area, and buyers are forced to use what is available. While this usually induces buyers to shift purchases to other zones, the opening bids may be stirred to surprising heights on low-quality furs.

In conclusion, while the hide jargon may vary from one district to another, tight definitions still describe what a top hide looks like. In fact, one of the characteristics of the professional hide buyer is the ability to keep a picture of the perfect hide clear in his mind. He must often be able to act quickly when he sees hides that meet that description, and bid accordingly. All good buyers retain a strong mental image of the kind of hide their business requires, and they want to get close to meeting those needs with each and every hide purchase.

The more a hide man knows about how hides are graded, what they are used for, and the economic conditions that influence his market, discussed in the next chapter, the better he can plan his efforts and benefit financially. It is crucial to the fur producer's success to have the same mental impression of the perfect-looking fur as the grader or buyer. The producer has to know what type of product the buyer wants and work toward providing that goal.

Chapter 17

Market Factors That Influence Price

In addition to the fine points of fur grading, other factors touched upon in the beginning of this book come into play that help set prices—the world economy, the state and technology of the fur industry itself, fashion trends, and the specific concerns the buyer must take into account if he is to reap a profit from his purchases. Understanding these influences will keep the hide man alert to changes that may affect his efforts and ultimately his bank account.

The industry has changed very markedly from the fur trade days covered so romantically in our history books. Today, all the fur produced and sold will be purchased by the garment industry. There was a time when some hides were used for such diverse products as paint brushes and shaving brushes, but the garment industry is now the only buyer for all the furs offered. This will influence the price, as there is no competition.

It also means that the prices paid will greatly reflect the state of the garment industry. In good economic times, when there is considerable discretionary income available to consumers, the demand for furs will be high. Higher raw fur prices will be the result. On the other hand, in times of poor economic performance, it takes little understanding of basic economics to realize that raw fur prices will be down. There may be a lag, in which

hide prices may continue high for a year or so because manufacturers are locked into production schedules and economies of scale, but ultimately, when the garment industry suffers, so does the hide man's pocketbook.

Foreign markets also influence the price. Japan, above all others, is a great consumer of raw furs, turning these into thousands of garments of varying quality. Foreign ability to purchase raw furs out of the North American production area is directly affected by the international exchange rate of the American dollar. When the American dollar is weak on the money markets, foreign buyers can afford more American dollars. Very simply, they are able to turn their money into equal or greater amounts of American dollars. They will then use this to bid up the price of raw furs as long as there is enough demand for their finished products. Interestingly, most of this demand comes from the United States and Canada. Under these conditions, fur producers prosper. This is exactly what happened in the last fur boom prior to the 1981-1982 recession.

Another factor, well known to hide men all over the world, is the historic demand for furs by the major fashion houses of New York and Paris. Fashion sets the basic demand for furs, and this lust for looks gets passed down into the garment industry.

Ed Sceery with a few well-prepared coyote, bobcat and fox hides. Proper handling enhances the value of all long-haired furs. Many hide men do not know what makes some furs more valuable than others.

For years after World War II, French designers kept American hide prices well above what could have been expected had the market been responding only to the industrial need for furs. Industrial need means anything that is not related to the fashion industry, such as paint brushes.

Anyway, it was not until the late 1960s that furs became less fashionable among the middle classes of America. Following the decline of what many might call the "Hippie Era," furs came back into fashion and hide prices began a slow upward climb that still persists.

Additionally, the introduction of "fun furs" helped to repopularize furs in fashion circles and rekindle the sybaritic tastes of the middle-class American consumer. The fun furs also did much to improve the technology of fur processing. The new dyes and better sewing techniques resulted in lower prices for fun fur products, and also had a ripple effect that enabled the true fur manufacturers to utilize smaller furs, control the dying processes better and still produce a product that was acceptable in the marketplace. In short, this translated into a renewed demand for real fur coats and fur products.

Changes in the kinds of furs consumers are willing to wear has also influenced the industry. At one time, coyote was not favored as a winter or long overcoat. However, in more recent times, it has become a popular article with a steady consumer demand. While less expensive than mink or muskrat, which is a real plus, it still makes a durable and stylish product.

The preference for coyote and fox fur has manifested itself in a new market for rustic articles. This includes things like vests, pouches and gloves, which are often made in a cottage-like industry where one or perhaps two individuals work on a full-time or near full-time basis. Here the quality of hide is almost unimportant, as little secondary processing is done. Few hides are dyed and the stitches are sewn so as to appear homemade. The point is that many of the hide grading factors necessary for sale into the large fur houses can be bypassed for this market. Indeed, almost any hide can be used and a beginning hide man should seek out these potential markets.

Another price-setting influence, perhaps not readily recognizable as such, should be understood. As mentioned, innovative fur technology has spilled over into an increased demand for fur products. This same technology has also changed the value of many factors currently used in fur grading. For example, size is no longer as important as it once was, simply because smaller hides and even parts of hides can be economically used in fur coats. Hides once considered too small or too damaged can now be used.

However, while size may not be as great a factor as it was once, hide buyers still continue to demand size, and still, accordingly, downgrade smaller hides. This is partly due to the tradition involved in hide grading and partly due to good business practices. So, although many of the factors are changing, the net effects are not yet realized at the hide buying/hide preparation end of the business.

A final, important concept to consider in the hide business is that without a doubt there will always be some demand for exceptional quality hides. This arises from the needs or whims of the extremely well-to-do, who, for centuries, have been interested in high-quality fur articles and have been willing to pay a premium for them. The hides needed to satisfy this special demand will most often be purchased by custom furriers or their brokers and used in the immediate trade. This accounts for the exaggerated prices paid for exceptional furs at some international market auctions.

When talking about hides of general quality, however, the same kind of demand does not exist. This is because the products made from these furs are sold to the average person. The large and diverse group of people known as middle Americans can pay only certain limited amounts for their furs. Thus, the furs required to meet this demand need only be good enough to manufacture a specific product, which will be worth no more than a given price, even if the fur is above average. In other words, the final product, regardless of quality, will bear a price that is fixed within a relatively narrow range.

In a nut shell, the quality of furs is many times in the eye of the beholder. An individual viewing one coat or another is often unaware of the steps and the difficulty needed to bring the garment to the store rack. The challenge for the manufacturer has always been how to make the best product with the widest market appeal from the resources available. In reaching this goal, hide quality, although important, becomes secondary to other factors.

The Buyer's Economic Concerns

The hide buyer is a businessman. This is the first, most important principle to digest. His goal is to purchase your hides for as little as he can and at the same time pay as much as he can to keep out competition and build his hide inventory. He must walk this tightrope because, in the final analysis, he must sell into that risk-laden fur market described earlier. It does not matter at what level the purchase is taking place. The same principle applies—buy low and sell high.

Distance to Resale Markets. One of the major factors determining how much a buyer will pay for a fur is the distance he has to ship his purchase for

Two picture-perfect fox hides in adult and sub-adult sizes. Exceptional quality hides will always be in demand.

resale. The distance to market will vary depending on where the buyer ships, but the principle will remain the same. In the continental United States, the major fur producing states are Louisiana, Wisconsin, Minnesota, Ohio, Illinois, Pennsylvania and Michigan. The major fur manufacturing houses are located in New York, St. Louis, Seattle and Minneapolis. In other words, the manufacturer's location is quite a haul from the fur producing areas of the U.S. Furs must be shipped across this distance and shipping costs are high. This cost is reflected in how much an area buyer can pay.

Different buyers have ways of working around this problem. The most common is to assemble large packets of furs and then take advantage of any economies that can be realized from having shipped such a large bundle. This may take the form of paid shipping when selling to a large manufacturer, or it could mean personal delivery of the furs to an auction house by truck or train. Most

A mixed bag of top-quality, prime, well-handled hides. It usually means good prices and high profits for those in the buying/selling chain.

buyers attempt to combine trips with loads of furs and return trips with another product that is later resold at a profit.

Why is the fur industry concentrated in places like New York when the furs are produced in the West and Midwest of the country? The answer is that America is actually a net importer of raw furs of all kinds. Argentina is the largest exporter of furs to the U.S., but furs also come from Canada, England, Europe and South America to be processed. Here, in the large fur centers (mainly New York), the partly processed furs are manufactured into fur garments for re-export.

Turnover Time. The largest fur trading firm in the world today is the Hudson's Bay Company. Established in 1607, the company still maintains hinterland trading posts throughout Canada's rugged Northwest Territories and the Yukon and is still the largest single buyer of raw furs today.

Large buyers can, of course, influence the price paid for furs and the cost of furs to manufacturers. In the past, the Hudson's Bay Company would hold furs in storage if the prices were too low. In the north, where refrigeration is seldom needed, this company built large storehouses where tons of any particular fur would be held in cold storage for years at a time. Bobcat and arctic fox were routinely held off the market by this fur marketing giant.

Today, such practices would be economically difficult to justify, although many individual buyers still hold furs over until the next season if the conditions are right and they have the necessary cold storage. Nevertheless, the practice of hoarding furs and releasing them at specific times was a factor in the pricing of furs at the wholesale level. It can be important today, but its influence is less because there is still such a high demand for raw furs— spread over numerous buyers and manufacturers.

This high demand results in a rapid turnover of furs, and this, of course, influences the wholesale price. An example would be selling 50 good coyote pelts for 10 dollars apiece within 14 days of having received the hides from the hunter. If these were bought for nine dollars each, a profit of 50 dollars would be realized. On an annualized basis, this would be equivalent to returning 24 percent on the dollar. If the same hides were kept for a year, it would be only a 10 percent profit. A rapid turnover

The buyer must also consider shipping costs, turnover time and opportunity cost if he is to make a profit dealing in hides.

means that a buyer can profit more quickly from his trades and assemblage of hides. In turn, he buys more hides and sells these quickly. The result is that a certain amount of money can be used to generate more money and the profitability of the firm grows. Clearly, then, the turnover time a buyer expects from his fur purchase will help determine how much he can pay for hides in a given market area.

Opportunity Cost. Another concept that greatly influences the wholesale price of hides is "opportunity cost." Economists define this as the sacrifice of doing something else. In short, the time spent assembling and buying hides has to be worth more to the buyer than if he spent that time performing some other task. This includes his cash outlays, his time and his effort. He may love to buy hides, but the effort must be worthwhile, or in the long run his business will not remain viable.

The impact of this economic factor is seen most clearly in the hide business when there are more buyers in an area at the time of high prices than when hide prices are low. The time spent buying hides becomes worth more than spending that time doing something else. It is a difficult economic principle to grasp; however, its importance to sellers of long-haired hides is clear.

It is for this reason that many hide buyers at the local level are gainfully employed at a variety of other jobs. Few local buyers are full-time hide men. For years the local hide buyer, for example, was also the junk collector. This is still seen in many parts of the country today. Aside from the seasonal requirement, the opportunity to purchase hides is not always secure.

The influence of the combination of factors detailed above has produced hide buyers that are very shrewd businessmen. They know that their economic livelihood is dependent upon the hides they buy and the prices they will finally receive for their efforts.

After looking at all the factors, it is easier for you to see just what is motivating a hide buyer anytime he decides to purchase a hide. He evaluates the risk of taking your particular hide against what he knows or believes he will receive from the next buyer up the ladder. Many times the conditions of the market can change before he has assembled all the furs he needs for the type of pack he had in mind. All things considered, there is great risk in being a buyer.

Now, are you ready to go out and peddle your pelts?

Chapter 18

The Hunter As Businessman

The possibilities of making money via hide hunting we know are very good. However, the hide man finds that the business side of things oftentimes interferes with his hunting endeavors, and usually his chief interest, for whatever reasons, is in the actual hunting and not so much the money end. But any hunter who sells 200 or 300 hides over the course of a season is as much a businessman as any other. He must have a working understanding of selling methods as well as how to keep accurate records.

Let's first take a look at various marketing techniques and the how, where and to whom of selling prepared hides.

Dealing With the Local Buyer

In addition to being shrewd businessmen, as discussed in the previous chapter, buyers have become very wary about from whom they buy. Many attempts to pass off poorly prepared hides and rough sewing jobs have made the buyer wise. Today, he is likely to downgrade a hide more heavily, and this, in part, accounts for some of the disparity in prices hunters will be offered for the same parcel of hides on the same day from different buyers in the same locality.

Long-hair hunters should pay particular attention to developing a good buyer-seller relationship. This is easily accomplished by presenting well-cared-for hides that are properly handled and sorted as to size and condition. Providing hides regularly is also wise. Condition and supply go a long way to making the buyer's decision much easier as he takes into account all the economic factors that influence the market.

Many local buyers will purchase a carcass with the hide still in place and either skin the hide themselves or have a skinner do it. Hides presented in this manner will naturally bring the lowest price. There are, however, distinct advantages to providing the local buyer with well-prepared hides. As mentioned before, it is possible to build up a good working relationship with the buyer in this way. Sometimes, too, a buyer will err your way, but over the long haul, prices usually will adjust to what the market will bear.

Also, a local buyer will most likely be more familiar with the quality of fur that comes from a given area. For example, some areas are better coyote producers in terms of hide quality, and this results in better prices for the buyer. This is passed on to the hunter.

The single biggest advantage of dealing with local buyers is that the money is paid at the time of the sale. And, after all, cash in hand is what it's all about. If the hunter is satisfied with what the local hide man can offer, then he has ended his risk in continuing to store the hides, transport them or otherwise protect them from damage.

Many times there becomes a limit to how many hides can be kept on hand. Let's face it, hides are difficult to store and protect. Besides, they take up a lot of room. Few of us have the luxury of an empty barn or an unused outbuilding on a farm where you can store hides safely and keep them away from mice and porcupines. In the city, the problem is even greater and may result in some health considerations as well as complying with local ordinances. Under these kinds of circumstances, selling to the local buyer can put an end to a lot of problems.

One disadvantage in dealing with a local buyer is that many times the prices may not be as high as those the big auctions or the sales organized by a trapper's association will bring. However, local buyers will often come out to where your furs are located. In the rural parts of the country, this can mean savings in time and travel costs.

How To Negotiate Price. An important element in dealing with a local fur buyer is the setting or negotiating of the final price of a given pelt. It is here that the hunter's knowledge of market conditions, the quality of the hide, and the factors acting upon the market combine to give him his best position. Many buyers and sellers will tell you that there is a deep psychology to arriving at a price. In everyday life, few items can now be bargained for and haggled over. The ones in which some bargaining can take place have a price set within a very narrow range. An automobile is a prime example of this type of item. Everybody tries to make the best deal possible, but in reality there is little room for the price to be lowered.

It is certainly not necessary to accept the first price quoted by the buyer. If the buyer does not know you, he will test your knowledge of the market and the hide by offering a price that tends to be on the low side of the current market. If he can buy the pelt for this price, it means less risk on future deals and a chance for greater profit. On the other hand, many hide buyers who know the hunter or are familiar with the kinds of hides the hunter is bringing in may offer on the high side of the prevailing market. The hope is for repeat business. In addition, clean, well-prepared hides, neatly stretched and well dried will bring a premium offer since the buyer does not have to bother with these steps in the dressing process. Other times a buyer will offer a hunter a reasonable price, with no room for further negotiation.

There is no harm in negotiating. Some people are shy about doing this sort of thing, but with a little practice you can soon become at ease with it. Begin by talking about the hide itself. Point out the desirable or salient features. Mention if it is larger than a normal hide. Compare your superior efforts against other hides that might happen to be in the shop. Focus on the condition of the fur, mentioning all the important factors such as the quantity of guard hairs, the thickness of the underfur, or the unique or special color. Most hide buyers will take a second look and many will up the ante a few dollars once they realize they are talking with a knowledgeable hunter. For them this is often good business, as they hope the hunter will bring in more hides. In your discussion, mention that you are a serious hunter and that you are spending considerable time at your craft. If there is a particularly large hide hanging on a stretcher in the corner of the shop, take an interest in it. Ask where it was taken and who the lucky hunter was. Remember, too, that most hide buyers have a deep interest in the outdoors and almost any form of hunting. Many times it is one of the main reasons they are in the business, and they like talking to fellow outdoorsmen and sharing the odd bit of gossip and lore. Many buyers are veritable fountains of information on the outdoors.

However, if showing an interest in the business and explaining the good qualities of your particular hide does not bring an increased offer, don't pursue the matter any further. Perhaps the buyer has offered all the hide is worth to him and there is no more debate to be had. If you are not satisfied with the price, thank the man for his time and move on to the next buyer. Remember, too, that you can always come back and take what was offered.

Although many hunters will not consider going back to a dealer who has offered a price below their expectations, there is nothing wrong with returning with the same hide later in the day. Remind the buyer of the price he quoted, and tell him you have thought it over and are willing to accept his figure. Most buyers will chuckle and hand you the money. Don't feel awkward about the transaction; they will know you've shopped around and checked with the local competition.

It is best to make your repeat visit to the buyer on the same day that he quoted the price. In a week or two, fur prices may have changed or other business factors may have altered. His accountant may have just told him he is not making any money, or his banker may have phoned to say he is overdrawn on his account. Anyway, a few factors may have changed and there is no guarantee that the price previously quoted carried any commitment longer than the time it took to say it. Under these conditions, take your money and leave further debate for another day.

Many buyers will quote a price on an individual hide, especially if there are only a few hides presented. With larger parcels, a buyer may want to quote a price "straight through," that is, the same price for each hide. This has advantages in that the transaction is usually done quickly and the hunter receives a substantial sum of money. However, sometimes the better hides are actually selling for less when this type of pricing is used. In theory, the price is supposed to average out over the lot of the hides, but the seller may feel he could make more money on the better hides. It is fair to ask the buyer to quote on individual hides or on the lot or any combination. In this way, three of your best hides could be picked out and a special price given for them. These are some of the kinds of negotiating techniques that can be conducted by the individual seller at the time of sale. Never feel bashful.

International Fur Auctions

At the opposite end of the scale is selling your hides into one of the international fur auctions. Most of the time large packages of well-prepared furs will sell better by this method than any other. On the other hand, small or irregular furs or those that have been sewn excessively or are obviously in bad shape will not sell and many times will not be returned to the shipper. This aside, for the hunter who amasses several hundred long-hair kills over the course of the season, selling into one of the international markets in New York or Winnipeg can be profitable. These auctions are the same ones the local buyers sell into, and it is plain that the prices paid at these auctions are the true market value of the hides at that point in time.

One of the most famous fur auctions is the Dominion/Soudack Auction in Winnepeg. American furs are sent through a custom broker. The one currently used is H.A. and J.L. Wood, Custom Brokers in Pembina, North Dakota. (See box.)

However, there are some serious drawbacks to using an international fur auction. Most important is that the hunter cannot get his furs back. Sometimes, although it has been rare lately, the pelts may not sell for years at a time. In the past, the fur houses would also simply unload lots of furs that were not selling. This occurs with long-hairs that have been poorly prepared. In short, unless your furs meet good standards of grading, it is possible that they will be ignored or sold at a low price.

The local country buyer and the high-pressure

LOCATING BUYERS/BROKERS

To locate fur buyers or brokers, contact:
Hudson's Bay Company—Fur Sales, Canada, Ltd. 65 Skyway Ave., Rexdale, Ontario, Canada M9W 6C7
(416) 675-9320. Telex 06-989411
Dominion Soudack Fur Auction Sales— 589 Henry Avenue, Winnipeg, Manitoba, Canada R3A 0V1

For furs shipped from the U.S. for sale in Canada:
Hudson's Bay and Annings—929 Watson Avenue, Madison, Wisconsin 53713
H.A. and J.L. Wood Custom Brokers— Pembina, North Dakota 58271

Or subscribe to:
Fur-Fish-Game—2878 East Main Street, Columbus, Ohio 43209
Predator Caller and Trapper—Box 550, Sutton, Nebraska 68979

international fur auctions are worlds apart. With the local buyer, the seller has control of his product right up until the time of sale, but with the auction this is not possible. On the other hand, the highest possible prices for well-prepared furs will be realized at an international auction. It is from the auction house that the furs go directly to the fur dresser's table and begin the long process into fur articles.

The large auctions, and many smaller kinds as well, offer the fur manufacturer an opportunity to examine the furs before bidding. Large auction houses may have three or four examination days in which the prospective buyers can prowl the fur parcels looking at the quality of furs available. The sale then follows and it may vary in length from one day to several, depending on the state of the market at any one time. Following the sale, the furs are packed and prepared for shipping. Finally, there is the "prompt" day, when the buyers must settle their accounts with the auction house and the furs are shipped to the various manufacturers.

Nothing is quite like an auction. Large fur auctions are exciting with frantic bidding by world-class manufacturers desirous of getting the best furs possible. It is, indeed, instructive and interesting for any hunter to take the opportunity to visit one of these auctions and see the old-fash-

ioned free enterprise market system in action. It is also worth seeing the quality of furs available and studying the way in which the furs have been prepared for market compared with your own techniques. Should you ever get the chance to take in a fur auction, you'll know what I mean.

Trappers' Auctions

A step down in size from the large international auctions are the local or trappers' fur auctions. Here buyers examine furs in much the same manner as is done at the large auctions. Indeed, much of the methodology of a large auction is used in the local trapper's sale. Many of these are organized into fur co-operatives where the auction facility and staff are paid out of membership fees and commissions on the sale of the furs. In essence, the members own their own facilities. Many hunters, and a lot of trappers as well, feel they receive their best deals through these types of sales. Many times the hunter can see his hides sold and it is not necessary to travel to distant fur auctions to see the same kind of action.

One of the big problems, however, is that when the market is down, few large buyers will travel to these auctions. During the early 1970s when the competition was keen for most types of furs, especially long-haired kinds, buyers would visit some of the smaller sales in the hope of collecting high-quality hides at lower prices. As hide prices continued to rise, the number of buyers working the circuit of trapper-run auctions actually increased. In essence, some of the keen competition that was usually reserved for the big world-class auctions was filtering down into some of the smaller trapper-run sales. The results were fantastic prices paid for some furs, especially bobcat, during this time, which, in turn, produced a positive ripple effect throughout the entire fur marketing chain. It helped some local auctions gain in status as reasonable places to ship furs, and it enriched the pocketbooks of local trappers and hide hunters. In the past when few bidders appeared at these auctions, the prices paid for good-quality furs tended to be less than might normally be expected, given the run of market conditions.

As is the case in any other type of auction market, there are the usual problems of shipping distance and travel costs. Furs received after certain receiving dates will miss the auction, and hold-over or storage fees may be assessed until the following auction. This, of course, comes off the price of the hide after commission. Again, as in other transactions where the seller is not present, poor prices may result on unwanted items.

The Fur Broker

Another avenue open to large-volume hide sellers is going through a fur broker. Basically, a fur broker acts like a real estate agent; he sells furs on your behalf and deducts a commission. Brokers are usually professionals in the hide business and prefer to deal in large quantities of furs. Some go so far as even specializing in the kinds of hides they will handle. The possibility of higher prices exists because a broker will assemble packages of hides and offer these for sale to a selected clientele. Under these conditions, good-quality hides will bring better prices and lower-quality hides will be passed off at lower numbers. Usually a broker knows the kinds of hides his potential buyer wants to see and he will move heaven and earth to meet these needs. This will yield premium dollars.

There are some disadvantages in dealing with a broker, most of which have to do with the remoteness of the hide hunter from the broker. Many horror stories are told about hunters who have never been paid. Storage and handling fees, as well as a commission at the time of sale, are part of the cost of doing business. Most of the time the hides cannot be returned and, if they are, there's a good chance they will be mixed up and not the ones originally shipped. Add on return shipping charges, too. Clearly, risks are present in dealing with a broker and any hunter who attempts this for the first time should approach with caution.

Other Selling Tips

Whichever route you travel in marketing your furs, be sure to check the reputation of the buyer you are dealing with. On a local level, it is fairly easy to check on the buyer. A few contacts will quickly give you an impression of the prices paid and the treatment you'll receive. The fact that someone is buying hides in an area usually means the prices are adequate, at least for the hunters or trappers working that particular venue. Buyers at a distance pose more problems. However, a few calls to local bank managers will soon tell you where the outfit banks, and a few frank words with the bank manager may reveal some interesting information. Also, the reputation a buyer has with local trappers is often a good indication of reliability.

Membership in a fur co-operative is also wise, especially if only a few hides are sold each year. Beginners are wise to join a co-operative, as the opportunities to learn about furs and fur grading are better there than anywhere else. As mentioned previously, many co-ops have their own fur marketing service and this will usually assure good prices to members.

If there are no local buyers in your area, try contacting the local taxidermist. Many are hide buyers on the side or can at least tell you where they market the hides they work with. Others may have contacts with tanneries that are looking for hides or know somebody who buys on behalf of a tannery.

The want ad sections of various outdoor publications routinely carry the addresses of buyers only too willing to purchase your hides. As well, the newsletters of the many state trapper's associations carry ads of nearby hide buyers.

Traditional trapper magazines such as *Fur-Fish-Game* have the names of many reputable hide buyers. More recently, a publication called *Predator Caller and Trapper* has a special section on where to sell furs. All major hide buying companies advertise in this monthly tabloid.

Again, buyers who receive hides by mail are, of course, carrying considerable advantage. There is little room for negotiation and the buyer need only contact the supplier by return mail with the price for the bundle. This is not always to the seller's advantage. However, in an area where there are no other ways to sell hides, sale by mail may be the only option.

Don't Overhold Hides. Many hunters feel that it is better to hold over hides or assemble large packages rather than sell a few hides at a time. Some hide men will overhold hides from one year to the next, hoping the price will rise. Such hides may become freezer burned, turn yellow and are ultimately downgraded. The lower grade and the cost of overholding usually wipe out any profit. Most times it is best to sell hides as soon as they are taken.

If two or three hides are taken every day, selling at the end of two weeks or so is best. On the other hand, if you plan to put together a large number for a broker or other agent, then holding can be recommended. If the hide take is small, then sell as soon as possible.

Never be afraid of offering mixed assortments of hides. There can be several coyote, half a dozen red fox and two or three bobcat. A buyer will actually prefer a good cross section of hides, as it gives him the opportunity to pick up a variety of hides on a single visit.

The next time you drop a parcel of furs on your buyer's steps, remember that there are dozens of factors operating together in varying degrees that will determine how much a buyer can pay for the raw furs. Markets can change dramatically from early in the season to later in the same year.

Remember, too, that there are several ways to market furs. Each hunter will have his own preference and reasons for so choosing. Also, when dealing face to face with a dealer, it is not necessary to accept the first offer quoted; negotiate.

As well as deciding the best way to sell your furs, pay attention to the current market and market conditions. When prices begin to rise, many more hunters take to the field. Watch the trends in fur prices by keeping in touch with your buyer and studying the prices quoted in magazines and trade journals.

Never be afraid to telephone buyers in other areas and ask what the going prices are for the long-hairs that day. It is not unusual for long-hair prices to increase slightly after the opening of the season as last year's held-over furs are disposed of and more prime pelts come onto the market. Keep in touch with your market, as sometimes it will be possible to sell some of your smaller or lower quality furs right at the initial surge in prices. Higher quality furs could then be sold later when few are coming to market in the hope of receiving even higher prices.

Remember, the fur pricing market is much like the stock market and, in fact, in many ways behaves exactly like the futures market. All the factors outlined in this chapter can operate together favorably at any one time. On other occasions, unrelated incidents and strange combinations of events can send prices plummeting. Indeed, the perishable nature of furs, the risk of changes in consumer preference and the unpredictability of supply have always made me wonder why there are no "fur futures" traded on the major stock exchanges. For my money, it would be no different and make about as much sense as the current trades in pork bellies and cotton. Anyway, keep in mind that the buyer is always attempting to gain some insight into what the market will do next. The hide hunter should be doing the same thing.

Read, study and listen. Be a smart, informed seller of furs and prices well above the average will be yours for the taking.

Keeping Accurate Records

Hide hunting is a business that generates cash and it is subject to taxation as any other business endeavor. It is for this reason that a few tips on record keeping for taxation purposes are outlined.

In the hide business, the return for effort can be extremely good. Basic business rule of thumb says

Remember that much outdoor gear directly related to hide hunting is deductible against income from the sale of hides. Keep accurate records of major purchases.

that every dollar generated through the sale of goods or services probably cost half of one dollar to produce or accomplish. In areas where hide prices are average and little travel is involved, the chance of making significant money is very real. Thus, every fox hide that sells for 40 dollars probably cost the hunter 20 dollars in expenses, time and effort.

Sorting out the profitability of the hunting effort means that good records are a must. The very nature of hunting makes this difficult, but with some effort record keeping can be learned the same as any other skill along the way to being a successful hide hunter.

The biggest problem is that hide hunting is most often a sideline to some other work, or at least is

something not always pursued on a full-time basis. This means that expenses associated solely with hunting have to be separated from the other costs. Hide hunting is also seasonal and very often hides are sold in a season other than the one in which they were taken. Hides taken in the fall and early winter are often sold during the late winter and sometimes in the spring. In addition, hides may be overheld from one year to the next, and this complicates the bookkeeping by resulting in high sales every two years or so, with low income and continued expenses in the intervening year.

The Shoe Box Method. Keeping track of bills and invoices need not be a problem, even for those not familiar with how to handle and process paper. The average hunter can keep track of his receipts by using the old shoe box trick. Anytime a bill or invoice is paid, the receipt is tossed into the shoe box. When it comes time to summarize the expenses, either on an annual basis, such as at the time of filing income tax, or monthly for a larger scale hide business, all the amounts can be easily totaled.

What is the difference between a receipt and an invoice or bill? A bill is a statement of charges for goods or services. An invoice is a list of goods shipped to a buyer, stating prices. A receipt is written acknowledgment that something has been paid. A bill marked paid is considered to be a re-ceipt. Many stores simply issue receipts or bills marked "paid," but businesses that supply or purvey goods issue invoices. Thus, when something is purchased and a bill or receipt is offered as a record of payment, be sure to record the item purchased on the back. Some stores will issue invoices on request, and while this helps maintain better records, the IRS will accept a bill with a hand-written notation detailing what was purchased. This may seem to be a fine point, but it is important when records and expenses are called into question.

Many items are allowable expenses. For most

Many items are not often thought of as deductible against hide income. Winter clothing, back gear, snowshoes, skinning knives and rifles are all articles that can be reasonably charged against income.

Buildings used for preparing hides and related outdoor gear can be depreciated. Accurate record keeping is a must. The amount of equipment needed to go after long-hairs will vary greatly with the effort needed and the conditions under which the hunting has to be done. However, remember long-hair hide hunting can be very profitable if the hunter runs his hunting business effort wisely.

hunters, the major expense is in traveling. Gasoline prices are certainly higher than ever before and it is doubtful that they will decline significantly in the near future. Other costs include vehicle insurance and upkeep, baits and lures, trespass fees, license fees, the cost of this book, hunting-related magazines, equipment such as game calls used on the hunt, ammunition, stretchers, knives, snowshoes, winter clothing, camouflage clothing,

and boots or rain gear. All these should be recorded and backed up with the appropriate bills and receipts. Postage and freight are also deductible.

Other important expenses include taxes, heat, light and water where a building or portion of a building is used in the hide hunting business. This could include the building used to prepare the hide or to store and dry the finished product. Remember, too, that a portion of telephone expenses are deductible, providing they were for business reasons. Calls made to fur dealers, buyers or suppliers should be noted on the monthly phone bill and added to the shoe box file. Membership fees in a fur co-operative, fur storage fees and royalties are likewise considered real expenses.

Knowing what expenses are deductible is the first step; obtaining receipts whenever making any hunt-related purchase is the second step in keeping good books. Gas is particularly difficult because many service stations do not routinely give receipts on purchase and it means a special request has to be made of the attendant. Most oblige, but some wonder about the hunter's sanity.

Vehicle expenses are often the most contentious for the IRS man. Most tax men have no idea what is involved in hunting and many have it firmly fixed in their heads that hunting cannot be a legitimate business anyway.

I remember attending a course on income tax where a local lawyer, an accountant, and an IRS expert were giving businessmen some advice on tax-deductible expenses. The IRS man boldly offered that for vehicle records to be accepted, the mileage must be recorded daily. The lawyer, beginning to chuckle, told the IRS fellow that the only people who did that were government employees and they were indeed paid to do it. However, monthly records will probably serve the seasonal hunter, providing the distances do not appear excessive.

A percentage of the miles driven over the total for the year will usually be allowed for expense purposes. Thus, a hunter using his vehicle to drive 30,000 miles in one year with records to show that 15,000 of those miles were driven in the course of hide hunting, could charge 50 percent of the vehicle expenses against income for that year.

The more obvious expenses like gasoline can be kept track of by using a credit card. Use the card for all the gasoline purchases made during the year and it will be easy to total the amount. Either this amount, or the appropriate percentage, can be used in determining the deductible expense. If a hunter is very active, it would be best to use a separate credit card for hunt-related travels and another card for personal expenses. The IRS likes this kind of accounting.

The second major area of expense is depreciation. Basically, depreciation is the loss in value of an item which occurs through use or obsolescence. At one time, businessmen considered depreciation as a way of building up a fund to be used to replace an item of machinery over a given period of time. This concept is now old-fashioned, as static rates of depreciation, inflation and high replacement costs make saving toward replacement nearly unattainable. However, the concept remains firmly entrenched in our tax system and any hunter would be permitted an allowance against his capital goods.

Items that are routinely depreciated include vehicles, snow machines, all terrain vehicles, buildings used in hide preparation, trailers used for hunting and sleds. Rifles are also a depreciable item, as is reloading equipment purchased solely for hide hunting purposes.

Depreciation is essentially determined by taking a percentage set out by the IRS for each item. Some items are depreciated at higher rates than others. This amount is totaled and added to the list of operating expenses.

Don't forget about the income side to all this figuring. It is required that the hunter keep track of all his income from hide sales. Income should be itemized and show the gross amounts received; other information should include the date of the transaction, name of the buyer and quantity. Sometimes a description like "one large cross fox" is also useful. If other items such as ginseng, claws, tails, urine, scent glands and internal organs are sold, record these as income to the hide hunting business.

When the expenses and depreciation are put together and subtracted from the income side, a statement of income and expenses results. Most businessmen keep a separate list of all their depreciable items, showing additions and deletions yearly. This schedule is also used for showing the amount of depreciation yet remaining.

Successful bookkeeping really means getting into the habit of keeping track of your expenses and income. Receipts are a necessary part of this, and taking care of these flimsy bits of paper need not be irritating. It is an essential part of running your hide business like a real business—in which looking at the bottom line means smiling at the monetary measure of your efforts.

Appendix

FUR HANDLING SUPPLIERS

Krofick Outdoor & Trapline Supplies
R.D. 2
Latrobe, Pennsylvania 15650

Mississippi River Trappers Supply
Rt. 1 Box 236-C
La Crescent, Minnesota 55947

Southeastern Outdoor Supplies
Route 3
Bassett, Virginia 24055

Harju Wood Products
Route 1 Box 98
L'Anse, Michigan 49946

Ludy and Mary's Trap Supply
Chelsea, Iowa 52215

Valentine Equipment Company
7510 S. Madison St.
Box 487
Hinsdale, Illinois 60521

Sandstone Fur Company
495 North Main
Amherst, Ohio 44001

Spinney-Eakins Distributors Ltd.
Box 310
Yarmouth, Nova Scotia
Canada B5A 4B3

S.I.R.
1863 Burrows Ave.
Winnipeg, Manitoba
Canada R2X 2V6

Woodstream Corporation
Lititz, Pennsylvania 17543

Northwoods Trapline Supplies
Box 25
Thief River Falls, Minnesota 56701

Aeschleman Fur Company
Box 388-B
Roanoke, Illinois 61561

Midwest Supply
803 Oak Terrace
La Crescent, Minnesota 55947

Index